ANTARCTICA'S
LOST AVIATOR

ANTARCTICA'S
LOST AVIATOR

The Epic Adventure to Explore the Last Frontier on Earth

JEFF MAYNARD

PEGASUS BOOKS
NEW YORK LONDON

ANTARCTICA'S LOST AVIATOR

Pegasus Books Ltd.
148 W. 37th Street, 13th Floor
New York, NY 10018

Copyright © 2019 by Jeff Maynard

First Pegasus Books cloth edition February 2019

Interior design by Maria Fernandez

Library of Congress Cataloging-in-Publication Data is available.

ISBN: 978-1-64313-012-5

10 9 8 7 6 5 4 3 2 1

Printed in the United States of America
Distributed by W. W. Norton & Company

For Annabelle, Bethany, Baxter, and Wes.
May they soar over new frontiers.

CONTENTS

AUTHOR'S NOTE

By the end of World War I, about five percent of the Antarctic landmass had been explored. A small wedge from the Ross Ice Shelf to the South Pole was the only area of the vast interior impressed by a human footprint, and less than one third of the coastline had been sighted. During the 1920s and 1930s, as new areas were added to maps, inaccurate names were sometimes assigned to them. For example, in 1928, when Sir Hubert Wilkins flew along what we now call the Antarctic Peninsula, he incorrectly reported it to be a series of islands. As a result, maps of the period showed it as the "Antarctic Archipelago." (The northern section was known as Graham Land and the southern section as Palmer Land.) In other cases, names were assigned, then altered as areas underwent more definitive mapping, or mapmakers chose to be more concise. Hearst Land moved and became Hearst Island. James W. Ellsworth Land was, for a period, Ellsworth Highland and is now simply Ellsworth Land. For consistency with quoted passages and maps, I generally adopt the names the explorers used, only offering an explanation when necessary to avoid confusion. I have also included maps, showing the known areas of Antarctica at the commencement of the Ellsworth expeditions, along with Wilkins's map of the Antarctic Archipelago drawn in 1930.

Navigation held special difficulties for polar aviators during the 1930s. Their instruments and methods were evolving from those used by mariners, who took sextant readings at sea level. So in addition to the difficulties associated with traveling at a much higher speed, navigators cramped in a cockpit also had to estimate their altitude, which was problematic over unexplored land, where the heights of mountains were unknown. Also, mariners sailed in lower latitudes, where meridians of longitude are farther apart and magnetic compass variation is less acute. Because I didn't want to slow the narrative with lengthy explanations, an overview of the methods employed by Lincoln Ellsworth to cross Antarctica is included as an appendix, along with the instructions, estimated positions, and compass variations for the flight, as compiled by Sir Hubert Wilkins.

For period authenticity, I have usually retained the terms and expressions that were used by the explorers. Hence, distances are in miles, length in feet and inches, and weights are generally quoted using imperial measures. The only exception to the use of imperial measures are gallons, which are U.S. I include the metric equivalent to weights, capacity, and distance where I feel it may assist understanding. Unless otherwise stated, miles are statute rather than nautical.

PROLOGUE

The surviving black-and-white film shows two men preparing for a flight beside a sleek metal airplane. Behind the plane, flat compacted snow stretches, like a theater backdrop, to a distant horizon of gently sloping hills. Scattered about the snow in front of the plane are drums of fuel, bags of supplies, and a lightweight wooden sled.

Both actors in the unfolding drama are tall men. Lincoln Ellsworth is the slimmer of the two. His youthful face and thick head of hair make him appear younger than his fifty-five years. Ellsworth is pulling a thick fur parka over his upper body and adjusting the hood. He smiles and briefly spreads his arms wide to present the accomplishment to the camera, then looks around the snow for something to load aboard the plane.

The other man is Herbert Hollick-Kenyon. He is wearing trousers, boots, a check woollen shirt, and aviator sunglasses, which hide his eyes. His solid build and receding hairline make him look older than his thirty-eight years. He ignores the camera as he suits up, deftly clamping the stem of a lighted pipe in his teeth, then transferring it to his hand. The dexterity is impressive and performed without a hint of self-consciousness.

Near the plane, the flags of the institutions with which Ellsworth has an association are held on bamboo poles, a horizontal strut ensuring each is clearly visible in the still air. The camera pans across the flags of the

National Geographic Society, Yale University, the New York Athletic Club, the Hill School, Pottstown, Pennsylvania, and, towering over them all, the flag of the United States of America with forty-eight stars. (In 1935, Alaska and Hawaii are not yet states.) Ellsworth smiles proudly at the camera again and, on the soundless film, goes through the carefully choreographed motion of pointing to each flag in turn.

The film jumps to the same scene a few minutes later. The flags have been packed away. Hollick-Kenyon is sitting casually on the snow, his pipe still in his mouth, strapping gaiters over his boots. He too is now wearing a fur parka.

Ellsworth is pacing anxiously in front of the plane. In his right hand he carries a leather cartridge belt, devoid of bullets. The wealthy Ellsworth who owns, among other things, mansions in New York and Chicago, a villa in Italy, a castle in Switzerland, and great works of art, considers this old cartridge belt his most precious possession. It is the good luck charm he will carry on the flight he hopes will write his name in the history books. The belt would have no value and no meaning were it not for the fact it was once owned by Ellsworth's hero, the western lawman Wyatt Earp. The belt has made a long journey from one frontier to another.

The film jumps again and bit players have walk-on roles in the performance. A mechanic checks the engine, more for the camera than mechanical necessity. Everything has already been checked and rechecked. Another man steps on the low wing and wipes the cockpit windscreen with a cloth. And it goes on until Hollick-Kenyon and Ellsworth are ready to climb aboard.

Hollick-Kenyon climbs in first, sliding the canopy to the rear and maneuvering his bulky frame into the narrow cockpit. He reaches up and pulls the canopy forward, over his head, so Ellsworth can climb into the seat behind him. Settled, Ellsworth grins at the camera and, reacting to some unheard direction, leans awkwardly forward, thrusting his head partway out of the cockpit, so his face is not in shadow.

A man closes the side hatches on the fuselage before walking out of frame. The streamlined silver metal plane is beautiful, even by modern standards. The large block letters along the side are clearly visible: ELLS-WORTH TRANS-ANTARCTIC FLIGHT.

Next, the shot is wider and the single propeller spins invisibly while snow is blasted rearward. The plane moves forward on wide flat wooden skis, gathering speed. It passes the camera, which is not panning, and the port wing appears to come dangerously close to the lens. The plane moves away as it taxis and gathers speed.

Finally, the plane accelerates across the snowfield, lifts off, circles once over the cheering men still on the ground, and flies out of the picture. The local time is 0800 Greenwich Mean Time (GMT). The date is November 23, 1935. The location is Dundee Island, near the tip of the Antarctic Peninsula. The wealthy and eccentric American explorer, Lincoln Ellsworth, after years of setbacks, misfortunes, and ridicule, is finally on his way to attempt the first crossing of the last unexplored continent on Earth.

The camera stops filming, but the activity continues. The man who has been operating the camera, the Australian explorer Sir Hubert Wilkins, organizes the crew to return equipment to the expedition ship, moored at the edge of the ice a few miles away. Men haul crates, tools, and empty fuel drums down the slope from the makeshift runway to the ship, which Ellsworth has named *Wyatt Earp*.

Already aboard the *Wyatt Earp*, the radio operator, Walter Lanz, is listening intently for messages from Ellsworth and Hollick-Kenyon. Lanz writes each message on his pad with a pencil and crew members relay the information to others working around the ship. At first the messages from the fliers are received clearly. They report the plane is flying slower than expected, but everything else is going according to plan.

At 1046 GMT, Hollick-Kenyon radios the right rear fuel tank is empty and he has switched to the front left wing tank. Aboard the *Wyatt Earp*, Sir Hubert Wilkins quickly makes his calculations. In two hours and forty-six minutes the fliers have consumed sixty-seven gallons of fuel at twenty-four and a half gallons an hour. At that rate, because the total fuel capacity of the plane is 466 gallons, they can fly for nineteen hours.

At 1115 GMT, three hours and fifteen minutes into the 2,200-mile flight, Lanz receives the message: "We too far east. Going to make compass course 190."[1]

A few minutes later he records: "IAS 110. Very slow."[2] The Indicated Air Speed (IAS) is only 110 miles per hour. The plane is capable of flying at 200 miles per hour and should be cruising at 150 miles per hour. There are mutterings aboard the *Wyatt Earp*. Why are they flying so slowly? Is there a headwind? Is something wrong with the engine? Wilkins makes more calculations. If they are only flying at 110 miles per hour the 2,200 miles flight will take twenty hours. They will not have enough fuel. The fliers should turn around and return to the ship.

Minutes later, Hollick-Kenyon radios that he and Ellsworth are still flying. The headwinds are increasing. Mountain ranges are in front of them. They will need to gain elevation, burning even more fuel. They have traveled 400 miles—too far to walk back to the *Wyatt Earp* if they are forced to land.

At 1241 GMT, Hollick-Kenyon radios they are flying at 13,000 feet and still climbing and still flying into a head wind. They have no intention of turning back to the safety of the ship. After eight hours, the radio messages are crackling and breaking up. Lanz writes on his pad:

> I estimate that we are at sevent . . . one . . . erabouts . . . my guess is . . . at . . . pect still clear . . . to s . . . ight dull . . . little no wind.[3]

Lanz waits for the next message, but nothing is heard. Hours pass and there is still nothing to record on the pad. The ice pack surrounding Dundee Island presses at the side of the *Wyatt Earp*. If the ship is not moved to open sea soon it will be trapped, perhaps for the winter.

Wilkins waits twenty-four hours for a radio message from Ellsworth and Hollick-Kenyon, but nothing disturbs the airwaves. By now the plane's fuel must be exhausted. But have the fliers landed safely? If they have, why have they not transmitted their position? Wilkins reluctantly radios a message to Buenos Aires, from where it is relayed to New York. The message explains that the American explorer, Lincoln Ellsworth, has disappeared. He departed, with pilot Herbert Hollick-Kenyon, on a trans-Antarctic flight expected to take fourteen hours. After eight hours radio contact was lost.

In New York, Ellsworth's lawyers and business managers fear the worst. Ellsworth has previously hinted at suicide. Could he have possibly done it? Could their client, who has battled depression for much of his life, who has endured taunts and snickers at rumors that he is gay, and who has repeatedly failed to demonstrate competence in navigation, finally realized his secret ambition to reach a remote frontier—the last frontier on the planet—and remain there permanently?

Aboard the *Wyatt Earp*, Wilkins receives frantic messages from New York asking what can be done. The experienced Antarctic explorer understands the answer is virtually nothing. Except for the fliers, and the small crew aboard the *Wyatt Earp*, which is now trapped by the ice, there is no one else on the continent and no other ship in Antarctic waters. The crew of the *Wyatt Earp* can only wait and hope. Lanz, often relieved by other crew members, strains his hearing to listen for the faintest signal from the radio. The waiting and listening continues for days, and then weeks.

Antarctica offers only silence.

Eighty years after Lincoln Ellsworth and Herbert Hollick-Kenyon took off to attempt their trans-Antarctic flight, I landed at the Gerald R. Ford International Airport, Grand Rapids, Michigan, searching for information about the man who had sent them on their way, Sir Hubert Wilkins. I was greeted at the airport by Mike Ross, a giant bear of a man in his seventies, who led me across the parking lot to his pickup truck, then drove me an hour north to the small town of Fremont. Mike was the son of the late Winston Ross, who had been Wilkins's personal secretary and, after the deaths of Sir Hubert and Lady Wilkins, had inherited their lifetime collection of correspondence, records, and artifacts. Initially, Winston Ross had been at a loss as to what to do with the enormous amount of material. Hoping to raise money to preserve it, he had sold certain correspondence to collectors of polar memorabilia. Then, in 1985, he had transferred much of the remainder to the Ohio State University's polar archival program. But after Winston Ross's death in 1998, his son Mike discovered still more boxes of material and, not knowing to whom he should give them, had stored them at his home in Michigan. I'd come to see what they contained.

When we arrived at Mike's rural property on the outskirts of Fremont, he led me into the workshop behind his home and showed me the stack of boxes. For the next week, either in my motel room, or amid the tools in Mike's workshop, I sifted through thousands of photographs, artifacts, letters, and documents, carefully copying them and taking notes. I found remarkable items, such as Wilkins's mention in dispatches from the Western Front in World War I, specially marked bars of soap from the airship *Hindenburg*, a proclamation from George V of England authorizing Wilkins to claim land in Antarctica, and autographed pictures from people such as Walt Disney, Amelia Earhart, Roald Amundsen, and Joseph Stalin.

I also found the records of the Ellsworth Trans-Antarctic Expeditions.

In the years I had spent researching Sir Hubert Wilkins I had read everything available about his time, during the 1930s, helping Ellsworth realize his dream of being the first person to cross Antarctica. But a lot of research had previously revealed very little, except that Ellsworth appeared to be apathetic, incompetent, and, for the most part, uninterested in his ambition. What motivated him to cross Antarctica was a mystery. Nor could I understand why Wilkins had spent so much time helping someone else achieve what he wanted desperately to do himself.

The Michigan boxes held the answers. They contained intimate letters between Wilkins and his wife, explaining the happenings aboard the *Wyatt Earp*. They revealed radiograms and telegrams, the crew's contracts, erratic instructions written by Ellsworth, receipts for purchases, press releases, the ship's papers, and more. In short, they revealed the story. Combined with the records I had already studied, the Michigan boxes opened an intimate window into one of the strangest episodes in polar history. It is this untold story I now present to the reader.

It is a story of men who came after the Heroic Age and how they competed for the last great prize in polar exploration—the first crossing of Antarctica. And it is the story of how the ammunition belt of a western frontier lawman came to be carried across the frozen continent, and how a lonely, insecure, fifty-five-year-old gay man triumphed where so many others had failed.

ANTARCTICA'S
LOST AVIATOR

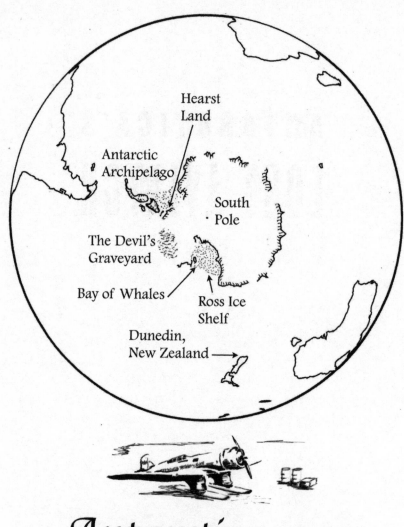

Hearst
Land

Antarctic
Archipelago

South
· Pole

The Devil's
Graveyard

Bay of Whales

Ross Ice
Shelf

Dunedin,
New Zealand ⟶

Antarctica 1933

The known coasts of Antarctica at the
commencement of the Ellsworth Trans-
Antarctic Expeditions. The Antarctic
Peninsula was believed to be a series of
islands and shown on maps as the
Antarctic Archipelago.

PART I

ALMOST HEROIC

So Skoal! Roald Amundsen:
The winter's cold, that lately froze our blood,
Now were it so extreme might do this good,
As make these tears bright pearls, which I would lay
Tombed safely with you till doom's fatal day;
That in thy solitary place, where none
May ever come to breathe a sigh or groan,
Some remnant might be extant of the time
And faithful love I shall ever bear for you.

—Poem written by Lincoln Ellsworth
on the death of Roald Amundsen

1

THE ELF CHILD

MAY 1880–OCTOBER 1924

Before 1924, Lincoln Ellsworth gave no indication he intended to be a polar explorer. To the contrary, he didn't like the cold and was susceptible to pneumonia. He detested discomfort and deprivation and, whenever possible, he avoided physical work. He had difficulty focusing on any subject for even a brief period and, when confronted with a challenge, he usually surrendered to apathy and sought an easier path. In short, if one were to list the personal attributes necessary for polar exploration in the first half of the 20th century, it would be difficult to recognize even a few of them in Lincoln Ellsworth. But at the age of forty-four, Ellsworth stumbled upon an opportunity to become an explorer and seized it, hoping the overt display of manliness might finally gain the respect of his domineering, emotionally cold father.

Lincoln Ellsworth was born on May 10, 1880, in a stately mansion on Ellis Avenue on the South Side of Chicago, Illinois. His only sibling was a sister, Clare, born five years later. Ellsworth was a sickly child, and a family friend later told him he was "too fragile to support the hard studies and hard games of other boys." The friend, writing a decade before

J.R.R. Tolkien published *The Hobbit* explained to Ellsworth, "one feared you were an Elf Child,"[1] and observed the condition was a great concern to Ellsworth's father.*

Ellsworth's mother, Eva, doted on her frail son until he was eight, when she died of pneumonia. The upbringing of Lincoln and Clare became the responsibility of their father, James W. Ellsworth, a powerful, overbearing businessman who had amassed a fortune mining coal to supply the insatiable needs of America's growing railway network. James W. Ellsworth was a God-fearing man who believed in hard work, discipline, and thrift. He once wrote that nothing is, "accomplished in our country but has begun with a puritanical spirit."[2] Ellsworth Senior sought to indoctrinate young men with his values by funding the Western Reserve Academy in Hudson, Ohio, and a former master at the academy said of him:

> There was no middle relationship possible. Either one fought him or served him; hated him or loved him. But even if one loved him, there was no intimacy. The unsmiling, forceful presence, tall, ramrod straight, impeccably groomed, held people at a distance.[3]

At the time Eva Ellsworth died, American railroads were rapidly expanding and coal production was trying to keep pace. The newly widowed James W. Ellsworth did not want to be distracted from his financial empire. He sent eight-year-old Lincoln and three-year-old Clare to be raised by nannies on the family farm in Hudson. What might have been, for many children, an idyllic upbringing of privilege and playful adventures, was hell for young Lincoln. He failed miserably at the local elementary school and recalled only ridicule. He readily admitted, "School was a horror. I couldn't do anything with school—always the dunce of my classes, always falling behind. It was to be this way throughout my school and college days."[4] Years later Ellsworth would realize he was not intellectually dull, but that

---

* Elves originated in Germanic folklore. They were small, took human form, and were mischievous. A common trick of elves was to sneak into a home and replace a human baby with one of their own, thus creating an Elf Child.

he needed something to interest him before he could absorb information. School never interested him, and he developed what he described as "the trait of indifference."[5] Ellsworth was shy, sensitive, and artistic. He read, wrote poetry, and tried to comprehend why he could never gain his father's approval. His one playmate was his younger sister, and he remembered scampering to hide under her bed whenever he felt frightened.

Ellsworth had barely reached his teens when he was dragged from the security of the farm at Hudson and packed off to boarding school. Lincoln's father selected the Hill School in Pottstown, Pennsylvania, as the appropriate institution through which Lincoln would continue his journey to manhood. The school's headmaster, John Meigs, believed the love, charity, and forgiveness of the Christian God was best instilled in young men using rigid discipline and physical punishment. Meigs, who a student once described as, "terrible as an avenging angel," wrote, "the religion of a boy means learning what duty is and caring much and always for it. All else is accessory; this is essence."[6]

For Ellsworth, the hell of his formal education continued. "At the time it seemed a sort of nightmare,"[7] he recalled. At the Hill School, his nickname was "Nelly,"* and Ellsworth's pale skin and soft features had him dress for the female roles in the glee club dramas. He spent his early teen years escaping to the world of books. In his loneliness, he constantly wrote to his father, pleading with him to visit the boarding school, or asking to be understood.**

Ellsworth finally graduated from the Hill School, two years later than most other young men his age. In 1900, his father's influence gained him entry into Yale University, where his continued inability to apply himself to academic study meant he survived less than a year before being asked to leave.

Ellsworth was twenty-one and, having struggled through a confused puberty, wanted little more from the world than to be left alone. In recalling

---

* The word Nelly does not appear in Webster's dictionary of the era. In English dictionaries its meaning is given as (i) silly or (ii) an effeminate, presumably gay, man.

** Lincoln Ellsworth often wrote letters and poems to his father from a young age, begging for understanding. Mary Louise Ellsworth (see Chapter 8) discovered the letters after Lincoln's death and, finding herself unable to confront the depth of emotion expressed, burned them and never revealed the contents.

his early life, he often described it as "horrific" and "hell," and explained it was so traumatic he could remember little of what happened before the age of thirteen. He never publicly admitted his depressive nature. That he suffered from depression can be ascertained by his actions and the writings of others who, in their correspondence, feared for Ellsworth's mental state and sometimes suggested he was suicidal. Neither did Ellsworth ever write about his sexuality. That he was gay or bisexual can, again, only be determined by his actions or what others wrote about him.

Shortly after being asked to leave Yale, sympathetic former classmates invited Ellsworth on a camping trip in Yellowstone National Park. "That brief trip did more for me than all the schools and teachers I had known, for on it I found myself at last," Ellsworth remembered and he, "brought back from Yellowstone Park a head full of daydreams of adventure in the wild and untrodden parts of the continent."[8]

After the trauma of his youth and formal education, the highly sensitive Ellsworth discovered refuge in the American outdoors. In particular, he came to love the silence and beauty of the North American deserts, writing:

> The grandeur of desert mountains and the glory of color that wraps the burning sands at their feet are beyond words to describe. To the seeing eye the desert is always revealing new beauties and wonders. To its lover it becomes an eternal fascination.[9]

As automobiles, airplanes, telephones, radios, and other inventions civilized America at the beginning of the 20th century, Ellsworth longed for the frontier way of life that was disappearing. He wanted to live in a world before his father—and men like his father—built roads, railways, and skyscrapers, or rounded up cowboys to herd them into factories. His favorite book was Theodore Roosevelt's *Ranch Life and the Hunting-Trail*:

> The whole book filled me with a passion for the West. I devoured that book like a man starved for reading, sitting until the small hours, night after night with it, rereading favorite chapters again and again . . . [such as] the one in which Theodore Roosevelt

tells how, as a frontier sheriff, he walked into a saloon filled with desperadoes, held them up, and cowed them with his gun, and herded them all into jail.[10]

As the world became increasingly crowded and noisy, Ellsworth dreamt of escaping to some untamed frontier where he could be a rough rider of the plains, whom Roosevelt described as, "brave, hospitable, hardy, and adventurous . . . he prepares the way for the civilization, from before whose face he must himself disappear."[11]

During his twenties, Ellsworth would interrupt his wanderings to make brief attempts to work for his father. He chose outdoor work, learning surveying and engineering, but never stayed at anything long enough to secure formal qualifications. Each enforced stay in one of Ellsworth Sr.'s businesses lasted, at most, six months, and Lincoln would find an excuse to go hiking and camping again, traveling as far as Canada or South America.

Much of the tension between father and son, created by each man having different ambitions, was relieved in 1907, when Lincoln was twenty-seven. Realizing his only son would never follow in his footsteps, or take the helm of the empire he had built, James Ellsworth sold his businesses and, at age fifty-eight, devoted his energy and wealth to acquiring art. He remarried, bought a castle in Switzerland and a villa in Italy, and traveled around Europe with his second wife, purchasing whatever caught his fancy.*

Lincoln was finally free of his father's expectations. He could daydream and wander the world. During his twenties and thirties Ellsworth legitimized his love for the outdoors by collecting fossils or relics from the Grand Canyon or the deserts, which he would donate to the American Museum of Natural History. The museum had little use for the repetitious trinkets, but as they were often accompanied by a generous check signed by Ellsworth Sr., the trustees had the good sense to accept them. Ellsworth also fancied himself a scientist, but never committed to any field long enough to do more than read a few books on the subject.

---

* Notable pieces in James W. Ellsworth's collection at the time of his death were Rembrandt's *Portrait of a Man* and a Gutenberg Bible.

When, in 1917, the United States entered World War I, Ellsworth enlisted in the U.S. Army as a private second class and traveled to France hoping to be trained as a pilot. In Paris, he was informed he was too old to be a pilot and, instead, was assigned to clerical work before a bout of influenza caused him to be sent home. He resumed his wanderings in America while the war ground to a conclusion.

Thus life meandered on for Lincoln Ellsworth until October 1924, when he was in New York, having just returned from a camping trip, and an item in the newspaper caught his attention. The famous Norwegian explorer Roald Amundsen was in town, trying to raise funds for a flight to the North Pole.

Roald Amundsen had devoted his life to polar exploration, and by 1924 it had left him bankrupt and bitter. Born in Norway in 1872, Amundsen had, during his teen years, resolved to unlock the secrets of the Arctic. In his youth he designed polar clothing, made his own equipment, and trained himself for his calling by regularly skiing cross-country in the depths of winter. After a trip to Antarctica on a Belgian research ship, then successfully negotiating the Northwest Passage in a small boat, Amundsen set his sights on the biggest prize in polar exploration—the North Pole. He borrowed a ship, the *Fram*, recruited a crew, purchased plenty of sled dogs, and was preparing to depart when, in September 1909, two men, Frederick A. Cook and Robert E. Peary, emerged from the Arctic claiming they had each reached the Pole.

Knowing he could not be first to the North Pole, Amundsen decided to make use of his fully provisioned ship and become the first person to reach the South Pole. That entered him in a race against Robert Falcon Scott, who was leading a British expedition to Antarctica with the express purpose of reaching the South Pole. At the end of 1910, Amundsen set up a base at what he called Framheim (home of the *Fram*) at the eastern end of the Ross Ice Shelf, Antarctica, where he waited out the winter. Scott set up his base at the western end of the shelf and did the same.

After the sun reappeared to light the high southern latitudes, Amundsen left Framheim with four companions and forty-eight dogs, and sledded across the shelf, up the Axel Heiberg Glacier to the Antarctic Plateau, and then to the Pole, which he reached on December 14. Scott and four companions reached the Pole on January 17, 1912, where they found a tent and letter left by Amundsen. Having been beaten to the Pole, Scott's party turned for home and the five men died on the return journey because of (depending on one's opinion of Scott) mismanagement, bad luck, unseasonably bad weather, or some combination of those factors.

Meanwhile, the *Fram*, with Amundsen on board, reached Hobart, Tasmania, on March 7. The world soon learned that he had reached the South Pole, but people had to wait almost a year for a relief ship to bring news of Scott. When it was revealed that Scott had perished, British people were particularly bitter toward Amundsen and his victory. His critics said he was a "professional explorer" and therefore not a "gentleman"; he had been underhanded in stating publicly that he was going to the North Pole, and then sneaking down to the South; he had not collected scientific data; and he had survived by eating his dogs. In truth, Amundsen's biggest mistake was that he had won. A small team of hardy and hardened men from Norway, with experience and careful planning, had upstaged the ambitions of the proud and mighty British Empire and the Empire did not like it.

Burdened by debt, made weightier by accusations of cheating, Amundsen again sought refuge on the ice, but his plans were interrupted by World War I. After the war, he made an attempt to sail the Northeast Passage, before deciding his future was in the sky. He gained a pilot's license and resolved to fly to the North Pole and across the Arctic Ocean. He took an obsolete plane to Wainwright, Canada, but crashed it landing on rough ground. Amundsen reasoned that what he really needed was a plane that could take off and land on water or ice: a flying boat. The best available at the time were the Italian-built Dornier Wal flying boats. But how to pay for them? Amundsen was forced to turn to the only way he knew to raise money: touring and lecturing. The money was in America, so that's where he went.

Thus, in October 1924, Roald Amundsen was holed up in New York's Waldorf Astoria Hotel, refusing to accept visitors lest they be creditors and "nearer to black despair than ever before," on a tour that, "was practically a financial failure":

My newspaper articles had produced but little revenue. As I sat in my room in the Waldorf Astoria, it seemed to me as if the future had closed solidly against me, and that my career as an explorer had come to an inglorious end. Courage, will power, indomitable faith—these qualities had carried me through many dangers and to many achievements. Now even their merits seemed of no avail.[12]

Then Lincoln Ellsworth returned to New York to read that the "Conqueror of the South Pole" was in town trying to raise money for a flight to the North Pole. Ellsworth saw an opportunity for adventure and telephoned the famous explorer, saying, "I am an amateur interested in polar exploration, and I might be able to supply some money for another expedition."[13]

2

THE KINGDOM OF DEATH

OCTOBER 1924–JUNE 1925

For Amundsen, the appearance of Ellsworth must have been a godsend. Here on his doorstep was an insecure middle-aged man, with a generous allowance from a wealthy father and a dream of performing a great feat of exploration. Amundsen flattered Ellsworth, who later recalled proudly "that first long talk I had with Amundsen in his room at the Waldorf developed many things, the most important being that henceforth we were to be partners in polar exploration."[1]

Ellsworth immediately felt an affinity with Amundsen, writing he "was like a child whose confidence has been betrayed so often that he finally trusts nobody. So he encased himself in a shell of ice."[2]

The wily Amundsen, the world's greatest polar explorer, and the eager but inexperienced Ellsworth, who had never strapped on skis, conceived a plan. Or more correctly, Amundsen revealed his ambition to fly across the Arctic Ocean via the North Pole, and skillfully ensured Ellsworth felt part ownership of the idea. Ellsworth enthused, "Our first ambition must be to fly clear across the Arctic. It interested neither of us to merely attain the North Pole."[3]

From the point of view of polar exploration, the idea had merit. The Atlantic side of the Arctic Ocean was reasonably well known, at least as far north as the Svalbard Archipelago, while Cook and Peary had both trekked north from Greenland. But the Arctic Ocean north of Alaska and Canada was still largely a mystery. Cook and Peary had each reported seeing land in the distance in that direction, and various scientists at the time were theorizing, based on the known drift patterns of the ice, that a continent, or at least large islands, existed in the Arctic. Amundsen wanted to fly from Spitsbergen, in the Svalbard Archipelago, to the Pole, and then over the top of the world into the large unknown area where he hoped he would discover "Amundsen Land." It would be the crowning achievement of his lifetime and not tainted with the accusations of cheating and unsportsman-like behavior that had dogged him since the South Pole.

Ellsworth's role was to raise the funds. He asked his father for an advance on his income by "pleading for myself as I never had before."[4] Lincoln's timing was fortunate. Ellsworth's Sr.'s second wife, Julia, had died three years earlier and since then he had withdrawn from the world. He was also suffering from declining health. Lincoln recalled:

> He was nervous and irritable, and the pressure I was putting upon him bothered him terribly. Wouldn't he at least see Captain Amundsen, I begged? Was that asking too much—to give himself the opportunity of meeting familiarly one of the world's historic men?
>
> "Bring him, then," my father finally cried. "Bring him."
>
> It was the first break in his defenses, the first time his iron opposition had even sagged.[5]

The meeting between James W. Ellsworth and Roald Amundsen took place on November 9, 1924, at the industrialist's house on New York's Park Avenue. Ellsworth Sr. was suitably impressed. In Amundsen he undoubtedly recognized the indomitable spirit and single-minded focus that had driven his own ambitions, and which were lacking in his son. When James Ellsworth agreed to back the venture, Amundsen reached into his bag, took out the binoculars he had carried to the South Pole, and presented them to the former businessman.* Having been promised the money he needed, Amundsen canceled his lecture tour and hurried back to Europe to oversee the organization of the expedition.

Lincoln Ellsworth began the more complex task of getting his father's permission to accompany Amundsen. It was a process that consumed three months as the two obstinate men tried to outmaneuver one another. Lincoln wrote, "[Father] paid over the money but began a desperate campaign, one that verged on the unprincipled, to keep me from accompanying the expedition."[6]

At first Ellsworth Sr. said he would permit Ellsworth Jr. to participate in the risky flight if he stopped smoking. Lincoln agreed, but wrote in his autobiography that he never intended to honor the promise. Ellsworth Sr. would sign a bank draft, give it to his son, then a day later instruct the bank not to make the funds available. The two men would confront each other, and Ellsworth Sr. would contact the bank again and change the instruction. Family friends were dragged into the bickering and implored Lincoln to be considerate of his father's age and failing health and not accompany the expedition, while other friends urged Ellsworth Sr. to let Lincoln have his way. Lincoln pleaded with his father to be allowed to go, writing in one letter, "I do not want worldly goods, castles or villas or money with which to purchase luxury. I do want the opportunity to make good and satisfy my inward self in the line of endeavor I have chosen."[7]

Ellsworth Sr. thought his son foolish to make such a choice, and threatened to stop his allowance. And so it went on until eventually Lincoln's sister, Clare, intervened:

> Clare loved me, yet secretly she was one of those sceptics who thought I was going to my death. But she knew that I would rather die than not go. She knew that if I did not go I would be crushed in spirit for the rest of my days. So she interceded with Father on my behalf. Father was furious with her, threatening

---

* Amundsen had scratched the date when he reached the South Pole on the binoculars. Lincoln Ellsworth later inherited them from his father and donated them to the American Museum of Natural History, where they remain today.

her with all sorts of dire things in the future because she had dared interfere. Yet she fought on for me, risking her own future as I was. In his frame of mind then, Father might well of cut off his children with a pittance and left all his money to the Western Reserve Academy. I think it was Clare's influence that made him give up in the end.[8]

The tired old man relented and released the funds. Lincoln Ellsworth hightailed it to Norway to catch up with Amundsen and ship their two flying boats to Spitsbergen. He wrote that his last meeting with his father was "a most dismal experience."[9] Father and son had disappointed each other all Lincoln's life. To his father, Lincoln was the sissy who never had the head or the heart to bludgeon some industrial empire into shape. To Lincoln, his father had neither the insight to understand his son, nor the compassion to see his desperate need for acceptance. "I could only express the nature God and circumstance had given me,"[10] Ellsworth recalled, perhaps hinting at his sexuality.

When Lincoln sailed from New York, his sister came to wave him off. "I had hoped that [Father] might come to the boat, but he didn't." Lincoln wrote:

> For a long time I stood at the rail with a heavy heart. The ship turned slowly in the stream, then moved toward the Battery, the procession of Manhattan skyscrapers marching majestically by. I watched until we were far down the bay and the New York spires had huddled together and shrunk.
> Then my depression dropped from me like a cloak.[11]

Ellsworth described his first expedition more than a decade after the event, but one can still hear the enthusiasm in his words, mirroring those of an excited schoolboy on his first camping trip away from his home and parents.

Ellsworth also felt a new sense of importance. At Oslo, Amundsen had organized a dinner to bid the expedition farewell. Ellsworth, because of an oversight, had forgotten to bring a detachable collar, in fashion at the time, for his shirt. Amundsen borrowed one from a waiter at the hotel where Ellsworth was staying and, after the dinner, returned it. When Amundsen and the waiter spoke in Norwegian, Ellsworth was intrigued and asked Amundsen what the waiter had said. Amundsen explained that the waiter intended to keep the collar as a souvenir. Ellsworth was thrilled:

> Can you imagine a New York bell-hop or hotel waiter preserving the collar worn by even a successful explorer, to say nothing of a prospective one? The Norsemen have been sea-rovers and discoverers for a thousand years. Exploration represents their national genius, as business organization does that of the United States or invention that of Italy. Venturers for discovery's sake take the rank in Norway that other countries accord only to their idols in sport or entertainment.[12]

Mocked and ridiculed since childhood, Ellsworth was suddenly finding himself respected.

At Tromsø, the northern port from which the expedition would depart, Ellsworth met the pilots and crew, who had been hired by Amundsen, and watched, not speaking Norwegian, while they prepared for the five-hundred-mile voyage to Kings Bay, Spitsbergen.* Two Dornier Wal flying boats were loaded, still unassembled in their crates, aboard the *Hobby*, a small steamer that plied the treacherous waters between Norway and Spitsbergen. A week later, at Kings Bay, Ellsworth again watched fascinated, as Amundsen oversaw the unloading and assembly of the flying boats. "It was all new to me," Ellsworth wrote. "We had the feeling of being the cynosure of the world's eyes, and it was to me, at least, tremendously exhilarating."[13]

The Dornier Wal flying boats had been built in Pisa, Italy to a German design. The boat-shaped Duralumin hulls were wide enough to negate the need for wing floats. The Dornier Wals could, hopefully, land and take off in narrow leads (open areas in the ice) of water. Each flying boat had

---

* Today Kings Bay is generally referred to as Kongsfjorden. It is located on the west side of Spitsbergen, the largest island in the Svalbard Archipelago.

two powerful 350 hp Rolls-Royce engines and were capable, should one engine fail, of flying using only the other. Neither flying boat was named. They were referred to by the manufacturer's designation: *N 24* and *N 25*.

Amundsen, with pilot Hjalmar Riiser-Larsen and mechanic Karl Feucht, would fly in one Dornier Wal (*N 25*). Ellsworth, with pilot Leif Dietrichson and mechanic Oscar Omdal would be in the other. Riiser-Larsen and Dietrichson were aviation officers in the Royal Norwegian Navy. Omdal was a Norwegian pilot/mechanic, while Feucht was German, sent from the Dornier Wal factory to maintain the motors.

The six-man expedition planned to fly 750 miles from Kings Bay to the North Pole and, if the engines were running smoothly, continue over the Arctic to the north coast of Alaska. If the flying boats were not behaving, they would turn around at the Pole and return to Kings Bay. They might, if Amundsen thought it advisable, land somewhere near the Pole to discuss their options. It was a vague plan, not helped by the fact they had no radios, so once they were airborne the two crews could only communicate by means of semaphore or making gestures with their hands.

By May 21, everything was ready and the weather promised to remain clear. The Kings Bay coal mines were closed for the day and the Norwegian miners were allowed to witness a national hero, Roald Amundsen, again going where no man had gone before.

At 4:30 P.M. the massive engines were started, the Duralumin hulls inched forward, increasing speed as they slid over the smooth ice and, in a deafening roar, both Dornier Wals lifted into the air.

"It was unreal, mystic, fraught with prophecy," Ellsworth wrote. "Something ahead was hidden, and we were going to find it."[14] Something hidden ahead there may have been, but for Ellsworth, equally, there was something he was leaving behind. As he sat in the nose cowling of the *N 24*, a new unknown world of ice and cold ahead of him, he was leaving behind a world of derision, exclusion, and shame. He later described the flight into the unknown north, saying, "I had accomplished the ambition of my life. I felt like a god."[15]

The two flying boats remained within visual range of each other and flew steadily north for seven hours, crossing the edge of the Arctic ice pack. Believing they must be nearing the Pole, Ellsworth began looking for open leads of water in the jumbled pack ice below, where they could land the flying boats. "I have never looked down upon a more terrifying place in which to land an airplane,"[16] he later wrote.

But then, surprisingly, Amundsen's flying boat dipped and began to descend. Without radios, there was no opportunity to question the reason. Dietrichson had no choice but to follow in the N24. Dietrichson skillfully dropped the flying boat into a narrow lead of water squeezed between jagged ice humps. Without room to taxi to a halt, the hull of the N24 smashed into an ice cake and immediately began sinking. Ellsworth, Dietrichson, and Omdal scrambled out of the doomed flying boat onto the ice. Ellsworth stared at his surroundings. Moments earlier he had felt like a god. Now he confronted a new reality. "In the utter silence this seemed to me to be the kingdom of death."[17]

On the ice, Ellsworth, whose job it was to navigate, handed his sextant to Dietrichson, who determined they were at latitude 87°44'N and longitude 10°20'W. They were 136 nautical miles (156 statute miles) from the Pole. Also, in navigating the expedition north, Ellsworth had not allowed for wind drift. They were twenty degrees off course. Commenting on Dietrichson's reaction to his navigational error, Ellsworth noted, "Great was the pilot's disgust."[18]

But why had Amundsen brought his flying boat down early? He was an expert navigator and surely he had been taking his own sightings and not blindly following the inexperienced Ellsworth. And where were the others from the N25? Ellsworth climbed to the top of an ice hummock and scanned the horizon with his field glasses. There was no sign of the others.

For the next few hours, Ellsworth, Dietrichson, and Omdal attempted to drag the N24 onto solid ice, to no avail. After they had salvaged some supplies, Ellsworth climbed to the top of a taller ice hummock and spied the N25 about three miles away. He could see the figures of Amundsen, Riiser-Larsen, and Feucht working near the plane. It took Ellsworth and his companions five days to transverse three miles of open leads and jagged ice. When they finally reached the other flying boat:

> Five days had wrought a shocking change in Amundsen. Sleep-
> less toil and anxiety had graven in his face lines that seemed

to age him ten years. In all his many adventures in the polar regions, I doubt if he had ever been in such peril as this or under such a strain.[19]

Ellsworth learned that Amundsen had not landed by choice. The engine of the *N 25* had cut out due to a leak in the air intake. Since landing, Feucht had repaired it, and the engine was functioning perfectly. Also, Riiser-Larsen had managed to land the *N 25* without damage. It was ready to fly.

The experienced Amundsen knew a danger facing the small group was the lack of discipline and focus, which would lower morale. He ordered a strict schedule of work, rest, and meals. The first task was to haul the flying boat out of the water and onto the ice, to prevent it being crushed should the lead close. Using wooden snow shovels, sheath knives, and an ice axe, the men hacked out a ramp and taxied the *N 25* onto a flat slab of ice. They had enough fuel to fly the *N 25* back to Kings Bay, but their issue was finding a long flat area of ice from which to get airborne.

On May 31, ten days after their forced landings on the ice, Amundsen held a conference and everyone agreed if by June 15 they had not been able to get airborne, then they would abandon the *N 25* and take their chances walking over the ice to Greenland. Although they did not voice their doubts, Ellsworth recalled that each man understood a journey on foot to Greenland gave them almost no chance of survival.

"But men fight for their lives to the last inch," Ellsworth wrote. "And we had to begin at once to prepare either for that journey or for a much longer stay on the ice than any of us had contemplated."[20]

With a renewed sense of urgency, the men fanned out from the *N 25* to look for an open lead of water or a suitable flat ice runway. The search continued for a week. Ellsworth wrote:

We had been on the ice for fifteen days, and our position was as hopeless as ever. No lead had yet exposed water broad enough for a seaplane's run. The ice of the frozen leads would not bear the weight of the ship. The plane could not reach flying speed on the snow.

Nine days to June 15, when we must make the supreme decision.[21]

On June 6, Riiser-Larsen and Dietrichson strapped their skis on and went searching for a runway again. They returned a few hours later and announced they had discovered a flat area of ice half a mile away. The daunting job now facing the exhausted men was to carve a road, sixty feet wide, through the ice hummocks, so they could haul the flying boat to the proposed runway. For the next nine days, with the strength of men whose only other option was death, they hacked their way through the hummocks, or filled crevices with blocks of ice and snow. Ellsworth worked as hard, or harder, than any of the others in that desperate effort, and Amundsen later credited him with saving the expedition.

Finally, on June 15, the six men climbed aboard the *N 25* and, with Riiser-Larsen at the controls, got airborne. "I experienced no particular elation," Ellsworth wrote. "But only a dull happiness when I felt the plane lift. We were all beyond sharp emotions."[22]

Dietrichson sat forward of the pilot and steered the course to salvation. Six hours later they sighted a small island in the Svalbard Archipelago. Their incredible good luck continued when, shortly after landing, they were spotted by a fishing boat and taken back to Kings Bay, where they learned the world have given them up for dead.

Ellsworth also learned that on June 2, while they had struggled on the ice, his father had died. Ellsworth worried that his disappearance had broken his ailing father's will to live, and he felt personally responsible for the old man's death. For the first time in his life Ellsworth had taken a bold risk and survived, but his father had died thinking his son had perished in the Arctic. It affected Ellsworth deeply. He would write in his autobiography, "If I did not have for him the warm affection a son feels toward a less austere and preoccupied father, I at least had an immense respect for him, and a great admiration."[23]

A week after they had reached Kings Bay, a larger ship was sent to fetch the *N 25* before the expedition returned to Oslo for an official welcome. Ellsworth recalled, "I wish I could describe that welcome and what it meant to me. I was entirely unprepared for its fervor." The six men taxied the *N 25* up the fjord, past a row of warships from many nations:

> The quays and wharves were black with humanity. Whistles of all sorts or river craft howled and shrieked; airplanes circled overhead. The guns of the fort began booming a salute, and a great throng was waiting at the landing.[24]

Ellsworth found it overwhelming, writing, "It was an intoxicating draught for one who has never known celebrity or the feeling of being treated as an important personage. It created an appetite that could never be once and for all appeased."[25]

Ellsworth swore to himself that he would continue his exploration and accomplish something that would make his late father proud. He may not be able to build a great business empire, but he would somehow immortalize the Ellsworth name.

3

NO LONGER THE ONLY AMERICAN

JUNE 1925–MAY 1926

The death of James W. Ellsworth meant that Lincoln and his sister, Clare, inherited a fortune—what today would be many billions of dollars. Ellsworth was in a position to finance any polar venture he cared to. While still at Kings Bay, the shrewd Amundsen pitched another idea to Ellsworth. He proposed they investigate making the flight across the Arctic in an airship. Encouraged that his brief time in the spotlight had people admiring him, the cash-rich Ellsworth pledged $100,000 on the spot, then hurried back to America to collect more fossils from the Grand Canyon.

Amundsen had already researched the available airships which, in 1925, could be loosely divided into three categories: smaller, lighter blimps, which had no frame within the "gas bag" or "envelope"; rigid German zeppelins with a full internal metal frame; and semi-rigids, which had a partially flexible spine within the envelope. Amundsen supposed the inflexible zeppelins were too large and cumbersome to survive the high winds of polar regions, while the blimps, which were mainly used as observation balloons for one or two people, were too small. The most suitable airship, Amundsen concluded, was a small semi-rigid dirigible. Such an airship had recently been built by an Italian air force officer, Umberto Nobile. Named the *N1*, Nobile's airship did not have the lift capacity of the huge zeppelins, but its flexible spine might withstand stronger winds, suggesting it was more suitable for Amundsen's requirements.

Shortly after the affairs of the 1925 expedition were wrapped up, Amundsen met with Nobile and discussed his idea of a trans-Arctic flight via the North Pole. Nobile was enthusiastic, welcoming the opportunity to demonstrate the advantages of his airship to the world. He immediately traveled to Rome to sell the idea to his boss, the Italian dictator Benito Mussolini.

At the time, Mussolini was absorbed in rebuilding Italy after World War I and intent on demonstrating the advantages of strong fascist leadership. After listening to Nobile, Mussolini graciously bestowed his support for the venture. What better way to show the efficiency and resourcefulness of the new Italy than to have an Italian airship fly across the Arctic? Nobile reported Mussolini's eagerness to Amundsen, who immediately became concerned, because he wanted to lead the expedition and have it fly under the Norwegian flag. He also wanted to claim Amundsen Land if he found it. But if the airship was coming from Mussolini and the money from Ellsworth, where did it leave him? Squeezed between the ambitious Italian fascist and the insecure American, Amundsen feared Norwegian eminence, and his role, would be diminished. To preserve his authority, he sought the help of Rolf Thommessen, president of the Aero Club of Norway, who was also the owner of Norway's daily newspaper *Tidens Tegn*. Thommessen agreed to throw some money, along with the resources of his newspaper and the Aero Club, behind the undertaking, to ensure it would be seen as Norwegian.

Pressing ahead, Amundsen wired Ellsworth in the U.S., asking if he would confirm his interest in the airship idea and raise his pledge to $120,000. Ellsworth replied that he would, but only if he was to be credited as a leader of the expedition.

Amundsen then traveled to Rome where he met with Mussolini and, after negotiating the details, signed a contract. The Italian government agreed to sell the dirigible airship *N1* to the expedition for $75,000 for the flight from Spitsbergen to Alaska, via the North Pole and, at the completion of the flight, would buy it back for $46,000 if it was still in good condition. It was a better deal than Amundsen had expected. Mussolini was being suspiciously generous.

With the airship secured, negotiations shifted to the duties and composition of the crew. Amundsen and his Norwegian backer, Thommessen, wanted to include as many Norwegians as possible, to satisfy national pride. For the same reason, Mussolini wanted lots of Italians. Additionally, Nobile, as the builder of the airship and the person best qualified to fly it, believed he should be airship commander.

While the discussions became bogged down in details, the problem arose as to what to do with Ellsworth who, thus far, had only demonstrated an ability to sign the check. Mindful that the "Norwegian expedition" had to assign a prominent role to the American, Thommessen announced in his newspaper that Ellsworth would share the responsibility of navigating the flight with Leif Dietrichson. Unfortunately, that didn't please Dietrichson, who immediately declared he would have none of it. He had been Ellsworth's pilot in the Dornier Wal and, based on that experience, believed the American would struggle to navigate his way through a hotel lobby. Dietrichson flatly refused to navigate if Ellsworth was going to take even partial credit. Amundsen was forced to promptly sack his old friend. It was easier to replace the navigator than the sponsor. Henceforth Ellsworth was listed as navigator, but everyone understood the role would need to be discreetly delegated to someone competent.

As the negotiations regarding crew members and roles continued, Thommessen cabled Ellsworth, asking him to forward the money. Ellsworth cabled back that he would only release it after it was announced in both the Norwegian and the American press that the expedition would be known as the "Amundsen-Ellsworth Trans-Polar Flight." Thommessen reassured him that it would be, made the announcement, and waited for the money to arrive. But the title upset Mussolini, who threatened to withdraw his generous offer to buy back the airship unless Nobile's name was also included. By that time, Thommessen, who was responsible for building the airship hangar at Kings Bay, had committed a sizeable amount of his personal fortune. He could not afford to have the Italians renege on their offer to buy back the airship, so he lengthened the title to

"Amundsen-Ellsworth-Nobile Trans-Polar Flight." That promptly upset Amundsen and Ellsworth, who could not understand why Nobile's name had to be included at all.

Nobile, meanwhile, emboldened by his elevation from obscure airship designer to national hero, demanded assurance that as commander of the airship he had the final say during the flight. If, for example, when they reached the North Pole, he felt it unwise to continue to Alaska, he expected the right to order the airship back to Kings Bay. To ensure that his authority went unchallenged he proposed that the entire crew, including the Norwegians, swear a solemn oath of loyalty to him. The Italian government sent a message to Thommessen saying that unless that request was met the Italians would withdraw from the venture altogether. Poor Thommessen, caught in the middle again, smoothed that situation out as well with a deftly managed compromise. He explained to Nobile that he would be commander and, as recognized by international law, had ultimate say in the control of the airship. In matters not related directly to flying, Ellsworth and Amundsen would be in charge. In reality, no one really knew who was in charge.

Other finer details were negotiated and contractually stipulated as well, such as the order in which the national flags were to be dropped at the North Pole (eventually agreed to be Norway first, America second, and Italy third), along with who had the right to say what to the press.

While Nobile was preparing the airship in Italy, and its name was officially changed to *Norge* (Norway), Amundsen traveled to the U.S. to deliver a series of lectures on the expedition. One of the lectures was attended by Richard Byrd, who was secretly preparing to upstage the forthcoming flight.

Richard Evelyn Byrd was born into a wealthy and influential Virginia family on October 26, 1888. He was raised carrying the high expectations of an ambitious mother until his poor academic record convinced her that young Dickie would not be following his alcoholic father and elder brother into politics. Disappointed, Byrd's mother packed him off to the U.S. Navy, where his handsome features and family influence, initially at least, saw him promoted quickly. But good looks and name could only get Byrd so far and, by the end of World War I, his career had reached a plateau and he was regularly passed over for promotion. Realizing his future options were limited, he left the full-time Navy to become a reservist, so that he could pursue private interests, yet still wear the uniform and maintain some Navy involvement. Byrd identified a future in aviation. He knew pioneering flights bought fame and that where fame went, fortune often followed. In 1924, like Amundsen, he hit upon the idea of making the first flight to the North Pole. He convinced the Navy to loan him three seaplanes, then accompanied an expedition to Greenland where he constantly argued with his leader and, after making short exploratory flights, returned to the U.S. determined that the next time he went north he would be in command, rather than a subordinate.

Byrd convinced the Navy to give him a ship, then recruited a crew of mostly volunteers and received sponsorship from leading businessmen. While he was putting the expedition together, he became aware that Ellsworth and Amundsen were also planning a flight to the North Pole, but using Nobile's airship, rather than an airplane. So as not to appear to be a rival, Byrd kept his intentions secret and instead announced that he planned to explore the unknown area of the Arctic between Svalbard and Greenland looking for Robert Peary's "Crocker Land." He knew the best departure point from which to fly to the Pole was the Norwegian settlement at Kings Bay, Spitsbergen, and realized that he needed to be there at the same time as Amundsen's and Ellsworth's expedition.

So when Amundsen was in New York to speak about the upcoming airship flight, Byrd seized the opportunity to introduce himself. Ellsworth, who was privy to the conversation recalled:

> . . . Byrd confided in us his plan to continue the search for the evanescent Crocker Land the following spring as an independent explorer, using airplanes. The Amundsen-Ellsworth airship expedition had been announced, so Byrd knew we would be at Spitsbergen. He asked us if we had any objection to his using Kings Bay at the same time, as a preliminary base from which to fly to the north coast of Greenland, where he planned to set up the permanent base for his search.

Said Amundsen heartily: "We will welcome you with open arms."[1]

At the conclusion of Amundsen's lecture tour, he and Ellsworth sailed to Norway and subsequently to Kings Bay, where they expected to rendezvous with Nobile, who would fly the airship from Rome. On April 28, 1926, while they were waiting, Byrd turned up, as promised, with a fully equipped expedition and a Fokker Trimotor plane fitted with skis. Since their meeting in New York, Byrd's true intentions had become public knowledge. Smelling another race (particularly one involving Amundsen) newspapers had begun loudly promoting the "Air Race to the North Pole." Who would reach it first: Amundsen or Byrd?

For Byrd, it was a race he could ill afford to lose. To fund his large expedition he had borrowed money and signed agreements with publishers and newsreel companies. If he reached the North Pole first he would make a profit. Should he come second to Amundsen and Ellsworth, he would be left in debt.

As his ship neared Kings Bay, Byrd learned that Amundsen's arms were not as open as he had suggested in New York. There was only space for one ship at the Kings Bay jetty and that was occupied by Amundsen and Ellsworth's ship *Heimdal*. Byrd radioed for it to be moved temporarily so he could dock and unload his plane. The *Heimdal*'s captain replied that it was not possible. Byrd came ashore in a lifeboat to confront Amundsen, who explained they were waiting for the *Norge* to arrive from Italy, via Leningrad (now St. Petersburg), and that the *Heimdal* needed to remain where it was. If the airship had difficulties en route the *Heimdal* might be needed to go to its assistance. The tense exchange was watched by a young Norwegian pilot, Bernt Balchen, who recorded the reactions of Ellsworth:

> Lincoln Ellsworth edges unobtrusively in from the kitchen. He and Amundsen had met Byrd in New York three months earlier, and they shake hands briefly. I am curious to see these fellow countrymen greet each other. They are courteous, of course, but there is no real warmth in their greeting, and a couple of times, glancing at Ellsworth as he slips into the background, I detect a

trace of annoyance in his face, as though he is piqued at the fact that he is no longer the only American explorer in Kings Bay.[2]

Byrd stormed back to his ship, furious that Amundsen would not allow him to unload his plane until after the *Norge* had arrived and, presumably, departed for the Pole. With his future riding on getting to the North Pole first, Byrd implemented a risky strategy. His crew lashed lifeboats together and, first the fuselage, then the wing, were carefully floated ashore on the makeshift raft. While Amundsen watched in dismay, Byrd had his plane assembled and ready for a test flight within twenty-four hours. And there was still no sign of Nobile.

Needing a runway for the big plane, Byrd's entire crew pitched in to dig out and flatten the snow-covered ground. A suitable runway was prepared within forty-eight hours, but on Byrd's first attempt to test his plane the metal skis fitted to the Fokker twisted. By that time, the young Norwegian, Bernt Balchen, had become friendly with Byrd's pilot, Floyd Bennett. Himself a ski champion, Balchen explained to Bennett that metal skis would not slide easily on an icy surface. What the Americans needed, Balchen continued, were wooden skis coated in tar. Not surprisingly, Amundsen reprimanded the naïve Balchen for his unbidden assistance, but nevertheless Byrd's crew hurriedly fashioned new skis for the Fokker. While they were doing so, Nobile, with his crew of Italians and Norwegians, arrived in the airship.

The relationship between Amundsen and Nobile was already strained as a result of the disputes over titles, rights, and the makeup of the crew. But after Amundsen learned of the events on the flight to Kings Bay, it came perilously close to breaking irrevocably. For the trip north, the Norwegian crew had wanted to wear warm polar clothing, but Nobile forbade it, saying weight had to be reduced. The Norwegians had therefore boarded the airship in lightweight street clothes, only to be greeted by the Italians clad in furs, mitts, and boots. The Italians enjoyed their flight to Kings Bay, while the Norwegians shivered through the intense cold. Amundsen interpreted it as a personal slight, writing later, "[Nobile's] arrogance and egotism and selfishness were unparalleled in my experience."[3]

Once on the ground at Kings Bay, Nobile informed the enraged Amundsen that he needed two days to repair a motor before the *Norge* would be ready for the Arctic flight.

Meanwhile, on May 8, Byrd had replaced his skis and was ready for his flight to the North Pole. When he attempted to take off, however, his new skis became bogged in the slush. Again, pilot Floyd Bennett turned to his new friend Balchen, who explained that Byrd needed to take off after midnight, when the snow was frozen hard, instead of during the day when it was soft. That night, at 12:37 A.M., Byrd and Bennett got airborne. They flew north with a full load of fuel and returned fifteen and a half hours later. Byrd emerged from the plane and announced he had reached the North Pole. He had, he claimed, circled the Pole for thirteen minutes and taken repeated sextant readings to prove conclusively he had made it. The air race to the North Pole was over. Byrd had won.

Amundsen and Ellsworth felt cheated. They had conceived their expedition first and selflessly made their plans public, whereas Byrd had misled everyone by stating that he wasn't flying to the Pole. He had extracted a promise from Amundsen to use the Norwegian facilities at Kings Bay, then worked around the clock to get airborne while he watched Amundsen and Ellsworth wait for Nobile to repair the *Norge*. Finally, Byrd had flown to the North Pole and back in a suspiciously short time—about an hour less than expected, given the flying performance of his airplane.* But Amundsen and Ellsworth could do nothing but congratulate their victorious rival.

Two days after Byrd returned from his Pole flight the *Norge* was ready. Nobile had replaced a broken crankshaft in one of the motors and repaired torn fabric on the rudder. He told Amundsen and Ellsworth their flight could take place as soon as the weather was suitable. But having lost the race, Amundsen now felt it was more important to let Nobile know who was in charge than it was to reach the North Pole.

On the morning of May 11, the weather was clear. Nobile had been awake all night overseeing the preparation of the airship and understood

---

* Byrd's flight notebook was discovered in 1997. Various experts have studied it, and the consensus is that Byrd flew well short of the North Pole, possibly by as much as 150 miles.

that it was crucial to get airborne while the temperature was cooler, so the envelope could be filled with more gas. With everything prepared by 5:00 A.M., Nobile sent word for Amundsen to quickly get Ellsworth and the Norwegians on board. Word came back that the Norwegians had not finished their breakfast. The Italians could wait. Amundsen and Ellsworth finally emerged after 9:00 A.M., having enjoyed a good night's sleep and a hearty breakfast, to lead the Norwegians on board. Bernt Balchen, who had advised Byrd on the use of skis for his airplane, was not among the Norwegian crew. He had been informed by Amundsen he could wait at Kings Bay.

The flight finally lifted off, much later than Nobile had wanted, at 9:50 A.M.

Nobile guided the airship to the North Pole, where it arrived safely at 1:30 A.M. on May 12. The national flags were dropped in the pre-negotiated order, but again Amundsen and Ellsworth received a surprise. Obeying Nobile's instruction to save weight, they both dropped flags the size of pocket handkerchiefs. They were then astonished to see the Italians produce an armful of flags, the largest of which was the size of a tablecloth, then ceremoniously throw them out a window.

For Ellsworth, finally reaching the Pole seemed an empty gesture. In his diary he recorded only the briefest details:

> The North Pole 90° 1:28 A.M. GMT. Fog cleared and sun came out. Came down to 130 metres & with hats off dropped our flags. Both the Norwegian and American struck landing. We circle once around.[4]

Aboard the *Norge* there was a noisy partisan celebration. The Italians spoke Italian and slapped each other on the back. The Norwegians congratulated each other in Norwegian. Amundsen shook hands quietly with Oscar Wisting, who had stood with him at the South Pole fifteen years earlier. They were the only two men who had been to the top and bottom of the world. Ellsworth was unable to share the moment with anyone.

The *Norge* headed past the Pole into the unexplored region of the Arctic, where experts prophesized undiscovered land. But aboard the *Norge* nothing was sighted because continual fog made observation difficult. What lay below the airship remained unknown. After an epic 72-hour, 3,000-mile flight, during which Nobile worked tirelessly to keep the *Norge* aloft and on course, they landed at the small settlement of Teller, Alaska. Safely on the ground, Amundsen and Ellsworth promptly headed for the nearby city of Nome, where they could find a comfortable hotel. Nobile and the rest of the crew were left to dismantle the airship and pack everything for freighting back to Italy. After three weeks at Nome, a ship arrived to take the whole expedition to Seattle, Washington.

4

JUST A PASSENGER

MAY 1926–JUNE 1928

I f Ellsworth thought he was sailing south to a hero's welcome, he was in for a rude surprise. He soon found himself in the middle of a bitter dispute and was forced to offer humiliating apologies. Before leaving Rome, Nobile had been promoted to the rank of general in the Italian air force and, ignoring his own orders to keep unnecessary clothing to a minimum, he and the other Italians had hidden air force uniforms aboard the *Norge*. Arriving in Seattle, General Nobile and his subordinates wore their ostentatious uniforms and, at every opportunity, posed for photographs giving the fascist salute—a raised clenched fist.

Soon after, the animosity between Amundsen and Nobile became public when Nobile wrote for an American newspaper, lauding the Italian technology and crew, but failing to make clear that Amundsen and Ellsworth were expedition leaders. Amundsen was no longer on speaking terms with Nobile, so he turned to Rolf Thommessen, demanding he instruct the Italian not to write any more articles or sign any press releases, as he was not a leader of the expedition and, more important, those articles and press releases would diminish the value of the book Amundsen and

Ellsworth were coauthoring. Thommessen pointed out that the official title of the expedition was "Amundsen-Ellsworth-Nobile Trans-Polar Flight." Amundsen responded to this impertinence by resigning from the Aero Club of Norway in a huff.

Rather than curtailing his boasting in the press, Nobile increased it. New York's Italian-American newspaper *Progresso Italo-Americano* wrote glowingly about the Italian achievement and Nobile's role. Other accounts highlighted Nobile as commander of the expedition and the person most responsible for its success. Amundsen countered these claims by writing that Nobile, "now pretends to be the presiding genius of the expedition,"[1] and that his statements were part of a "mass misrepresentation of the facts which has been poured forth by Italian propaganda."[2] But the Italian bragging was unrelenting, so Amundsen started attacking Thommessen for not ensuring the world knew it was a Norwegian achievement.

Thommessen needed to sell the *Norge* back to the Italians to recoup some of his expenses, and the Italians had informed him they would not honor their agreement unless they received what they considered their rightful share of the glory. Mussolini personally cautioned Thommessen, saying that if he wanted the money, he had to get Amundsen to shut up. Hopeful of calming the situation, Thommessen appealed to Ellsworth to act as a mediator between Nobile and Amundsen. Ellsworth invited the two men to his New York apartment, but the meeting descended into a shouting match. Amundsen would recall:

> Nobile thereupon burst into a tirade which revealed fully the schemes and ambitions which had been boiling in his mind from his first connection with the expedition. This emotional oration disclosed that he had from the very beginning harbored "illusions of greatness." His vanity, feeding upon his ambition, had built up in his own mind an idea of his importance in the matter, which bore no relation either to what he had been told by us when we employed him or to the plain facts of his written contract. In his mind's eye he had seen himself throughout as a great explorer, who had been seized with a vision in which he had invented the idea of a flight across the Arctic Ocean, who

had then designed the ship in which the flight was to be undertaken, who had then joined forces (for reasons unexplained) with two relatively unimportant persons named Ellsworth and Amundsen, and finally flown triumphantly across the North Pole with the eyes of the world upon his daring exploit.[3]

Evidently, there would be no patching things up between Amundsen and Nobile. Worse, by stepping between them, Ellsworth found himself in the crossfire. Mussolini accused Ellsworth of stirring up trouble by insisting that Nobile was not a leader of the expedition, when clearly its official title verified that he was.* Thommessen, still needing to indulge the Italians, also attacked Ellsworth, describing him as bitter and incapable of navigating or being able to take meteorological observations. According to Thommessen, Ellsworth was not only unnecessary, but he got in the way. Nobile joined in, criticizing Ellsworth in the *New York Times*:

> As captain of the airship every person on board depended on me during the flight. Riiser-Larsen, second-in-command of the airship, was appointed navigator by me. All preparations for the flight were made under my initiative and direction, and for this I worked, with the other Italians, about nine months, while Mr. Ellsworth was in America without knowing or asking anything about the expedition.
>
> I tried always to be nice to Mr. Ellsworth, but now I cannot help but tell what is known by everybody, that Mr. Ellsworth on our expedition was just a passenger whom I took on board at Spitsbergen and left at Teller.[4]

It all hit Ellsworth hard. After continuing criticism in the press he was humiliated into issuing a public apology to the Italian people. Shattered and depressed he sought escape with another pilgrimage to the Grand

---

* Ellsworth and Amundsen collaborated on the official book of the expedition, *First Crossing of the Polar Sea*, the rights of which had already been sold. Nowhere in the book is the official title of the expedition mentioned.

Canyon and begged Amundsen to come with him. "Will never forgive you if you don't spend the month of November [1926] at Grand Canyon," Ellsworth cabled Amundsen. "Paying all expenses."[5] But Amundsen was fully occupied writing the book he hoped would set the record straight, and declined Ellsworth's offer.

Neither was Ellsworth having much luck getting the recognition he craved from the American people. Six weeks before he had returned to New York, Richard Byrd had arrived to a hero's welcome. Byrd received a ticker tape parade down Broadway, before he and pilot Floyd Bennett were rushed by special train to the White House, where President Calvin Coolidge presented them both with the nation's highest civilian award: the Congressional Medal of Honor. By the time Ellsworth had reached New York, the publicity value of polar aviation was exhausted. Few people were interested in the man who came in second, and Ellsworth was forced to write letters, or get friends to lobby Congress to honor him. Vice President Charles Dawes (who was Ellsworth's father's cousin) supported the idea, but the legislators were unmoved. The flight of the *Norge*, most of them argued, was predominantly an Italian-Norwegian affair.

In the meantime, everyone had received medals for the *Norge* flight except Ellsworth. The Norwegian government honored the Norwegians. The Italian Government struck special medals for the Italians, and even Nobile's dog, Titina, which he had taken on the flight, received a medal. But there was nothing for Ellsworth.

Ellsworth's answer was to award medals to himself. He formed what he called the Polar Legion, and stipulated that membership was only open to someone who had led an expedition to either geographic pole. Ellsworth invited Amundsen and Byrd to a dinner in New York and inducted them into the Polar Legion. Robert Scott and Robert E. Peary were inducted posthumously and medals sent to their widows. Nobile was conspicuously absent. Next, Ellsworth had special *Norge* medals struck. Gold ones for Amundsen and himself as leaders of the expedition, bronze ones for the crew. He sent a bronze medal to Nobile who, insulted at being relegated to a crew member, promptly sent it back.

Following the establishment of the Polar Legion, Ellsworth retreated into his private world. He had invested in two polar expeditions. The first had failed to reach the North Pole, and his father had died, believing his son was dead. The second had ended in bitterness, and Ellsworth was left disgraced and being described as a passenger. Disappointed that his efforts to gain public adulation had left him humiliated, he returned to the Grand Canyon, where he picked up fossils and camped under the stars. He wrote that he constantly returned to the Grand Canyon because:

> . . . like the sojourners to Mecca, I come from afar to worship
> and meditate at this Shrine of Nature, and in its silent depths
> to find peace and relaxation from the din and strife and super-
> ficiality of modern civilization.[6]

A year after the flight of the *Norge*, Amundsen released his autobiography, *My Life as an Explorer* and "din and strife and superficiality" found Ellsworth, and forced him, once more, into the public eye.

Half of Amundsen's new book was a recap of his adventures in the Arctic and Antarctic. The other half was an attack, not only on Nobile but, in places, on the Italian people. According to Amundsen, Nobile was incompetent, a liar, and a hysteric, while Italians, because of their "Latin temperament" were not suited to polar exploration. Amundsen wrote it was his duty to inform:

> . . . this strutting dreamer, this epauletted Italian, who . . .
> before had no more thought of Arctic exploration than he had
> of superseding Mussolini as Chief of State . . . [of the] piti-
> able spectacle he would have presented on the polar ice if the
> *Norge* had by chance been forced down, and how preposterous
> would have been his claims to effective leadership under those
> conditions.[7]

Amundsen even managed to infer that Catholic priests had conspired with Nobile to rob Ellsworth and Amundsen of their rightful recognition.

The criticism was so harsh, personal, and public that Mussolini, and even King Victor Emmanuel of Italy, encouraged Nobile to answer it. Nobile wrote more articles, contradicting Amundsen's claims, then personally wrote to Ellsworth, asking him to let the world know the truth. Ellsworth, still hoping to avoid the ongoing controversy, responded with a vague reply, denying there was any animosity, then wrote privately to Amundsen, reassuring him that Nobile would never come between them, and adding, "I am so sorry you had to return home for I miss you, as I always do, when you are away. I guess I will never have two such wonderful years again [as] we had together."[8]

After writing his articles, which had the effect of throwing more fuel onto a fire, Nobile felt honor-bound to answer criticism with deeds. He would, he announced, return to the Arctic to make an all-Italian airship flight to the North Pole.

Amundsen, having vented his anger and frustration, withdrew from public life, while Ellsworth rambled in the Grand Canyon, hoping his years as a polar explorer would soon pass from public memory.

Nobile completed his new airship, which he named *Italia*, and with an all-Italian crew returned to the Arctic. After short exploratory flights, he left Kings Bay and reached the North Pole on May 25, 1928, but the *Italia* crashed on the return flight. Seven men were killed, while nine, including Nobile, were stranded on the ice north of Svalbard. Nobile's unsuitability as a polar explorer, as predicted by Amundsen, immediately became apparent as he dithered, barked irrational orders, became depressed, and told the surviving men to do whatever they wanted. Three tried to walk to land (one died and two were eventually rescued), while the remaining men set up a makeshift camp and waited for the Italian government to rescue them. That was another mistake.

Mussolini was embarrassed by Nobile's failure and wanted the men stranded on the ice to stay there. Repeated radio signals from the survivors to the Italian support ship at Kings Bay were ignored, but the men on the ice stubbornly refused to die. They continued to send out their distress signals from a radio with fading batteries until, finally, an amateur radio operator in Russia picked up their faint signal and relayed the news to the world—members of the *Italia* crew were alive on the ice somewhere north of Svalbard.

Dragged out of retirement by the disaster in the Arctic, Amundsen wired Ellsworth asking him to come to Norway to help with the search. "Fifty thousand dollars needed relief expedition. How much will you contribute? When can you come?"[9]

But the crash of the *Italia* had left Ellsworth feeling even less appreciated. Four days after the news of the crash, while the fate of the crew was still unknown, the United States Congress voted to award a gold medal to Nobile. Ellsworth could not understand it. Two years after the successful flight of the *Norge*, his own country had still not honored him, but within days of Nobile disappearing, Congress had rushed through a medal for the Italian. The depressed Ellsworth never responded to Amundsen's plea for support.

The Italian government, meanwhile, announced there was no need for any assistance, because Italians would rescue Nobile. Despite the government assurances no help was needed, a frenzy of aviators, explorers, and adventurers rushed to Kings Bay to join the search. Without Ellsworth's money, Amundsen had difficulty finding anyone to give him a plane. Thommessen was still angry with him, so no planes were forthcoming from the Aero Club of Norway. And the Italians would not give him a plane because the last thing Mussolini wanted was Amundsen rescuing Nobile.

Finally, the democratic French, eager to upstage the fascist Italians, lent Amundsen a plane and a French crew. Amundsen (along with Leif Dietrichson, whom Amundsen had reluctantly fired from the *Norge* after he refused to share navigation duties with Ellsworth), plus two French pilots, left Tromsø, Norway, on June 18, and flew toward Spitsbergen. The plane and the crew disappeared.*

Meanwhile, one pilot did eventually manage to reach the stranded *Italia* crew, but he only had space to fly one person back to Kings Bay. Foolishly, Nobile climbed aboard and was rescued first, gifting Mussolini the ammunition he needed to discredit him. The government, which Nobile had fanatically supported, turned on him. Nobile was arrested and accused of incompetence, cowardice, and deserting his crew. Eventually, a Russian icebreaker rescued the remaining trapped men.

---

*   Wreckage from the plane later washed up on the coast of Norway. Amundsen and the crew of the plane have never been found.

"With Amundsen passed the heroic age of polar exploration,"[10] Ellsworth wrote, unknowingly coining the term that today distinguishes the era of Scott, Shackleton, and Amundsen. With Amundsen too passed Ellsworth's "partner in polar exploration" and a friend he admired so much he followed him into the unknown.

5

NO OTHER WORLDS TO CONQUER

JUNE 1928–NOVEMBER 1929

Following the death of Amundsen, Ellsworth wrote that his brief foray into polar exploration was over.

> The voyage of the *Norge* was a far cry from my youthful vision of polar exploration—the painfully established bases, the bitter journeys with sleds and dogs, the heroic battles against the elements. The *Norge* and its crew were but a machine in which the explorer could sit at ease and watch unroll the panorama of the unknown . . . With the completion of the *Norge* flight, I thought that my days in the polar regions were over . . . There seemed to be no other worlds to conquer.[1]

But commitment was such a challenge for Ellsworth he could not even commit to giving up. He remained restless and unsatisfied. He toyed with more ideas and never followed through. Nobile had criticized him for being unable to navigate, so Ellsworth decided to take lessons. His former rival,

Richard Byrd, was acknowledged as the most accomplished aerial navigator of the time (and was co-inventor of the bubble sextant), so Ellsworth wrote to Byrd asking to be taught aerial navigation. He even suggested that he and Byrd mount a joint expedition to fly over the unknown areas of the Arctic, looking for land. Byrd however already had plans and explained that he was about to leave on an expedition to Antarctica.

Next, Ellsworth approached Dr. Gilbert H. Grosvenor, president of the National Geographic Society, explaining he would put up $85,000 for a flight from Greenland to Alaska to settle the Crocker Land question once and for all. He was careful to explain to Grosvenor he wanted no part in organizing the expedition—he expected the society to do that. But if Grosvenor found an expedition ship, a plane, a pilot, and crew then Ellsworth would consider coming on board, just before the expedition sailed, to assume command and be flown across the Arctic. Not surprisingly, Grosvenor declined.

With no one willing to organize an Arctic expedition for which he could take credit, Ellsworth told friends he intended to live in Africa where he would collect artifacts for the American Museum of Natural History.

Alarmed at the increasingly despondent tone of Ellsworth's correspondence, his business advisor, Harold Clark, became concerned about his client's state of mind. Clark had helped manage Ellsworth Sr.'s business empire and, for many years, was privy to the strained relationship between father and son. He understood the importance of finding things to interest Ellsworth to draw him out of his dark moods. Desperate to find such an interest, Clark contacted Isaiah Bowman, director of the American Geographical Society, who was aware that Ellsworth was looking to sponsor an expedition he could "lead." The problem was finding something suitable. Bowman wrote to Ellsworth, suggesting he join an expedition to the Patagonian Andes, but Ellsworth never responded. Bowman followed up by writing, "if we are to help you, we must have communication with you."[2]

Clark continued to push Bowman for suggestions, so Bowman sent Ellsworth maps of Antarctica, suggesting he could explore some of its unknown coasts, but Ellsworth asked who would organize the expeditions on his behalf. To that, Bowman had no answer. Bowman wrote to Clark after his suggestions had been rejected:

I want to stay in touch with Lincoln for I feel that he needs friendship of disinterested men who can advise him as to his best interest. He has a great stock of energy that should be turned to good account. Moreover, I find him a likeable character.[3]

While Ellsworth suffered another period of despair, Vice President Dawes proposed to the Smithsonian Institution that both Ellsworth and Byrd be awarded the Langley Medal, which the institution bestowed for outstanding contributions to the science of aeronautics. After reviewing the two nominees, the Smithsonian rejected the suggestion that the medal be awarded to Ellsworth. It did, however, award it to Byrd.

Since his dubious flight to the North Pole, upstaging the *Norge*, Byrd had been busy. In 1927, he attempted to be the first person to fly nonstop across the Atlantic Ocean. When he was narrowly beaten by Charles Lindbergh, he sought another aviation "first." Diminishing opportunities in the northern hemisphere forced Byrd's gaze south and he announced he would fly across Antarctica, via the South Pole. Such a flight would achieve many firsts. Byrd would be the first to fly in the southern continent, the first to cross it, and the first to fly to the South Pole. Polar history books would bulge with the name Byrd.

Shortly after he began planning his new expedition, Byrd realized that setting up bases on both sides of the continent would be difficult and expensive, while no plane was capable of flying across Antarctica and back without refueling. He dropped the idea of the trans-Antarctic flight and, instead, focused simply on a flight to the South Pole and back. He could, he calculated, follow the route Roald Amundsen had used in 1911–12. Byrd would take expedition ships, with airplanes, to the Bay of Whales in the Ross Ice Shelf. Then, like Amundsen, he would unload his men, equipment, and airplanes, erect a base, and wait out the winter. When the sun returned in the spring, he would fly to the South Pole and back, then pack up and return triumphantly to the United States as the first man to fly to both Poles.

Byrd's expedition left for Antarctica in September 1928. By the end of the year, while Harold Clark and others were trying to shake Ellsworth out of his lethargy, Byrd's base on the Ross Ice Shelf was under construction.

◆

At the beginning of 1929, a second death dealt Ellsworth a severe personal blow and heightened the concern of his friends for his emotional well-being. On February 22, Ellsworth's sister Clare died of pneumonia. Ellsworth considered Clare "the staunchest friend I had in the world."[4] She had been his one companion throughout a desperately lonely childhood. Furthermore, she had stood up to their father when Ellsworth had wanted to join Amundsen in 1925. Following Clare's death, people close to Ellsworth feared he might commit suicide. Fairfield Osborn, president of the American Museum of Natural History, wrote to Harold Clark expressing his concerns and saying, "It seems more important than ever that [Lincoln] should be able to have some definite scientific occupation in addition to his business affairs."[5] But the problem, as always, was to find an expedition that someone else would plan and organize, yet allow Ellsworth to assume the role of leader.

A few months after the death of his sister, while his friends and business associates tried to find a solution, Ellsworth decided to inspect the Swiss castle he had inherited from his father.

Lenzburg Castle evolved from fortifications built atop a hill in the 11th century. The German monarch Friedrich Barbarossa owned it briefly in the 12th century. It expanded and changed hands many times until 1911, when James W. Ellsworth came calling. Lincoln's father had heard there was a table in the castle dating from the period of Barbarossa and he wanted to buy it. The owner wouldn't separate the table from the castle in which it had sat for eight hundred years, so Ellsworth Sr. bought the castle and used it as a repository for the European art he collected.

Lincoln had owned Lenzburg Castle for four years before he decided to pay his first visit in June 1929. In typical Ellsworth fashion he didn't announce his impending arrival. He wandered the streets of Lenzburg alone, before shuffling up the hill to the castle's gate and ringing the bell. When one of the staff answered he said simply, "I'm Mr. Ellsworth."[6]

In his gloomy castle, the gloomier Ellsworth pondered his future. Everyone he cared for—everyone whose respect he had hoped to attract—was dead. What was left for him to do? What great thing could he accomplish that would finally lift him from mediocrity to the lofty heights of greatness and have him stand shoulder to shoulder in the history books with Amundsen, Scott, and Peary? More important, who could he find to organize the logistics of such an expedition, and still let him take all the credit? To Ellsworth, the future appeared hopeless. "I lost my father and I lost Amundsen—two men who looked at things with the same eyes as mine—so I guess I shall have to travel it mostly alone through the rest of my life,"[7] he confided to Harold Clark, a week after arriving at Lenzburg.

But in June 1929, Isaiah Bowman had a new proposition. He had just learned that Australian explorer Sir Hubert Wilkins, was recently back from Antarctica, and trying to mount an expedition to travel in a submarine under the Arctic ice to the North Pole. Wilkins was not only seeking sponsors, but people to travel with him. Perhaps this, Bowman informed Clark, might appeal to Ellsworth. Clark was only too pleased to relay the suggestion to Ellsworth, who agreed to meet Wilkins, should he care to come to Switzerland.

George Hubert Wilkins was born on October 31, 1888, in a remote farming community in South Australia. During childhood, he observed his strict Methodist parents put their faith in God and prayer to bring much-needed rain to their crops. Their faith was not rewarded and, in 1903, after a particularly devastating drought, his aging parents surrendered their farm and took the teenage Wilkins to Adelaide to learn a trade. Wilkins studied electrical engineering before becoming interested in cinematography. In 1911, he carried his movie camera to England, where he was employed filming newsreels for Gaumont. In 1912, when war again broke out in the Balkans, Gaumont despatched Wilkins to Constantinople (now Istanbul) to film the conflict from the Turkish side. Wilkins later described his first experience of war, when he rode with a cavalry charge into a Turkish village:

> We went down that slope like rolling thunder, every one of us mad with exultation. We didn't know what we were charging into. We didn't care. All we wanted was to kill. We charged into the rabble of Turks—foot soldiers and peasants. The Turkish

cavalry charged into their own people and cut them down. Cut them to pieces—men, women, and children. The very horses were screaming with blood lust. It was all I could do to keep from pulling my revolver and killing everything in sight. The madness of that charge got all of us.[8]

Wilkins had witnessed war and was horrified by it, but he was also horrified by something he had seen within himself: a lust to kill when swept up in the madness and rush of a mob. It both frightened and fascinated him. How could so-called civilized men hack women and children to death? How could he, an educated, caring person with a strong Christian upbringing, descend so easily to barbarism? If civilization was so fragile—so easily trampled under boot and hoof—what hope was there for Man's future?

In the midst of that self-examination, Wilkins turned to the German philosopher, Friedrich Nietzsche who, in *Thus Spake Zarathustra*, suggested that Man was continuing to evolve intellectually and would eventually become Übermensch or "supermen." Having declared that God was dead, or at least that Man's need for gods was no longer necessary, Nietzsche had proposed that people could leave superstition behind and, through science, continue the process of mental evolution that began millions of years ago, to reach a new state of understanding and enlightenment. The next step in that journey of human self-discovery was increased scientific understanding. As he pondered the future of human civilization, the Nietzsche-reading Wilkins began to envision his purpose in life.

In the decade following his experience in the Balkan War, Wilkins spent three years in the Arctic, two years at the Western Front in World War I, joined an expedition to Antarctica in 1920, and again in 1921, then lived with indigenous Australians for two years in northern Australia. The experiences helped him further define his role in the ongoing progress of civilization. If, Wilkins concluded, manned stations could be established in the Arctic and the Antarctic, scientists would be able to better understand and forecast the weather. That would allow farmers and primary producers to plan ahead, avoid droughts, and exploit times of plenty. By producing more food, the world's population would be relieved of the need to fight for survival, wars could be avoided and therefore:

. . . if we are able to establish freedom from anxiety as to future physical welfare . . . I am sure that we would soon experience a more rapid cultural and spiritual development and take steps toward a better civilization.[9]

By the beginning of 1926, Wilkins's efforts to improve civilization had turned to the Arctic and he was committed to finding land close to the North Pole suitable for his proposed weather stations. At the same time the *Norge* was flying from Kings Bay to Teller, with Ellsworth, Amundsen, and Nobile on board, Wilkins managed to make short flights out over the Arctic ice, from Barrow, Alaska. The following year, Wilkins and pilot Carl "Ben" Eielson flew 150 miles north from Barrow and landed on the ice. They took depth soundings and were astonished to discover the water beneath the ice was 18,000 feet deep. That would mean the Arctic was a deep ocean and that islands suitable for weather stations were unlikely to exist, at least in that area.

Wilkins returned to the Arctic in early 1928. On April 15 (while Nobile was preparing his new airship, *Italia*, at Kings Bay), Wilkins and Eielson took off from Barrow in their tiny Lockheed Vega single-engine plane and flew nonstop for twenty hours to land on a small island near Spitsbergen. They discovered no new land.

Unlike Ellsworth, Wilkins had no trouble being honored for his flight across the Arctic. In June 1928, he was knighted by George V of England and chose to be known as Sir Hubert, rather than Sir George. But even with the knighthood, and accolades that came from around the world, Wilkins remained focused on his mission to raise humanity to a higher state of civilization by establishing weather stations in the polar regions. Having discovered the area surrounding the North Pole was a deep ocean, he wrote:

This brought me to the conclusion that we would eventually have to use an island of our own construction, a mobile one in the form of a submarine, in order to set up an Arctic floating station. It would be useless to fly a party out to the spot and land [scientists] on the ice . . . [because] we know the ice is continually drifting. No base on the ice would remain stationary long enough to be of service in our meteorological plan.

But since water is water, no matter where it is, a submarine could operate in water under the Arctic ice just as well as under water in the Atlantic. And so it could be used to reach the spot to be occupied by the scientists.[10]

Wilkins declared his next goal was to explore the Arctic by submarine.

Almost immediately, he was presented with an opportunity to raise the money for an Arctic submarine expedition. Byrd (in mid-1928) was preparing to leave for Antarctica so he could fly to the South Pole. Importantly, Byrd was sponsored by the *New York Times*, which was paying for exclusive reports from the expedition.

Publisher William Randolph Hearst, who owned the rival *New York Journal*, was looking for someone to hurry down to Antarctica and fly to the South Pole before Byrd. Wilkins had flown across the top of the world and landed in the middle of a newspaper war. A Hearst representative approached the now-famous Australian and explained that if he could fly to the South Pole before Byrd, then Hearst would pay $50,000. Naturally all the publicity rights would go to Hearst's papers.

Wilkins quickly formulated a plan. He and pilot Ben Eielson would hitch a ride south with the whalers, who traveled to Antarctica each summer. The whalers could take them to Deception Island, which was on the opposite side of Antarctica from Byrd's proposed base on the Ross Ice Shelf. From Deception Island, Wilkins and Eielson would fly across Antarctica, via the Pole, to Byrd's base. The distance was twenty-two hundred miles, the same as their Arctic flight. At the completion of the flight, Wilkins and Eielson could simply drop in on the Americans, who would be setting up their base, then hitch another ride to New Zealand on one of Byrd's supply ships. Simple, efficient, and Wilkins would not only be the first person to fly to the South Pole, but the first to cross the continent as well. And he could be back to America to arrange his submarine expedition while Byrd was still preparing to wait out the winter.

The plan was implemented and the Wilkins-Hearst Antarctic Expedition reached Deception Island on November 7, 1928, where things began to unravel. When Wilkins had first visited Deception Island in 1920, the harbor had been frozen and he had observed it would make an ideal runway. But in 1928, unseasonably warm weather meant the harbor was not frozen, so there was no long flat runway from which to get airborne with a full load of fuel. Undeterred, a rough runway was hewed out of the rocky surrounding land and Wilkins and Eielson managed to get a plane aloft for some short flights: the first ever made in the Antarctic. On December 20, they even managed to get airborne with half a load of fuel to fly along the coast of Graham Land and Palmer Land to where a huge, previously unseen landmass spread out before them. Having consumed half his fuel, Wilkins named the area Hearst Land, before he and Eielson returned to Deception Island.

With only the short rocky runway available, the flight across Antarctica was considered impossible. A disappointed Wilkins returned north, reaching New York in March 1929. Hearst paid him $10,000 toward his expenses, but not the $50,000 bonus for the South Pole flight.

Still needing sponsors for his Arctic submarine venture, Wilkins approached Isaiah Bowman who had the ideal candidate. Lincoln Ellsworth was looking for an expedition he could sponsor and, more importantly, lead.

After an exchange of telegrams, Wilkins sailed to Europe and met Ellsworth at Lenzburg Castle where, spreading his maps across Barbarossa's table, he explained his vision for a series of polar weather stations. The first step, he explained, was to prove Arctic submarine travel was possible. Wilkins offered Ellsworth a place on his proposed submarine expedition. Ellsworth was impressed by the audacity of the idea:

> As he outlined the scheme to me, I grew enthusiastic for it, but was even more struck by Wilkins himself. He was a man, I discovered, exactly to my taste. I have often told him since that had he lived in our West during the pioneer days he would most certainly have been a frontier marshal two-gunning some wild district into law and order.[11]

Ellsworth was enthusiastic enough to sign a check for $20,000 on the spot, but explained it was unlikely he would accompany the expedition because, "I had firmly resolved never to go again into the polar regions except as the head of my own expedition."[12]

The two men did, however, discuss Antarctica and Wilkins's recent attempt to fly across the southern continent. The discussion planted a seed in Ellsworth's mind. He later admitted, "I had not yet thought seriously about the Antarctic, knowing little about it." But after listening to Wilkins, "[I] gained the impression that if I ever cared to organize an Antarctic expedition, Wilkins would be willing to enlist as my adviser."[13]

With Ellsworth's check for $20,000 safely in his pocket, Wilkins returned to America to seek more financial backers for his submarine. Again, his timing was fortunate. William Randolph Hearst was sponsoring German Hugo Eckener, who was planning to fly the *Graf Zeppelin* airship around the world. Hearst suggested Wilkins go along and report on the technical aspects of the flight. Sensing there was still money to be had from such a wealthy sponsor, Wilkins agreed to participate.

Sometime during the twenty-one-day round-the-world flight, which commenced on August 8, 1929, Wilkins and Eckener discussed their respective ambitions. Wilkins explained he wanted to mount a submarine expedition in the Arctic. Eckener explained his vision of a German airship service that could transport passengers worldwide. Airships, he understood, were perceived as fair-weather vessels. He and Wilkins would have discussed the crash of Nobile's *Italia* the year before, and how the tragedy had left people with the impression that airships were dangerous in polar regions.

During their discussions, Eckener and Wilkins came up with a bold plan that would serve both their aspirations. Eckener could fly the *Graf Zeppelin* to the North Pole and rendezvous with Wilkins's submarine. They could exchange mail and passengers and create a sensation that would make all previous polar expeditions pale by comparison. It would prove that submarines were the ideal way to explore the Arctic, while showing that airship travel was safe and comfortable anywhere in the world. Wilkins and Eckener agreed to pitch their idea to Hearst.

At the completion of the *Graf Zeppelin* round-the-world flight, Wilkins made a second attempt to collect the $50,000 bonus for a flight across Antarctica. Learning that Byrd had not yet managed to fly to the South

Pole, Wilkins returned to Deception Island with the whalers in October 1929, only to find the harbor was still not frozen over. On the second trip, he took a small tractor with him, hoping to bulldoze a smoother runway on the rocky ground at Deception Island, but the tough volcanic rock proved obstinate and Wilkins was not able to get his plane airborne with a full tank of fuel.

On the other side of the continent, Byrd had successfully established a base, which he called Little America, and waited out the winter. On November 28, 1929, while Wilkins was trying to bulldoze a runway on Deception Island, Byrd flew to the South Pole with Bernt Balchen* as his pilot.

Another polar first had been accomplished.

---

*   After assisting Byrd with his skis at Kings Bay in May 1926, Balchen had traveled to America, so that he could fly the latest airplanes. Recognizing Balchen's skill as a pilot in polar conditions, Byrd had invited him on his expedition to Antarctica.

6

THE SACRIFICE I MUST MAKE

DECEMBER 1929–MARCH 1931

n December 1929, while Byrd and Wilkins were in Antarctica, Ellsworth returned to New York, still without a clear idea of what he wanted to do. Noticing Ellsworth's despondency, Gertrude Gavin, the daughter of railway magnate James J. Hill and a friend of the Ellsworth family, proposed a canoeing trip in remote Labrador, Canada. Even better, Gavin suggested her godson, Beekman Pool, a young Harvard student, was willing to go along as company. Ellsworth responded to Gavin's offer with his usual vacillation:

> I should like to go on that Labrador trip and may yet, but that submarine trip looms big with me. I want to go back to the Arctic just once more. Wilkins returns from the Antarctic [on] April 1st and then it is yes or no. Until then I must remain undecided.[1]

While he was making up his mind, Ellsworth traveled to the Grand Canyon and collected more fossils. However, he took with him a copy of Dillon Wallace's bestseller, *The Lure of the Labrador Wild*, and returned eager to go on the canoeing trip. After informing Clark, "my future plans must remain dark until autumn,"[2] Ellsworth traveled to Canada to meet Beekman Pool, who would later become his biographer.

"I first set eyes on [Ellsworth] when we met in Quebec City," wrote Pool, the young man plucked from his penultimate year at university to accompany Ellsworth on a trip to Labrador:

> There flowed from him the same spirit of enthusiasm he had expressed in his letters. Of slight build, he had a friendly smile, graying crew-cut hair and very blue eyes with crinkles at the corners. His nose was slightly crooked—the result, I later learned, of tumbling from a high-wheel bicycle when he was a youngster. He was dressed in an old-fashioned belted jacket with matching trousers. He had always wanted to see Labrador, he told me.[3]

Pool and Ellsworth spent two months on a journey that was, according to Ellsworth, "as uncomfortable but in some ways as interesting as any I have made."[4]* Pool would later observe:

> [Ellsworth] found himself at middle age with vast amounts of money and noble aspirations, yet with every dream seemingly thwarted or somehow turned into disappointment. After an unhappy childhood and a disastrous relationship with his father, he yearned to gain inward solace through accomplishment, as well as public recognition for some significant achievement entirely his own.[5]

In early 1930, at the completion of their respective Antarctic expeditions, Wilkins and Byrd returned to a different America. They had left

---

* I interviewed Beekman Pool in 1999 as part of my ongoing research into Sir Hubert Wilkins. Pool was still completing his biography of Ellsworth. It was clear throughout the interview that he idolized Ellsworth. Pool was unable to stop tears welling up in his eyes when he recited the poem "Who Has Known Heights." He incorrectly believed the poem had been written by Ellsworth.

during the Roaring Twenties. They returned, in early 1930, to the Great Depression. Factories were closing, not only across America, but around the world. One in four American workers was without a job. Never again would two hundred thousand people line the streets to wave as aviators drove by in a ticker tape parade. Never again would companies offer big money to sponsor aviation or polar firsts. The bubble had burst and people had more serious issues to deal with.

Hearst bought the idea of a rendezvous between the *Graf Zeppelin* and a submarine, and agreed to a performance-based contract, which meant Wilkins would receive $175,000 if he reached the North Pole and exchanged passengers with the airship. For a rendezvous near the Pole, or no rendezvous at all, lesser amounts would be paid. Needing more money, Wilkins asked Isaiah Bowman if there had been any word from Ellsworth about accompanying the expedition, or increasing his sponsorship. Bowman replied that Ellsworth was canoeing in Labrador and it would be weeks, possibly months, before he could be contacted.

Hoping that the money would eventually be forthcoming, Wilkins turned to the man he had entrusted to modify a submarine for an under-ice voyage, Simon Lake.

Erratic submarine designer Simon Lake was born in Pleasantville, New Jersey, on September 4, 1866, and had begun experimenting with submarines while still in his teens. His first "underwater boat" was constructed from canvas and wood, and propelled by hand. It had wheels, because Lake believed it would be possible to drive along the seabed, in the same manner that cars drive along a highway. In 1894 Lake considered the trials of the boat, and the associated publicity, to be so successful he set about building a bigger version: the thirty-six-foot-long *Argonaut*, which was powered by a gas engine. When it was underwater, the *Argonaut* used a tube to the surface to draw in fresh air. It also had wooden wheels, so that it could roll along the ocean floor. Lake tried to interest the U.S. Navy in his invention but the Navy ignored him, so Lake resorted to taking celebrities and journalists for short rides underwater. His third submarine, which he named *Protector*, was larger still. The U.S. Navy was still unimpressed, so Lake sold it to Russia, which was at war with Japan at the time. Lake continued to compete for U.S. Navy contracts, but was usually beaten by his competitor, John Holland, who built more practical undersea craft.

During World War I, when the U.S. Navy was desperate for submarines, Lake was finally commissioned to build three "L," four "N," and three "O" Class boats to Navy specifications. Lake's Navy contracts ended with the hostilities and, by 1924, the Lake Torpedo Boat Company had closed its doors. Finding himself at loose ends Lake started refurbishing a submarine he had built in 1906; the *Lake XV*, which still had wooden wheels. He renamed it *Defender*, and intended to take tourists for rides at Coney Island. But before the *Defender* could be employed competing with the Ferris wheels of New York's beachside playground, Sir Hubert Wilkins had flown over the Arctic and announced he wanted to reach the North Pole by traveling under the Arctic ice. Lake contacted him and suggested the *Defender* was the ideal submarine for the voyage. Wilkins unwisely expressed interest.

When Wilkins returned to America early in 1930, after his second unsuccessful attempt to beat Byrd to the South Pole, Lake had reconsidered. Perhaps the antiquated *Defender* was not the ideal submarine to take to the North Pole, he informed Wilkins. Lake had learned that the U.S. Navy was scrapping several World War I submarines, and two O-class boats he had built were among them. In Wilkins's absence, he had convinced the Navy to loan the expedition the *O-12* for the nominal sum of $1. Wilkins followed Lake to the Philadelphia Naval Shipyard where, seeing his vision for the future of mankind expressed in grease and corroding steel, he was appalled. Nevertheless, Wilkins reluctantly agreed to accept the *O-12* and Lake began converting it for an Arctic voyage.

Simon Lake had spent his life trying to introduce unusual designs to submarines: wheels for rolling along the sea floor, drop weights for lowering the boat underwater, telescopic conning towers, and many other ideas that submarine development had shown were unnecessary or unworkable. At the Philadelphia Naval Shipyard, Lake was in charge, so no one could question the contraptions he dreamed up. Rather than concentrating on the vital components of a submarine—the hull, engines, and ballast tanks—Lake perched before his drawing board and contrived a host of impractical ideas.

For under-ice travel he decided the ideal thing would be a wooden superstructure on top of the *O-12* in the form of a large upside-down sled. The

O-12 would not submerge using negative buoyancy. Instead it would force its way down by sliding on the underside of the ice. It was a harebrained idea, without foundation in fact or experience. It was, regrettably, the first of many. Added to the upside-down sled, Lake designed a long hydraulic arm that could be raised and lowered, and at the end of the arm he placed a wheel. Supposedly, the arm could be raised, pushing the *O-12* deeper, while the wheel rolled along the underside of the ice. He also wanted collapsible drills for making holes in the ice to get fresh air, a hydraulic battering ram at the bow for punching a path through the ice, as well as a "jack-knife periscope." Eventually Lake cooked up thirty-two "special features," along with more than seventy modifications to the *O-12*. The majority were superfluous.

While Wilkins was promoting his submarine expedition, and Lake was overseeing the modifications to *O-12*, Ellsworth returned from his trip to Labrador, seemingly having lost interest in the upcoming submarine voyage. "I am unspeakably weary of basking in the limelight of someone else's notoriety and long for the solace that the Great West always gives me until I can start something of my own,"[6] he wrote to Harold Clark. Then he traveled to Death Valley, later explaining:

> My affection for the West had gradually centred upon two objects: the Grand Canyon and Death Valley; but if anything I loved Death Valley the better. Deserts had grown upon me with the years. I was always discovering new beauties in them. I never tired of the gaudy sunrises and sunsets of Death Valley or of studying its inconspicuous but teeming life, each species a triumph of adaptation.[7]

While Ellsworth was in Death Valley, the work at the Naval Shipyard became hopelessly bogged down in red tape and confusion. When the *O-12* had been rented from the U.S. Navy, Lake had estimated that the conditioning and outfitting would cost $50,000. Wilkins believed he could successfully raise that amount through sponsorship and publishing rights. But Lake was soon firing off telegrams to Wilkins explaining the job was going over budget. (Modifying the *O-12* would eventually cost $187,351.)

On January 18, 1931, Wilkins wrote to Isaiah Bowman, asking if there had been any word from Ellsworth who, by that time, had tired of Death Valley and was back in Switzerland. Bowman contacted Ellsworth and passed on his vague response: "He definitely declines to join this year, but talks of submitting alternative proposal for next year."[8]

At that point, perhaps again fearing the suicidal tendencies of Ellsworth, Harold Clark stepped in. On January 29, Clark wrote a five-page letter to Ellsworth urging him to become involved in Wilkins's submarine expedition. Clark, more than anyone, knew how to motivate Ellsworth. The letter was a masterpiece of flattery and persuasion. Ellsworth's name, according to Clark, would be "carried through the centuries" along with those of Scott and Amundsen. His father's money had made possible the flights of 1925 and 1926, so Ellsworth had a duty to continue the work this great legacy had started. Wilkins needed $50,000 to save his expedition from collapse and to Ellsworth that amount was a "mere bagatelle." More than just an expedition of exploration, it was a chance to do something for the good of mankind. The opportunity to become involved in such a bold venture was similar to Ellsworth contacting Amundsen when Amundsen was broke and holed up in the Waldorf Astoria hotel in 1924. It was, Clark implied, Ellsworth's destiny. And so it went on until Clark concluded, "Fifty thousand dollars, or several times that sum if needed, would mean nothing to you, and would bring the happiness that comes from having a stake in something that is filled with vitality and romance."[9]

Ellsworth was persuaded. A day after receiving the letter, he signed a second check, this time for $50,000, and Wilkins changed the name of the expedition to the "Wilkins-Ellsworth Trans-Arctic Submarine Expedition." At the top of the new stationery, Ellsworth's name sat below Wilkins's, who was listed as "Commander." Ellsworth was listed as "Director of Research." The *New York Times* summarized the official press release:

> The association of Lincoln Ellsworth, the American explorer who was co-leader with Roald Amundsen and Umberto Nobile in the transpolar flight in the dirigible *Norge* in 1926, with Captain Sir Hubert Wilkins in organizing and possibly

accompanying the latter on his projected submarine voyage under the North Pole next summer, was announced yesterday.

Mr. Ellsworth said: "I like Wilkins because he is of that virile pioneer type of the old American West that I have always so admired—men of great faith, courage, and simplicity, who said little and did much. That is why I like him and have joined forces with him."

[Wilkins] said: "It seems indeed fitting that the man who first carried the American flag over the North Pole in an airship should also be the first to carry it under the North Pole in a submarine."[10]

Ellsworth had a new friend. And while he didn't worship him in the manner he'd worshipped Amundsen, at least he enthused over the association. He wrote in response to a letter of thanks from Wilkins:

Probably it all gave me just as much pleasure as it did you. I do feel though that the honor of association is weighted more in my direction than it is in yours. It is an honor indeed to be associated with you. Just to have our names together. Why? Because for sheer audacity in the attainment of one's ideals, I know of none your equal, unless possibly it was Nansen's *Farthest North*.

. . . from boyhood I have dreamed of manly effort in the far lands of the North, and in whatever way I can aid I am well repaid for any effort I may expend, therefore thank you many times over for the opportunity to be of service.[11]

Ellsworth, as he often did, then sought to ratify the friendship by possessing some personal item that belonged to Wilkins:

Can I have something of yours that you have carried in your travels—such as a pocket knife, any old thing in fact that will stand wear and that I can carry in my pocket—even those gold studs you wore the other evening, if you haven't the other . . . I have an old pipe and pocket knife, besides a match box of

Amundsen's that went to the South Pole, and I treasure them beyond all value. I should like something of yours to carry on my own journey.[12]

Ellsworth also revealed that he was still considering the idea they had discussed eighteen months earlier. "There is nothing I would rather do than make that flight from the Weddell Sea to the Ross Sea," he wrote, but at the same time conceded his inability to organize an expedition himself, or do any of the logistical work:

. . . but it doesn't look promising at the moment. Chartering ships and going into the supply business in order to reach the base does not seem commensurate to the objective in view because it places too much reliance on someone else who is but vaguely interested in the thing itself.[13]

While Ellsworth hoped an expedition to cross Antarctica might magically materialize before him, Wilkins was relieved to have another $50,000 to top up his budget, because Simon Lake was still improvising at the Philadelphia Naval Shipyard. When crew wages and equipment were added to the cost of modifying the submarine, the budget ballooned to $250,000. A month after Ellsworth had committed his money, Wilkins was forced to ask him for a further $30,000. Ellsworth wrote back:

I wish to impress upon you the sacrifice I really must make in order to contribute further to the submarine expedition. But as I said, if it must be done, it must. I cannot see why Leeds is not willing to contribute and if [Harold] Clark is so interested, why doesn't he also?[14]

Ellsworth paid another $30,000, taking his sponsorship to $100,000, but his tone revealed the honeymoon had been short and he was losing interest in the expedition that bore his name.

7

THE THRESHOLD OF GREATNESS

MARCH 1931–NOVEMBER 1931

While Wilkins worried about the mounting costs, and Lake's partner, Sloan Danenhower, recruited a reluctant crew, Hugo Eckener was in Germany preparing the *Graf Zeppelin* for the still-expected rendezvous at the North Pole. Eckener's contract with Hearst was, like Wilkins's, performance-based. If the submarine and the airship met at the North Pole, Eckener would receive $150,000. If they met somewhere in the Arctic, Eckener would only receive $30,000. If they did not meet at all, Hearst would pay nothing. When Eckener learned that work on the submarine was behind schedule, he realized the rendezvous was becoming less likely. He needed other ways to raise money. Hearing that Ellsworth was writing checks for Wilkins, but unlikely to travel on the submarine, Eckener approached him and asked if he'd care to come on the airship flight for a fee of $8,000. As a sweetener, Eckener offered him a title that would appeal to his ego. Ellsworth accepted, announcing enthusiastically:

> . . . out of the clear sky came an invitation to me to join the
> *Graf Zeppelin* as Arctic navigation expert on a projected flight

into the far north. I snapped at the opportunity, going, too, as explorer for the American Geographical Society.[1]

Ellsworth quickly switched his allegiance to the flight of the airship, and expressed his disappointment in the increasingly expensive submarine expedition to the man who had convinced him to support it, Harold Clark:

> What benefit of any sort can be derived from [the submarine expedition]; what new data can be collected which can be beneficially utilized? Who cares seriously about the Arctic depths of unnavigable waters? And as for determining the set and drift of Arctic currents . . . I do not believe anything practical or useful can be obtained by diving under the ice.[2]

Eckener also approached the Russian government, which was planning a scientific expedition off its northern coast, and it was agreed that, for a fee, the *Graf Zeppelin* would carry Russian scientists and meet the Russian icebreaker *Malygin*, somewhere in the vicinity of Franz Josef Land.

With the modifications to the submarine falling further behind schedule, Wilkins ordered it to be moved to the Mathis Shipyard at Camden, New Jersey, where it could be completed by private contractors. Upset at being overruled, the petulant Lake, who had made a mess of it for more than a year, washed his hands of the venture and announced he would have nothing more to do with it. Wilkins was left to direct the remaining work on the submarine alone.

The *O-12* finally left the Camden shipyard and was towed to New York where, on March 24, 1931, more than 800 people, including Ellsworth, gathered to witness the christening of the world's first Arctic submarine. Wilkins named it *Nautilus*, claiming he was making a reality of what Jules Verne predicted in his novel *20,000 Leagues Under the Sea*, when Captain Nemo sailed amid the ice at the South Pole.* Ten weeks later, the Wilkins-Ellsworth

---

* Neither the North nor South Pole was explored when Verne wrote *20,000 Leagues Under the Sea*, and he imagined the Antarctic to be a deep ocean.

Trans-Arctic Submarine Expedition sailed. Ellsworth was not on hand to see the *Nautilus* commence its trip across the Atlantic Ocean.

Despite the fundamental components of the *Nautilus* having been overlooked in favor of Lake's inventions, Wilkins believed it might still be possible to rendezvous with the *Graf Zeppelin* somewhere in the Arctic. But shortly after reaching open sea the diesel engines began to give them trouble. It was also discovered the hull was leaking and the electrical generators, which charged the batteries, were partly underwater. In a short time, the port engine and both generators were out of commission, which meant the batteries were dying. Radio operator Ray Meyers tapped out a faint SOS. After eighteen hours the battleship USS *Wyoming*, which was en route to Sweden, heard the call. It steamed to the aid of the *Nautilus* and towed the crippled submarine one thousand miles to Ireland. The *Nautilus* was then towed to England, where it spent a month being repaired and many of the crew took the opportunity to resign. Any chance of a rendezvous with the *Graf Zeppelin* was gone, but Wilkins still wanted to get under the Arctic ice to prove it could be done. He sailed the *Nautilus* from Devonport to Bergen, Norway, but on that voyage the steering gear gave them trouble and the submarine drifted helplessly while it was repaired. At Bergen, three more crew resigned.

Four days before the *Nautilus* left Devonport, the *Graf Zeppelin*, with Ellsworth on board, had lifted off from Friedrichshafen, Germany, to commence its Arctic flight. It flew to Russia, where it was refueled, and lifted off again on July 26, heading for the Barents Sea. It crossed the Arctic Circle before Eckener headed for Franz Josef Land, where visual contact was made with the icebreaker *Malygin*. Eckener brought the airship down until it floated gently, just above the sea. Fearing sparks from the smoke stacks of the icebreaker might ignite the hydrogen in its twelve massive gasbags, the *Graf Zeppelin* was settled six hundred feet away, on an inflatable skirt that surrounded the gondola.

As a rubber raft was launched, the crew saw a tender from the *Malygin* coming toward them, crammed with weather-beaten men clad in furs. Watching from the raft, Ellsworth remembered:

> In the stern sheets was a vaguely familiar figure waving to greet
> me. When he came aboard the *Graf Zeppelin* and shook hands

I had to look twice to recognize him. It was Umberto Nobile, whom I had not seen since our *Norge* flight in 1926. He had aged visibly since then. The *Italia* disaster had made a different man of him.[3]

The strutting Italian fascist general, who had been raised to the status of a national hero after the successful flight of the *Norge*, was cut down following the crash of the *Italia*. The Italian government, along with the Italian people, had turned savagely on Nobile. Mussolini forced him to take his family and flee to communist Russia, where he now lived in exile. Staring at the disgraced airship commander, someone from the *Graf Zeppelin* muttered, "My God, how the man has aged." Ellsworth and Nobile shook hands and embraced. Any animosity between them was forgotten.

Eckener wanted to waste no time dangerously floating amid the ice floes. As soon as the mailbags were exchanged, the order was given to lift off. The tender from the *Malygin* returned to the ship. Ellsworth was moved by his reunion with Nobile, and wrote, "As he left in the bobbing boat of the *Malygin*—waving goodbye as he stood unsteadily in the stern—the scene had an element of pathos that I can never forget."[4][*]

The *Graf Zeppelin* was soon aloft and the next day it was over Severnaya Zemlya (Northern Land) of which only a small section of the east coast had been mapped. For six hours Eckener flew the airship at four thousand feet, discovering that the land consisted of two islands, not one as previously thought. On board, while the passengers dined lavishly and listened to music, Ellsworth wrote proudly, "This was real exploring, despite the luxury."[5]

By July 30 they were back at Leningrad. A day later the *Graf Zeppelin* returned to Friedrichshafen, having flown over eight thousand miles.

Wilkins was still stuck in Bergen. He had hoped to reach Spitsbergen by May 15, but after continual setbacks he finally arrived there, three months behind schedule, on August 15. The submarine was barely operable, most of the unnecessary equipment designed by Lake did not work, and

---

[*] Nobile moved his family to America in 1939. He returned to Italy after World War II and died in Rome in 1978, age 93.

Danenhower, along with the crew, wanted to call the whole thing off. But Wilkins refused to give up. Two days after arriving at Spitsbergen, with the *Nautilus* refueled, he headed north.

During the afternoon of August 19, the submarine reached the edge of the ice pack. When the crew prepared for diving Wilkins's final hopes of a voyage under the Arctic ice were dashed. The horizontal stern diving rudders were missing. Originally the *Nautilus* had horizontal diving rudders at the bow and stern, designed to steer the submarine up or down, in the same way that vertical rudders steer a boat left or right. The bow rudders had been removed at the naval dockyard because Lake believed the *Nautilus* would travel under the ice by sliding on its smooth wooden superstructure. The stern diving rudders, however, had been left in place. (No explanation of what happened to the rudders has ever been given. Wilkins later accused the crew of sabotaging the submarine at Bergen to avoid continuing.) Wilkins called a meeting and discovered, without exception, everyone wanted to abort the expedition, but Wilkins needed to salvage something from the expensive disaster. A week went by before the sea was calm enough to flood the forward ballast tanks and partially raise the stern. Wilkins gave the order to drive the submarine at the ice, in an attempt to slide under it. But without diving rudders to relieve the pressure on the bottom of the floe, and with the projecting ice drill and other deck obstructions gouging their way through the ice, the *Nautilus* was almost impossible to maneuver. Wilkins ended the brief incursion beneath the ice and ordered the *Nautilus* back to Spitsbergen, where it arrived on September 7.

A rumor spread among the crew that the expedition was broke and various members confronted Wilkins to demand their money. He drew on all his savings and came up with almost $22,000, which was still not enough to meet his obligations. He had no choice but to radio Ellsworth asking for extra cash. Ellsworth, according to the balance sheet, "loaned" the expedition $20,000, while Harold Clark, who had encouraged Ellsworth's participation in the first place, felt compelled to loan it $5,000. The crew was guaranteed their money and the *Nautilus* returned to Bergen.

Wilkins's original agreement was that the submarine should be returned to the U.S. Navy at the end of the expedition, but getting it back across the Atlantic would be difficult and expensive, so Wilkins asked if it could be scuttled off Norway. The Navy replied that it could, as long as it was in international waters, at least 1,200 feet deep.

It took a month to find an area off Bergen where the water was sufficiently deep. Finally, on November 20, 1931, the *Nautilus*, followed by a flotilla of onlookers, was towed to sea and its valves opened. Wilkins was not on hand to see the vessel, which was intended to help mankind reached a more advanced state of civilization, slowly turn on end and slip beneath the waves. He was already back in New York. His proposed lecture tour was canceled and the media attention that followed his departure had evaporated before his return. Wilkins's noble ambition had left him shattered and broke.

And the third Arctic expedition to carry Ellsworth's name had ended in failure.

Meanwhile, Ellsworth was back in his castle, after the *Graf Zeppelin* flight, with renewed enthusiasm for exploration. "The sight of the Arctic ice and unknown lands had fired me with a zeal for exploration such as had not burned within me since my first meetings with Amundsen,"[6] he wrote. But what could he do? What great polar achievement remained to be obtained? To Ellsworth, it became increasingly clear. There was, fortunately, still a polar first to be claimed. As yet, no one had managed to cross Antarctica from one side to the other. His biographer Beekman Pool would later write:

> [Ellsworth] was fifty-one years old. For almost two decades, on the threshold of greatness, he had endured the frustration of seeking personal fulfilment in a world of exploration that no longer existed. But the lure of fame still drew him like a magnet, and his path was clear. The Antarctic area over which he planned to fly was the last major portion of the entire Earth that remained unknown—a vast empty white area on the map. Whoever was first in revealing its secrets would earn a permanent place on the roster of great explorers.[7]

Ellsworth looked to Antarctica but, as he had done all his life, he procrastinated, trapped by his inability to lift himself from his lethargy. If he was to leave his seclusion, he needed someone to inspire him and lead him. Amundsen had done it, but Amundsen was dead. Ellsworth needed a new hero.

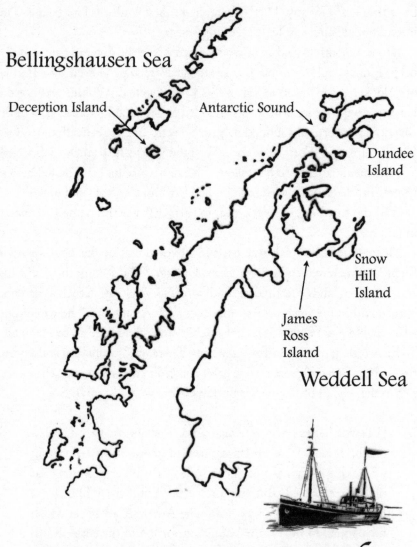

Antarctic Peninsula

The northern end of the Antarctic Peninsula as it is known today. Sir Hubert Wilkins had previously failed to find flat islands in the Bellingshausen Sea, suitable for runways. After the harbor ice in Deception Island was found to be too thin to support an airplane, Ellsworth was forced to take the Wyatt Earp into the treacherous Weddell Sea.

PART II
WYATT EARP LIMITED

Half a dozen persons who saw the four men on their journey down Fremont Street have described them. The recollections agree strikingly in detail. No more grimly portentous spectacle had been witnessed in Tombstone. The three stalwart, six-foot Earps—each with the square jaw of his clan set hard beneath his flowing, tawny mustache and his keen blue eyes alert under the wide brim of a high-peaked, black Stetson—bore out their striking resemblance, even in their attire; dark trousers drawn outside the legs of black, high-heeled boots, long skirted, square-cut, black coats then in frontier fashion, and white, soft-collared shirts with black string ties to accentuate the purpose in their lean, bronzed faces. Doc Holliday was some two inches shorter than his three companions, but his stature was heightened by cadaverousness, the flapping black overcoat and the black sombrero above his hollow cheeks. Holliday's blond mustache was as long and as sweeping as any, but below it those who saw him have sworn Doc had his lips pursed, whistling softly. As the distance to the O.K. Corral lessened, the four men spread their ranks as they walked.

—from *Wyatt Earp: Frontier Marshal*
by Stuart N. Lake

8

THE LONE EAGLE

OCTOBER 1881–JUNE 1932

The gunfight at the O.K. Corral lasted less than a minute. During that time about thirty shots were fired, three men were killed, and the legend of an obscure frontier gambler and part-time law officer, Wyatt Earp, was born. The fight took place on October 26, 1881, at Tombstone, a mining town in the Arizona territory. At the time of the famous gunfight, Tombstone boasted more than one hundred saloons, fourteen gambling halls, three newspapers, countless brothels, one bowling alley, and an ice cream parlor. Cowboys who worked the surrounding plains, along with miners who worked the silver claims, came to Tombstone to spend their money on alcohol, gambling, and women.

Virgil Earp was the town's marshal and a deputy U.S. marshal for the region. By all accounts, he tried to uphold the law and sided with the townspeople. The county sheriff (a law officer with similar authority, but for the surrounding area rather than the town) was John Behan. Behan was more inclined to side with the cowboys, a loose group of which Ike Clanton was a leader. As cattle rustling went unchecked, along with a series of stagecoach robberies, Virgil Earp believed Behan was not doing his job, so he intended to run for county sheriff himself. When Earp had to leave town he would often deputize his brothers, Morgan and Wyatt, to look after matters. The rivalry between the two groups was not helped by the fact that Wyatt Earp, although married, had recently begun a relationship with Behan's de facto wife, Josephine Marcus.

On September 8, 1881, seven weeks before the famous gunfight, the stagecoach from Bisbee was robbed and Virgil Earp arrested two of Clanton's friends. In the following weeks, threats, usually made under the influence of alcohol, were exchanged. Siding with the Earps during these verbal confrontations, was John Henry "Doc" Holliday, a former dentist turned gambler and gunman.

Matters came to a head on the evening of October 25, when Clanton and Tom McLaury rode into town wearing their guns. A local ordinance required everyone except peace officers to check their guns at designated locations on the city's outskirts. Clanton had a noisy argument with Holliday that evening, then settled down in a saloon to pass the night drinking and gambling. The next morning Virgil Earp pistol-whipped Clanton and disarmed him. A short while later, Wyatt Earp did the same to McLaury. Rather than go away and sleep off their intoxication, Clanton and McLaury gathered their kin and began making noisy threats against the Earps. Alarmed citizens saw the cowboys congregate, carrying guns, on Fremont Street. Clanton, still drunk, was proclaiming loudly how he was going to kill all the Earps. Everything was set for the showdown.

Virgil, Wyatt, and Morgan Earp were joined by Doc Holliday, and the four men walked west along Fremont Street to where the cowboys had been last reported. The three Earps carried a revolver either in their hand, pocket, or jammed into their trouser belt. Doc Holliday, the only experienced gunfighter in the group, carried a revolver in a holster on his belt and a shotgun concealed under his overcoat. By whatever means the Earps carried their pistols, it was certainly not in belt-mounted holsters. Part way along Fremont Street, Behan rushed forward and told the Earps and Holliday that there was no need for a gunfight. Wyatt Earp later testified in court that:

> I heard him [Behan] say to Virgil Earp, "For God's sake, don't go down there, you will get murdered!" Virgil Earp replied, "I am going to disarm them." He, Virgil, being in the lead. When I and Morgan came up to Behan he said, "I have disarmed them." When he said this, I took my pistol, which I had in my hand, under my coat, and put it in my overcoat pocket. Behan then passed up the street, and we walked on down.[1]

The confrontation happened at approximately 3:00 P.M. Clanton's gang was standing on Fremont Street, in front of a photographic studio owned by Camillus Fly. (The O.K. Corral was a block away on Allen Street. A laneway from the rear of the corral led to Fremont Street.) Morgan, Virgil, and Wyatt Earp, along with Doc Holliday, faced Ike and Billy Clanton, Frank and Tom McLaury, and Billy Claiborne. The two groups were standing about six feet apart. History is contradictory as to what, exactly, was said and who fired first. Virgil Earp called on the men to throw up their hands and be disarmed. Profanities were exchanged and someone started shooting. Thirty seconds later Frank and Tom McLaury, along with Billy Clanton, were either dead or dying. Ike Clanton, who had been the most vocal in his threats, hightailed it down the lane, past the famous corral, and didn't stop running until he was well clear of Tombstone's city limits. Billy Claiborne wasn't far behind him. Doc Holliday was grazed on the hip by a bullet. Virgil was shot through the calf, and Morgan was shot in the shoulder blade. Wyatt was unhurt.

At the end of the fight, Sheriff Behan emerged to arrest the Earps and Holliday for murder. After a monthlong trial they were found not guilty. What followed was known as the Earp Vendetta as cowboys tried to kill the Earp brothers. Virgil Earp was shot two months after the gunfight and lost the use of one arm. He eventually died of pneumonia in 1905. Morgan Earp was shot in the back and killed while playing billiards in 1882. Doc Holliday died of tuberculosis in 1887. Of the two men who ran from the fight, Claiborne was killed in a gunfight a year later, while Clanton was shot dead stealing cattle in 1887.

Wyatt Earp outlived them all. He took up with Josephine Marcus, the former partner of Sheriff Behan. For the next forty-six years they traveled together, with Josephine becoming a chronic gambler and Wyatt's fortunes rising and falling as he attempted to make a living through mining, gambling, or occasionally working as a peace officer.

The decorative leather gun belts, which combine cartridge belts and smooth "quick-draw" holsters tied to the thighs and adorned with ornaments, are the stuff of Hollywood. Peace officers, cowboys, and workers in the Old West saw their firearms as tools. Holsters for pistols were separate to cartridge belts and sometimes made with a loop or with slits so they could be attached to a belt or strap. It was common practice to wear an ammunition belt around the waist, yet carry a pistol tucked into the trousers or loose in a pocket. Wyatt Earp was casual about his firearms. Once, in 1900, when he had followed the gold rush to Alaska, he checked a pistol into the marshal's office at Juneau, and never bothered to retrieve it. (The pistol is on display at the Red Dog Saloon in Juneau.) He also wore a cartridge belt, loaded with ammunition, but without a gun holster. When describing how, in March 1882, he was trying to get on his horse during a gunfight he said:

> When I tried to get astride I found that it [the cartridge belt] had fallen down over my thighs, keeping my legs together. While I was perched thus, trying to pull my belt higher with one hand, the horn of the saddle was shot off.

The *San Francisco Examiner*, which carried the report, then went on to describe how Earp, ". . . saved himself and at the same time gave a jerk at the cartridge belt. Then he leapt in the saddle and got away."[2]

Sometime around 1910, Wyatt and Josephine settled in California. Wyatt continued to work as a freelance peace officer, but had as many encounters on the wrong side of the law as on the right. He ran card games, was often arrested for being drunk and disorderly, and tried to make various mining claims return a dividend. Josephine, by this time, was a hopeless gambling addict.

Wyatt Earp might have passed into oblivion, along with the gunfight that is synonymous with his name, were it not for novelist Stuart N. Lake.*

---

* I have established no family link between author Stuart N. Lake and submarine designer Simon Lake.

During the 1920s, Lake interviewed and wrote about another Old West gunfighter, William "Bat" Masterson, who continually spoke about the bravest man he ever knew, Wyatt Earp. Wanting to record as much western folklore as he could, Lake sought out Earp and asked to write his biography. Earp agreed and Lake conducted a series of interviews.

Wyatt Earp died peacefully at his home on January 13, 1929. Josephine did not attend the funeral. After forty-six years together, during which Wyatt drank and Josephine gambled, the two were barely on speaking terms. Nor did either of them have any money.

Wyatt Earp: Frontier Marshal was published in October 1931, when the *Nautilus* was waiting to be scuttled off Bergen, and Ellsworth was considering flying across Antarctica. Lake's biography glorified not only Earp, but also the Old West in a way that no one had glorified it before—steely-eyed gunfighters facing down desperados, the roaring boom towns that stood ready for carousers at the end of the cattle trails, the wickedness of the gambling halls. And in the middle of it all stood Wyatt Earp, larger than life, the bravest man who ever lived. It was largely escapist fiction, but the world in the grip of the Great Depression lapped it up. Here, in the Old West, was America's golden age. Here, in Lake's book, was a new American mythology.

And for Lincoln Ellsworth, here in Wyatt Earp was a new hero. He immediately became an enamored fan, later writing:

> I am frankly a hero-worshipper and sentimentalist. For years I have made almost a cult of the memory of Wyatt Earp. I have spent much time collecting every souvenir and trinket I could find associated with that unbelievably brave man.[3]

While most of the world worried about where its next meal was coming from, Ellsworth dreamt of glory, gunfights, and standing side by side with the man who tamed the West. For the sensitive and solitary Ellsworth, Earp was everything he wanted to be. He summed up his admiration by writing:

> What appeals to me most about the career of Wyatt Earp was his domination over men . . . On the buffalo range, in cow

towns, in Dodge City, Deadwood, and Tombstone he altered the course of Western history by his domination over men and events . . . Wyatt Earp has done more for me than any other figure who ever lived.[4]

Ellsworth always sought objects he could possess in the vain hope that somehow the strength or power of their previous owner would be transferred to him. So immediately after he read Simon Lake's book he wanted something that had been owned by Wyatt Earp. He visited Josephine at her home in California and found her eager to sell her husband's artifacts.* The first things Ellsworth purchased were a cartridge belt and Earp's wedding ring. Had the belt been worn at the gunfight at the O.K. Corral when Earp had put his pistol in his overcoat pocket? Was it the same cartridge belt that slipped around his legs when he attempted to mount his horse while being shot at? No one knows. In fact, if Wyatt Earp could be interviewed from beyond the grave, it's doubtful he would know, such was his casual attitude to guns and their accessories. But the belt was certainly owned by Josephine and most likely by Earp, and it served to embolden Ellsworth.

Armed with new symbols of strength and manly vitality, Ellsworth felt ready to stride back into the public glare. He could walk tall and proud again, like the Earps marching down Fremont Street, ready to challenge anyone who stood in his way. And, in Sir Hubert Wilkins, destiny had delivered his Doc Holliday.

Following the unsuccessful voyage of the *Nautilus*, Wilkins's ambitions were still firmly focused on getting another submarine and returning to the Arctic. But when Ellsworth asked him to organize an expedition to cross Antarctica, Wilkins was in no position to refuse. Whether or not he legally owed Ellsworth money, Wilkins certainly felt he owed him a moral debt for sponsoring the *Nautilus*. Plus Wilkins had no money and was finding it difficult, during the Depression, to get crowds to pay to hear him speak

---

* Some historians suggest that Josephine was not above buying items from pawn shops and selling them as once belonging to Wyatt Earp. As Ellsworth was the first to visit her, it is likely that the items he purchased were genuine.

and show his films. Wilkins agreed to help Ellsworth fly across Antarctica and set his mind to accomplishing the task.

Wilkins had previously traveled to Antarctica four times, with a view to either crossing it in an airplane, or exploring its interior from the air. On the first expedition, in 1920, Wilkins had learned the importance of having the whalers on his side and using their established bases whenever possible. On his second trip south, aboard *Quest* with Sir Ernest Shackleton, the most important lesson Wilkins had learned was to have a sturdy ship, capable of a long voyage through stormy seas. *Quest* had been totally unsuitable. On the Wilkins-Hearst Antarctic Expeditions, Wilkins's two attempts to fly across the continent had been thwarted by the lack of a suitable flat surface from which to get a fully laden plane airborne. Both times Wilkins's airplane was capable of flying 2,500 miles and both times the steep mountains, rocky ground, or thin bay ice had reduced his flying to short distances.

But in 1928 and 1929, while Wilkins had been on the Graham Land side of Antarctica seeking a suitable flat runway, Richard Byrd had been on the Ross Sea side, repeatedly getting his large three-engine planes airborne from the ice shelf. Although Wilkins had never seen the shelf, it seemed a safe bet to provide a flat runway. He also knew that airplane design had progressed in the five years since his Lockheed Vega had been built, and some were now capable of flying 4,000 miles without refueling.

A further consideration was the weather. Wilkins was aware that, because of the strong winter winds, the earliest he could get a plane airborne from either side of Antarctica was the middle of November, while getting a ship through the ice pack at the edge of the Ross Sea was difficult before December. Byrd, Amundsen, and Scott, on their expeditions, had only been able to set out for the South Pole earlier than December because they had spent the previous winter in Antarctica. But Wilkins had no intention of spending a winter. He wanted to go south, let Ellsworth fly across the continent, then return north as soon as possible, so he could concentrate on getting another submarine. A large expedition that established bases and wintered there was out of the question.

A bold plan began to form in Wilkins's mind. A plan that, he believed, would get Ellsworth down to Antarctica, across it, then back north in one southern summer. Wilkins would take a ship, with a small crew, a pilot, and an airplane to Dunedin, New Zealand. Once Ellsworth came on board, the ship could then be sailed down to the Ross Ice Shelf in mid-December. Wilkins would not waste time establishing a base. Instead the crew would eat and sleep on the ship. The plane could be unloaded onto the flat ice of the shelf, Ellsworth and a pilot could take off, fly across the continent to the edge of the Weddell Sea, then without landing simply turn around and fly back. The total distance, if Ellsworth only flew as far as the edge of the Weddell Sea, would be 2,900 miles, while the flight time would be approximately twenty hours. At the completion of the crossing they could load the plane back on the ship and return north, arriving back in New Zealand in February, or March at the latest. Wilkins explained the plan to Ellsworth who, having no alternative, instructed him to get on with it.

Wilkins, first and foremost, needed a ship. He went to Norway where, after looking at various vessels, he settled on the *Fanefjord*. It had been built in 1919 as a fishing boat at a time when fishing in Norway required a stout vessel capable of withstanding crushing pack ice. It had a large hold in which to store a catch and Wilkins noted it could also store a small plane, if the wings were removed. The *Fanefjord* boasted a 350-brake horsepower, four-cylinder semidiesel engine, which was supplemented by sails. With a fuel capacity of one hundred tons of oil, while burning it at a rate of one and a half tons per day and traveling at seven knots, the *Fanefjord* had a range of around eleven thousand nautical miles. Wilkins felt it should do the job nicely, and cabled details of his proposed choice to Ellsworth, who told him to buy it. The price was 75,000 kroner (about US$15,000).

The *Fanefjord* was modified and its hull reinforced. Two-and-a-half-inch oak sheathing covered the forward part of the hull, with twelve-gauge galvanized iron covering the remainder. The hull was additionally sheathed in three-quarter-inch iron plating. All sturdy enough, it was hoped, to act as an icebreaker if necessary. The forward hatch was widened to facilitate the loading of a plane, additional tanks were added to hold another ten tons of oil, new masts and sails were fitted, along with new water tanks and a host of minor equipment upgrades.

For a plane Wilkins turned to Jack Northrop, the innovative designer of his successful Lockheed Vega. Northrop's breakthrough design on the

Vega had been the monocoque body. Rather than a frame over which a lighter material, such as canvas, was stretched, the Vega's body provided strength from its shell. On the Vega, Northrop had achieved this strength by stressing sheets of plywood over concrete molds and fixing the panels together. Since designing the Vega, Northrop had left the Lockheed Company, formed the Northrop Corporation with Donald Douglas and replaced plywood with metal. His first plane with Douglas was the Northrop Alpha. It carried six passengers inside a sleek metal fuselage while the pilot sat at the rear in an open cockpit. Alphas went into service carrying passengers across America—something unheard of only a few years earlier. Northrop followed the Alpha with the Gamma, which was a streamlined, single-engine plane designed for high speeds over long distances. The first model was purchased by Frank Hawks, a noted pilot of the era, who immediately proved its efficiency by setting a record from Los Angeles to New York (over 2,400 miles) flying at an average speed of 180 mph. A pertinent feature of the Gamma was its low wing. Landing on snow, Wilkins reasoned, the wing could sit flat on the surface if the wheels were dug in, and therefore reduce the chance of the plane being lifted and blown away in a blizzard. Wilkins believed the Gamma would be the ideal plane for Ellsworth and ordered one. Northrop began building a second Gamma, the main difference from the first being that Ellsworth's plane would be a dual cockpit model, so Ellsworth could sit behind the pilot.

For the pilot, Wilkins knew the best man for the job was Bernt Balchen, who had returned to America after flying Byrd to the South Pole in 1929. Balchen's relationship with Byrd had become strained. "For a leader he is too prone to listen to gossip and flattery,"[5] Balchen said. Balchen was fed up with Byrd's mood swings; friendly one moment, aloof or angry the next. He didn't believe Byrd had made it to the North Pole and thought the record of his 1926 flight was a hoax. Shortly after returning to America from Antarctica, Balchen had planned an around-the-world flight, but was unable to raise sponsorship. After that he got married, became an American citizen, and struggled to support his wife in a world in the grip of the Depression. In 1932 he found work teaching Amelia Earhart navigation and advanced flying skills. He modified a Lockheed Vega, then flew it and Earhart to

Newfoundland, from where she flew the plane solo across the Atlantic. Then Balchen began looking for another opportunity.

On Wilkins's recommendation, Balchen talked with Ellsworth, who explained plans were well underway for a flight across Antarctica. Balchen agreed to be the pilot if he was paid $800 a month plus his expenses, for the length of the expedition. For a successful flight across Antarctica he would receive a $14,700 bonus. It was a lucrative contract at a time when professionals, such as doctors, were earning $60 per week and production workers were lucky to manage $17.

Balchen traveled to California, met with Jack Northrop, and inspected the plane. When it was completed, in August 1932, Balchen flew it successfully from California to New York to test its fuel consumption. Ellsworth wired that he wanted it named *Polar Star*. At the completion of the test flights, the *Polar Star* was disassembled and crated for shipping. Balchen, his wife Emmy, their baby son, and the *Polar Star* sailed to Norway, where Balchen met with Wilkins and inspected the *Fanefjord*. He made small models of the plane and ship to see if the plane could be stored below decks. It could.

Meanwhile, Ellsworth had grown fond of his castle. After his first visit, he adopted the habit of vacationing there each year. In the northern summer of 1932, while Wilkins was having the *Fanefjord* modified and Balchen was testing the *Polar Star*, Ellsworth traveled to Lenzburg to "keep my rendezvous with the ghost of Frederick Barbarossa."[6] After a brief stay he aimlessly traveled to Paris where he booked a passage to New York, planning to "buckle down to the concrete job of organizing my expedition."[7] But before he sailed he changed his mind and, on a whim, decided to improve his photography. Ellsworth had carried a Leica 35mm camera for years, but was unhappy with his results. Perhaps, he thought, he should take lessons. Typically, Ellsworth didn't want lessons from just anyone, or worse, to apply himself to time-consuming study and practice. As he often did when faced with a challenge, Ellsworth sought the best expert in the field and offered them money. So instead of returning to America, Ellsworth took a train to Zurich and introduced himself to a renowned pilot and photographer, Walter Mittelholzer who, for a fee, gave him lessons on how to use his simple camera.

While at Mittelholzer's airfield, the fifty-two-year-old Ellsworth met Mary Louise Ulmer, a fellow American, twenty-five years his junior, who was taking flying lessons. Ulmer was the daughter of an industrialist, Jacob Ulmer (who had died in 1928) and Eldora, who was fulfilling her duty as the wealthy, idle socialite mother of a plain, awkward, and painfully shy daughter. Eldora was dragging her child around Europe in the hope of finding a suitable husband. When Ellsworth and Mary Louise met at Mittelholzer's airfield, Eldora instantly knew she had hit the jackpot. Ellsworth was older, equally shy, and, she may have suspected from his bachelor status, gay. But he had two qualities that made him an ideal son-in-law: he was incredibly wealthy and he was well practiced in doing what he was told. Beekman Pool, who interviewed Mary Louise for his biography on Ellsworth, wrote that at the time of their meeting, "she was not pretty, but had verve."[8] Ellsworth invited mother and daughter to visit his castle and, ten days after they met, Ellsworth proposed marriage to Mary Louise. She accepted. In his autobiography, Ellsworth gave little hint as to why he chose to marry, explaining of the period:

> I protracted my camera instructions for two weeks, greatly to my technical and domestic advantage. My Leica shots of the Antarctic mountains were as good as I could wish; and at the end of my two weeks in Zurich, I, a lone eagle for fifty-two years and almost a creature of the womanless parts of the Earth, was engaged to marry Mary Louise Ulmer.[9]

Having succeeded in her safari to the continent to hunt down a husband for her daughter, Eldora's next task was to return to America to display the trophy. Any fleeting attention Ellsworth might have given to his polar expedition was redirected to surviving the less forgiving environment of a society wedding.

9

THE MAYOR OF ANTARCTICA

JUNE 1931 – JULY 1933

The primary achievement of Richard Byrd's first expedition to Antarctica (1928–30), by far the biggest and most technologically advanced to have reached the southern continent, was that Byrd had flown to the South Pole and back, following the route previously mapped by Roald Amundsen. He had also made a short flight east, glimpsing an area that he named after his wife, but that was it. Except for Marie Byrd Land, and a mountain range within it seen from a distance, little was added to the map or the knowledge of Antarctica. (Byrd named the range the Rockefeller Mountains to acknowledge John D. Rockefeller, a major sponsor of his first Antarctic expedition.)

At the end of his expedition, more than ninety percent of Antarctica's landmass remained unseen, while the main questions remained unanswered. What was beyond the threatening ice packs that guarded Antarctica? Was it one large continent, two smaller continents, or a series of islands? Did the mountains that stretched north along the Graham Land and Palmer Land until they almost touched South America continue in the opposite direction to reach the plateau that Shackleton had first climbed and that Scott and Amundsen had partially crossed to stand at the South Pole? By the beginning of the 1930s much was still unknown.

After his first trip to Antarctica, Byrd had been welcomed home as a hero again. He was promoted to Rear Admiral—the youngest in the U.S. Navy— and his belief in his own self-importance continued to climb unchecked, so that he considered himself above censure and reproach. Even Byrd's most admiring biographer, Lisle A. Rose, (who, against all evidence, still claims that Byrd reached the North Pole in 1926) was forced to admit that after his first trip south Byrd enjoyed more adulation than any person should have. He had "mastered" the frozen continent, but it had also "mastered him." Antarctica became the focus of all Byrd's ambition and came to define him as a man trapped inside his own self-image as a heroic polar explorer. According to Rose, anyone who wished to succeed in Antarctica first needed Byrd's permission to explore it. "Antarctica was his, he insisted; he was mayor of the place. That conceit became his curse and his burden."[1]

It was inevitable that Byrd would want to return to Antarctica. He had tasted fame and become addicted. Only by returning to Antarctica could he hope to taste more. But the bubble known as the Roaring Twenties had burst and wealthy sponsors were scarce. Byrd, like most men who surrender to an addiction, attacked the problem with all the skill, cunning, charm, and deceit he could summon.

In the mood of gloom and despair that gripped the American people, Byrd cleverly made his proposed return to Antarctica appear like an effort to lift the nation from the doldrums. America was having a rough time of it, and so was he, he convinced the public, but together they could make the nation strong again, as long as everyone put their faith in Byrd. No one questioned why he wanted to go back. No one asked what could be achieved that could not have been achieved on the first expedition. Byrd had already been south, with three planes, two ships, and eighty men. No one asked why the scientific data collected on the first expedition languished unpublished. If it had been about science, then surely he should correlate and publish what had already cost a million dollars to secure. But of course, it wasn't about science. It was about what Byrd unashamedly called the "hero business," and he cleverly promoted himself as a struggling American trying to survive the Depression and haul America up by its bootstraps.

Naturally, Byrd couldn't simply return to Antarctica and repeat his flight to the South Pole. He had to come up with something new and spectacular; something that would capture the public's imagination and thrust him into the headlines once more. He needed something bold that would answer the question, "Why?"

Byrd decided he would be the first to cross Antarctica.

During June and July 1931, while Wilkins was coaxing the *Nautilus* north and Ellsworth was flying in the *Graf Zeppelin*, Byrd began secretly sounding out sponsors about a second expedition south. By August he had convinced himself it was possible and commenced the enormous task of bringing together another major polar undertaking. Throughout the latter half of 1931, the paranoid Byrd continued to plan, plot, and procure until he felt sufficiently confident of success to make public what he was doing. The official announcement was made on January 16, 1932.

At the time of the announcement, Ellsworth had still not revealed his plans. Byrd had heard rumors from Isaiah Bowman of the American Geographical Society, and wanted to know if he had a competitor. He wrote to Ellsworth, asking him what his intentions were. Ellsworth wrote a vague reply saying he was considering an expedition to Antarctica. On April 16, Byrd wrote again pleading, "Will you please let me know what you decide to do?"[2] Ellsworth didn't need to reply personally to the second inquiry. Two days after Byrd had typed his letter, the *New York Times* announced that Ellsworth would travel to the Ross Ice Shelf and from there, with a radical new plane, he and Bernt Balchen would fly to the Weddell Sea and back.

Byrd was furious. Not only was Ellsworth going to make the flight he desperately wanted to make first, but Ellsworth had hired Bernt Balchen, the man who had been Byrd's pilot on the South Pole flight and clearly the most experienced and capable man for the task. To Byrd, it was a betrayal of trust. He wrote to Ellsworth, querying why he was out to "undercut" him, and explaining tersely that it had always been his intention to return to Antarctica:

> All during the winter night [of 1929] the members of my expe-
> dition [which included Balchen] knew that I was going back

and that my main objective was the flight to the Weddell Sea from Little America, and this fact became very widespread.[3]

But Ellsworth never bothered to respond to the letter.

Byrd, who was still in debt to the tune of $100,000 from his first expedition, signed agreements with Paramount Pictures promising his second expedition would, "face more ice, do more flying, and create more news than the first."[4] To create the headlines he was under contract to produce, Byrd understood he would not only have to fly across Antarctica, but he would have to do it before Ellsworth. He wrote to Ellsworth again, pleading, "Regardless of the way other explorers have hated each other, cut each other's throats and messed up each other's lives, let's you and I play the game."[5]

Still Ellsworth's replies were vague or nonexistent. He let Wilkins sort out the details, while he prepared for married life. Desperate, Byrd tried again:

This letter will reach you somewhere abroad. I really wish now that I had seen you before your departure. I wanted to tell you that I dislike very greatly to attempt to do something that you want to do. I want to emphasize this point. What I would like to have done would be to explain why, on account of the past and for the future, it is absolutely necessary for me to attempt to do this.

It goes mightily against the grain to be in this competition with you. I have racked my mind to find some way out of it, but so far without success. I must attempt to do this thing or give up entirely any further trip to the Antarctic. My job from Little America is only half finished. I cannot go into all my reasons for the necessity of my doing this in a letter. I just want to get this point over to you and want you to remember it.

The Depression has got us all by the throat and our going is most doubtful. I have not even yet selected a plane. The value of a dollar is so great now it seems a pity to have to spend money on this expedition at this time. Unless you have been able to collect some money from outside sources, I am afraid you are going to find your expenses are going to be terribly high. Ships are frightfully costly, as I have always found, and the *Bear* is costing me a pretty penny.

But warnings about expenses had no effect on the super-wealthy Ellsworth. What people thought of him did, however, and the devious Byrd even managed to imply the public would not look kindly on Ellsworth's expedition: "I doubt if the public will approve of any single expedition going down now and, if two go together, I don't know what the result is going to be."[6]

Ellsworth still wasn't bothered. He had all the money he needed and didn't have to send out letters begging for donations. He had Sir Hubert Wilkins, a man experienced in organizing polar expeditions, who had flown across the Arctic Ocean and in the Antarctic. He had Bernt Balchen, the best pilot for the job, and to top it all off, Ellsworth had a long-range airplane ideally suited to polar flying. It soon dawned on Byrd that there was nothing he could say to dissuade Ellsworth. His only chance was to beat him across Antarctica, or upstage him, so Byrd set out to do just that.

Byrd's first problem was an airplane. Ellsworth could afford $37,000 for a new Northrop Gamma. Byrd could not. Unlike five years earlier, manufacturers were not lining up to sponsor polar expeditions. Byrd wrote of his attempts to acquire supplies for his second expedition south:

> We proved ourselves, if nothing else, the world's hardest working beggars. We wrote innumerable times and called up manufacturers and firms specializing in things the expedition required. Approximately 30,000 [letters] were despatched hither and yon, having for their theme, "Please sir, would you be so kind . . ." And there were almost as many replies saying, in a word, "Sorry, gentlemen, but business conditions are such . . ."[7]

Finally, a wealthy businessman, William Horlick, paid for a Curtiss Condor which, with a full load of fuel, was capable of flying approximately 1,300 miles. It wasn't ideal because its range was insufficient to fly from the far side of the Weddell Sea to the Ross Sea, but it was the best that Byrd could get. Realizing he had an inferior airplane, Byrd studied maps of the known coastlines of Antarctica and concocted a plan. His expedition ships, *Bear of Oakland* (generally referred to simply as *Bear*) and *Jacob Ruppert* (usually *Ruppert*), would leave New York and enter the Pacific Ocean via the Panama Canal, before sailing down the west coast of South America, from where Byrd would reach Peter I Island in the Bellingshausen Sea. Byrd would fit his plane with floats, so it could take off from water, then fly to the Ross Ice Shelf. Byrd would then wait at Little America, in the base he had abandoned three years earlier, for the *Bear* and the *Ruppert* to arrive. It wasn't a complete crossing of Antarctica, but it would cover an unexplored section of Ellsworth's intended route and certainly diminish the news value of his flight.

Byrd continued to scheme. He knew there was no guarantee he could get airborne from near Peter I Island. He needed more than just the flight on which to build the publicity for the Byrd Antarctic Expedition II (BAE II). He wanted adventure to keep an audience enthralled. Ever the canny publicist, Byrd knew improvements had been made in radio transmissions in the five years since his previous trip to Antarctica. Families in America were gathering around their radio sets in the same nightly ritual that, thirty years later, families would devote to their televisions. Byrd wanted to be able to transmit weekly broadcasts that brought the excitement of his heroics into American living rooms. Early in the planning of BAE II he had an inspired idea. He would have his men transport a small hut to the interior of Antarctica. Then, with the hut stocked with enough food for the winter, Byrd would do what no one else had done before. He would spend the winter, not on the edge of Antarctica, but in the heart of it: on the plateau close to the Pole. To heighten the drama, he would spend the winter alone, sending out radio broadcasts, via Little America and Buenos Aires, to Big America.

Let Lincoln Ellsworth go south and fly across Antarctica. By the time he had, Byrd would have already flown much of the route and found anything worth discovering. Then, while Ellsworth was returning to America to claim whatever crumbs of glory could be salvaged from his flight, Americans would be listening to their hero, Admiral Richard Byrd, battling the cold, alone in a hut, high on the Antarctic Plateau, bravely making scientific observations for the good of humanity everywhere. It was a masterstroke of self-promotion.

Ellsworth and Mary Louise were married on May 23, 1933. A few days later, Ellsworth cabled Wilkins that the ship's name should be changed from *Fanefjord* to *Wyatt Earp*, and it was thus registered, after duly being inspected by authorities, at Ålesund on June 26. Ellsworth, on the advice of Harold Clark, who always kept a steady eye on his whimsical client's affairs, deemed it necessary to keep his private interests separate from the expedition and form a Norwegian company. On July 1, Wyatt Earp A/S Limited was formed in Norway. (A/S denotes *Aksjeselskap*, a Norwegian business entity requiring a minimum level of capital and limiting liability.) Ten thousand shares were issued at a price of one kroner per share. The law required a Norwegian national to hold the majority shareholding in any Norwegian company and so Aksel Holm, a local shipping agent, held 6,000 shares, Ellsworth 3,000, and Wilkins 1,000. Ellsworth had still not seen his ship nor, with the exception of Wilkins and Balchen, met any of his crew. Yet, of the yearlong preparations he would boast:

> I finally selected a staunch single-deck, motor-driven Norwegian fishing boat of 400 tons. She was built of Norwegian pine and oak in 1919. I sheathed her with oak and armor-plate for service in the pack ice. Her engine was of the semi-Diesel type, and I installed tanks for fuel sufficient for cruising 11,000 miles at a speed of seven to eight knots.[8]

Having ensured he would protect his business interests, Ellsworth needed to ensure he also protected his place in the history books. While the *Wyatt Earp* was still in Norway, every member of the crew, including Wilkins and Balchen, signed an agreement that stipulated they would not make any broadcasts, grant any interviews, distribute any photographs, or write any articles without Ellsworth's consent. Wilkins signed an additional agreement that he would write, "detailed articles while on the vessel *Wyatt Earp*; said articles to appear only under the name Lincoln Ellsworth." Nor, when Ellsworth returned to the United States in triumph, did he want

Wilkins to be seen or photographed with him. The victory was to be his alone. The additional agreement signed by Wilkins also stated, "Sir Hubert Wilkins will remain with the *Wyatt Earp* after her return from Antarctica . . . and will not return to the United States until two months after Mr. Ellsworth." Ellsworth would have imposed the same condition on Bernt Balchen to keep him out of the spotlight, except that he needed Balchen to fly the *Polar Star* on a promotional tour, so Balchen's contract included the stipulation that Ellsworth would return to America alone, and Balchen "will then join him to make the flight to either Washington or New York."[9] Ellsworth expected a successful flight across Antarctica would have him summoned to Washington to receive the Congressional Medal of Honor on the White House lawn, just as Byrd had been honored.

Two days after Balchen, Wilkins, and the crew had signed their agreements the *Wyatt Earp* was ready to sail.

10

CLOUD KINGDOMS OF THE SUNSET

JULY 1933–DECEMBER 1933

Finding himself suddenly married, the newlywed Ellsworth deserted his bride and traveled alone to Death Valley where, holed up in the luxurious Furnace Creek Inn, he informed Mary Louise that he might like it so much in Antarctica, he would stay there. "It's inconceivable to me that my life should not lie with yours," Mary Louise responded. "It was very saddening to find your letter so different from the others."[1] But Ellsworth, for the moment at least, was content in the desert and expressed his feelings in a letter, not to his wife, but his niece, Clare:*

> It is though I were formed of two beings from different spheres. The one is satisfied merely with the work and activity of the day. The other craves something else, something that is to be found somewhere in the west in the cloud kingdoms

---

* Before Ellsworth's sister Clare died, she had married Bernon Prentice and they had a daughter whom they named Clare.

of the sunset, or in the dreamy splendor of the moon, or farther away in the trembling stars.[2]

When he was informed by Wilkins that the *Wyatt Earp* was preparing to sail from Norway, Ellsworth ceased his stargazing, returned to New York, collected Mary Louise and her mother, and prepared to rendezvous with his expedition in New Zealand.

The *Wyatt Earp* sailed from Norway on July 29, 1933. It was a sunny day and all morning people had been gathering on the quay at Bergen to see the brave little ship set out on its gallant voyage. By mid-afternoon the moorings were slipped amid a chorus of cheers, while nearby ships hooted their sirens in encouragement. Hundreds of small boats escorted the *Wyatt Earp* as the crew lined the rails to acknowledge the well-wishers. From the top of the foremast the American flag fluttered proudly above the flags of scientific societies, schools, and clubs with which Ellsworth had a connection. Flapping alone at the stern was the Norwegian flag: a quiet reminder that this, despite its cowboy name, was a Norwegian ship. It might have been bought and paid for by a wealthy American, but to the Norwegian people the *Wyatt Earp* was still their ship, crewed by sturdy Norwegian men, courageously sailing south in the wake of Roald Amundsen. At the Inner Lighthouse, the Norwegian flag was dipped three times and three long blasts of the ship's siren bid farewell.

The *Polar Star* was stowed in the hold with its wings detached and wrapped in oiled paper to prevent corrosion.

In open sea, the *Wyatt Earp* was hit by a gale that lasted two days. It pitched and rolled, as it was prone to do, but otherwise proved seaworthy. Wilkins wrote to his wife,* "The ship rolls a great deal but it is not a viscous crazy roll, just swaying from side to side. We get used to it." After the gale abated, the crew enjoyed fine weather to Cape Town and became confident their small ship would be more than capable in the stormy Southern Ocean. "The captain and crew have turned out pretty good," Wilkins wrote. "There

---

* Wilkins had married Suzanne Bennett, an Australian actress working on Broadway, on August 30, 1929, shortly before the around the world flight of the *Graf Zeppelin*.

is a good spirit on board—the cook has cleaned up everything in the galley and mess and the food is good."[3]

Of the men on board Wilkins was the only Australian. Bernt Balchen, born a Norwegian, was a naturalized American citizen, while Chris Braathen, the mechanic, and Walter Lanz, the radio operator, were Americans. The rest of the crew were Norwegians and, with the exception of a young doctor, had all crossed either the Arctic or Antarctic Circle. The *Wyatt Earp* had an experienced captain, Baard Holth, at the helm.

Among the Norwegians was twenty-year-old Magnus Olsen, who was serving as first mate. Born in Norway in 1913, Olsen had been raised by his grandfather, who instilled in him a love of ships and the sea. He had graduated from the Norwegian Naval Academy in March 1933, just four months before the *Wyatt Earp* sailed. Olsen was also a flier, and he had been included in the *Wyatt Earp*'s crew to act as a reserve pilot for Balchen. Olsen would later publish the only Norwegian account of the first three voyages of the *Wyatt Earp*.[*]

The trip to New Zealand gave Balchen a chance to assess Wilkins. The perceptive Balchen was not impressed. "He is a strange fellow, fiddling around by himself all the time," he wrote to his wife. "Whatever he does, it usually ends up wrong."[4]

The *Wyatt Earp* had to stop for ten days at Cape Town, South Africa, while Balchen had his tonsils removed. Testy that the expedition was wasting time, Ellsworth sent a telegram wanting to know why the ship was delayed, emphasizing that they needed to get to Antarctica quickly, and reiterating, "under no consideration will I winter."[5] That Ellsworth had no intention of wintering in Antarctica was not news to Wilkins, and he urged the crew to proceed with haste. He was also pleased to report to his disinterested wife that "The crew are quite a deal better than those on the *Nautilus*":

> One or two on board are not ideal but they are not so bad while at sea as in port. Not many of them get drunk, but one went out the first night in port, had one drink at a cheap pub. The

---

* *Saga of the White Horizon* by Magnus L. Olsen, Nautical Publishing Company, London, 1972.

drink was doped and the sailor woke up on the wharf near the ship minus his false teeth, his collar and tie, and his hat. He has no recollection of what happened to him after the drink.[6]

The expedition left Cape Town on September 28, and six weeks later was greeted by Ellsworth in the southern New Zealand city of Dunedin. "How proud I was of my little ship, thus soberly and faithfully finishing her long voyage,"[7] he later wrote.

At Dunedin, the practical Balchen went hunting, and shot four wild pigs that were then hung from the rigging. He also wrote to his wife, "Wilkins has become much nicer now that Ellsworth has joined us."[8]

Ellsworth, for whom exploration was supposed to be about "the painfully established bases, the bitter journeys with sleds and dogs, the heroic battle against the elements,"[9] had sailed first class on a liner to New Zealand. He, along with Mary Louise and her mother, had arrived in Auckland earlier in September, insulted most of the local dignitaries, then, learning the *Wyatt Earp* was still held up in Cape Town, sailed to Pago Pago where it was warmer, before returning to New Zealand. Wilkins observed of the newly married couple:

> They have been having a wretched time in New Zealand. They don't care for the place at all and find the people uninteresting. However that is all their own fault for I hear from several quarters that people—the Governor and all the others in society out here, have been making many plans for the entertainment of the honeymooners . . . but they won't fall for the society stuff.
>
> To the Governor's invitation to call at Government House, they have not even answered, neither has Lincoln replied to a letter telling him that the people of Dunedin were affording him the freedom of the port—a saving to him of two or three thousand dollars. These little things I can now fix up, but it hasn't made the job much easier for me in this town.[10]

Having greeted his ship at Dunedin, Ellsworth learned it would be a month before it would depart for the Antarctic. Not wanting to spend any more time than necessary in the provincial city, he and Mary Louise found a comfortable hotel a few hours' drive north in the larger city of Christchurch.

In Dunedin, Wilkins oversaw the coaling of the *Wyatt Earp* and the loading of supplies, while receiving a stream of telegrams from Ellsworth, instructing him not to imply that he was somehow organizing the expedition on Ellsworth's behalf. Wilkins confided to his wife:

> [Ellsworth] sends me repeatedly, telegrams asking me not to accept luncheon engagements or speak or be seen in public any more than I can help for fear people will think that I am managing his affairs. Yet that fact cannot be but obvious because he has just as much trouble making up his mind what to do or what he wants, as ever, and it inevitably remains for me to finally say that he must do this and that, and then do it for him.[11]

Two days after the *Wyatt Earp* arrived at Dunedin, while Ellsworth sat in his hotel room at Christchurch, he received a disturbing radiogram from his old rival, Richard Byrd. "We are headed for Wellington [New Zealand],"[12] Byrd announced triumphantly, then continued to ask that if Ellsworth reached the Bay of Whales first, would he be good enough to supply Byrd with weather reports. To Ellsworth it must have seemed like the North Pole all over again: Byrd arriving with his large expedition to steal the glory and media attention.

Richard Byrd's second Antarctic expedition included two ships, the Curtiss Condor, two smaller planes, and an early form of helicopter known as an autogiro. Those were in addition to the two planes he had left at Little America in 1930. (He had taken a third in 1928, but it had been blown away in a gale.) The slower of the ships, the *Bear*, had sailed from the U.S. on September 25, 1933. The *Ruppert*, with Byrd on board, left on October 11. Byrd's original plan had been to first reach Peter I Island, a tiny landfall lying within the Antarctic Circle, southwest of Cape Horn. But for reasons he never explained, on the same day that the *Wyatt Earp* had reached Dunedin, Byrd changed his mind, postponing the idea of flying from Peter

I Island, and ordered his ship to sail directly to New Zealand, where the crew could stock up on alcohol at beautiful, friendly, and prohibition-free Wellington.* New Zealand's *Auckland Star* observed:

> Apparently there is a race between the Ellsworth and Byrd expeditions to reach Antarctica first. The expeditions are entirely independent of one another, but it is known that Mr. Ellsworth is not desirous of being headed in reaching the Ice Barrier. A message from the *Jacob Ruppert* has already indicated that Rear-Admiral Byrd is anxious to speed up his trip south and not delay the ships in New Zealand waters.[13]

Meanwhile, frustrated that Ellsworth's instructions were ambiguous, vague, or contradictory, Wilkins drove to Christchurch to speak to him directly. He found Ellsworth mired in depression and having second thoughts about the whole expedition. Mary Louise, after six months of marriage, was equally frustrated. Wilkins revealed to his wife:

> She does not know how long it will last. Mary does everything she can to please Lincoln . . . but she does not dare express very forcibly all her desires in order not to embarrass Lincoln. She told me that she has got him to promise to "go out"—step out, she said, twice a week when they return to the cities after the expedition. She has discovered that Lincoln does not like parties—luncheons, teas, or dinners or the theater, except vaudeville. He seems to like vaudeville shows so she expects their stepping out will be practically confined to the Hippodrome and such like.

Mary Louise also confided in Wilkins that she and Lincoln were sleeping in separate rooms, and Wilkins confirmed:

---

* Low-alcohol beer and wine were made legal in the United States in March 1933, partially ending Prohibition. The Eighteenth Amendment was not repealed until December 1933, making spirits, such as whisky, legally available.

. . . Mary's tale, and what I have heard from the keeper of the hotel where they have been staying, that separate bedrooms, sometimes the length of the corridor apart, are the vogue, seems to lack indication of lovers canoodling.[14]

Wilkins left Ellsworth holed up alone in his hotel room at Christchurch, and returned to Dunedin to continue preparing the *Wyatt Earp*. In the following weeks, barges plied their way around the ship and supplies were hoisted aboard to be stored in the holds. Magnus Olsen, the young Norwegian, recalled he was helping load the ship when:

. . . a mysterious box was then hoisted up. It so happened that I was the one to receive it, and as I stood looking at it, the little boat turned swiftly and chugged back to shore. As the sound of the engine died away, I began to hear strange noises coming from within the box itself. I wondered at first if the box contained a dog but by listening more intently I realized that the noises were the grunts of a pig![15]

Olsen adopted the pig, which had been donated by an anonymous farmer, and built a small home for it out of packing crates. Over the door he painted "Miss Piggy's Cottage," and observed that the pig continually soiled the deck, until a tray of sawdust was provided for it. The ship's cat, on board to keep the rat population in check, began using the litter tray and, remarkably, Miss Piggy followed its example. Soon she was trotting around like a house-trained puppy and was a welcome addition to the expedition.

Ellsworth also sent on board forty bottles of whisky for his personal consumption, in addition to the whisky and beer taken on board for the crew.

Finally, on December 5, the *Wyatt Earp* left Dunedin. At Port Chalmers, the last landfall near the mouth of the Otago Harbour, Wilkins scribbled a hasty letter to his wife:

We are away from the port and you should have seen the "awaying." Lincoln and Balchen full to the gills. Balchen followed by a Swedish blonde who immediately fastened herself to Ellsworth (who was in tears for an hour after the departure of Mary Louise, who went away an hour before we sailed) and you should have seen the snogging going on. The girl was very affectionate and apparently enjoyed kissing, and Lincoln didn't seem to mind it in the least.[16]

Other crew members had also brought girls on board for the short trip down the harbor from Dunedin to Port Chalmers, where Wilkins hustled them all ashore. With the girls gone, and Ellsworth and Balchen passed out drunk in their bunks, the *Wyatt Earp* chugged out into the Southern Ocean on its quest to achieve the last great first in polar exploration. Ellsworth's grand voyage of discovery was underway, and he later recalled proudly:

I don't suppose any vessel ever sailed before so filled with the presence of the figure whose name it bore as was the *Wyatt Earp* when it set out for the Antarctic. In the ship's library were two books about Earp: *Wyatt Earp, Frontier Marshall*, by Stewart N. Lake, and *Tombstone*, by Walter Noble Burns. Everybody on board read these two volumes, the Norwegians who understood English translating to those who didn't. On one of my fingers I wore a plain gold wedding-ring which the widowed Mrs. Earp had given me in memory of her famous husband. Wyatt Earp wore this ring during his Tombstone days, and he in turn had received it from his father. The ring, therefore, saw three generations of pioneers.[17]

II

THE UNIVERSE BEGAN TO VIBRATE

DECEMBER 1933–JANUARY 1934

A day after the Ellsworth Trans-Antarctic Expedition sailed, the Byrd Antarctic Expedition II arrived in Wellington, New Zealand. Byrd soaked up a round of social engagements while the crew hurriedly restocked their supplies and purchased alcohol. Asked to comment on the "race" to reach the Ross Ice Shelf, Byrd replied magnanimously:

> Mr. Ellsworth is an old and very great personal friend. Mr. Ellsworth asked my permission to operate from Little America and to take with him Mr. Balchen, who was with me on my last expedition and who is one of the greatest pilots in the world. That permission was readily given.[1]

When the comment was relayed by radiogram to the *Wyatt Earp*, it succeeded in annoying both Ellsworth and Balchen, neither of whom felt they needed Byrd's permission to do anything. Matters were not helped a day later when another radiogram, sent by a reporter, asked Ellsworth if he cared to comment on the announcement that Byrd intended to beat

Ellsworth to the Bay of Whales by flying from his ship, partway across the continent. Wilkins replied courteously on behalf of Ellsworth:

> Statement from Ellsworth—with a definite plan in view I am not in race to reach the Antarctic first. The Antarctic is a big territory and there is room for many expeditions. In my mind cooperation rather than a race should be the real incentive. I do not know Byrd's plans and it has never been my intention to use Little America.[2]

Less than a week after the *Wyatt Earp*, with its tiny crew, had left New Zealand, Byrd followed with the largest expedition yet to assault the southern continent. In addition to his ships and airplanes, Byrd's second Antarctic expedition included ninety-five men, 135 dogs, three cows (one of which was pregnant), and enough supplies to maintain a small community for three years. Among the fifty-two page inventory were three hundred pairs of overalls, fifteen stoves, fifteen hundred pounds of tobacco, six cases of chewing gum, three thousand books, six step ladders, seventy-two brooms, and two kitchen sinks. The Norwegian explorers had learned to adapt to the ice. The Americans would remake it in their own image.

After his brief visit to New Zealand, Byrd did not follow the *Wyatt Earp* to the Bay of Whales but, instead, headed back to the unexplored Pacific Quadrant, in search of headlines. Byrd still harbored hopes of upstaging Ellsworth by making significant flights of discovery from the area.

Between 80° West and 150° West no one had seen the coast of Antarctica or knew where the land—if indeed there was land—ended, and the ice began. Was there, in the Pacific Quadrant, another enormous ice shelf? Or a mountain range? Or islands? No one had been farther south than Captain James Cook, on his second great voyage of discovery (1773–74) when his path had been blocked by a wall of massive icebergs, stretching from horizon to horizon.

Byrd's plan was to thread his way through the icebergs as far as possible, lower the Curtiss Condor, which had been fitted with pontoons, onto clear water, then search for land. Seven days out of Wellington, after storms and rough seas had slowed progress, the *Ruppert* crept past Cook's southernmost point to enter the icebergs. Hundreds were counted, many three or four miles wide. Byrd named the area the Devil's Graveyard, because of the constant threat of being crushed.

A day later, the crew took depth soundings but could not find bottom at 300 fathoms (1,800 feet). Evidently, land was not nearby. A day later again, an ice-free area was found for the Curtiss Condor, so with pilot Harold June at the controls, Byrd flew south along the 150° West meridian. One hundred and eighty miles south of the *Ruppert*, he could still see nothing but icebergs. After flying past 69° South, more than one hundred miles farther south than Cook had sailed, and having used half his fuel, Byrd turned back.

On the *Ruppert* he faced a choice. A radio message from the *Wyatt Earp* informed him that Wilkins and Ellsworth were still battling their way through the ice pack to reach the Bay of Whales. Should he, having failed to find the coast on his first flight, now head west for the Bay of Whales and get his ship unloaded, so his men could start building Little America II? Or should he sail east to make another flight in an attempt to find land? He decided to go east, and for two frustrating weeks the *Ruppert* picked its way precariously through icebergs. The Devil, Byrd learned, had a large graveyard.

On January 3, 1934, near 116° West, and just below the Antarctic Circle, another open stretch of water was found and the Curtiss Condor was lowered to the sea. Again, Byrd flew south in the hope of discovering land, but shortly after takeoff, fog enveloped the plane. When the fog cleared Byrd saw the horizon was black with snow-covered squalls. They were flying into a storm. They had reached 72° 30' South and the coast of Antarctica still eluded them. Byrd flew back to the ship.

Byrd waited twenty-four hours to attempt another flight, but the weather only worsened. He ordered the *Ruppert* north and, after threading its way through the icebergs, it emerged into clear water on January 6. A day later Byrd received a radio message reporting the *Wyatt Earp* had reached the Bay of Whales.

The *Wyatt Earp* had a rough trip south. In heavy weather it would roll fifty degrees to each side. From being heeled over to port, rolling though one hundred degrees to starboard, then back to port, took only four and a half seconds. Anything not secured would be catapulted about the cabins with dangerous velocity. The entire trip was hell for the claustrophobic Ellsworth, who had never known such sailing or the confines of a small ship. He rarely emerged from his cabin and when he did, he managed to alienate the crew. On one occasion, he ordered Miss Piggy be slaughtered, so he could have fresh bacon for breakfast. Shortly after, First Mate Olsen knocked on his door, presented him with a pistol, and told Ellsworth if he wanted bacon, he was to get it himself. Miss Piggy's Antarctic adventure continued.

Extending several hundred miles from the edge of the Ross Ice Shelf was the dreaded "pack," a constantly moving maze of tabular icebergs slowly floating northward to melt in warmer waters. Fortunately, Captain Holth had been to the Antarctic previously and understood there was no quick or easy way to negotiate the pack. He spent three weeks threading the *Wyatt Earp* though the icebergs, before the expedition confronted the Ross Ice Shelf.

When Captain Sir James Clark Ross, the British explorer, discovered the shelf in 1841, and named it the Barrier, he observed there were few opportunities to unload a ship and scramble onto the ice along the four-hundred-mile wall that rose sharply from the water to, in some places, 150 feet. Ross did record that at the eastern end of the wall of ice, there was an indent, like the entrance to a narrow harbor. Robert Scott, on his first Antarctic expedition, found the same indent sixty-three years later. With the benefit of coal-fired steam propulsion, as opposed to a sailing ship at the mercy of the winds, Scott nosed the *Discovery* into the inlet to have a look around and took advantage of the low ice to disembark his men to practice their skiing. After going aloft in a tethered balloon to get a better view of the extent of the shelf, Scott named the indent Balloon Bight. Shackleton arrived next in January 1908 and renamed the indent the Bay of Whales, for "it was a veritable playground for these monsters."[3] Despite being able to unload their ships at the bay, neither Scott nor Shackleton thought a floating ice shelf was a safe place to set up their winter headquarters. Both continued to the western end, where they could build their huts on firm ground.

By the time he sailed south on the *Fram* in 1910, Amundsen had read Scott's and Shackleton's accounts of their respective expeditions and noted that the Bay of Whales was a permanent fixture:

For seventy years then, this formation—with the exception of the pieces that had broken away—had persisted in the same place. I therefore concluded that it could be no accidental formation. What once, in the dawn of time, arrested the mighty stream of ice at this spot and formed a lasting bay in its edge, which with few exceptions runs in an almost straight line, was not merely a passing whim of the fearful force that came crashing on, but something even stronger than that—something that was firmer than hard ice—namely solid land.[4]

Amundsen realized the Bay of Whales was formed by land farther south, impeding the northerly flow of the glacial ice. That unseen land, he reasoned correctly, would stabilize the surrounding ice shelf and make it safe on which to erect his hut. The bay was also a degree of latitude higher than the islands at the western extremity of the shelf, and therefore he could start his trek closer to the South Pole than Scott. Amundsen's gamble ultimately paid dividends.

In 1928, Byrd followed Amundsen and chose to build Little America at the Bay of Whales, because the flat surface of the surrounding ice shelf offered a vast ready-made runway for his airplanes.

On January 7, 1934, the *Wyatt Earp* entered the Bay of Whales. An area where the ice was level with the ship's deck was soon located. Balchen examined the surrounding shelf, approving its suitability as a possible runway, then he and mechanic Chris Braathen, who had also been at Little America with Byrd, strapped on skis and went in search of what had been their home four years earlier. Twelve miles south they found radio towers, chimneys, and the rudder of Byrd's Ford Trimotor protruding from the snow. Balchen burrowed down to the cockpit of the plane that he had piloted to the South Pole and discovered everything as he had left it. He sat in the pilot's seat and memories of the historic flight flooded back. He reached down and, on the floor, found the small pocket slide rule he had lost. Nothing had changed. Little America was frozen in time.

"Little America is as you left it with the planes in good condition except for digging out," Wilkins radioed to Byrd as a courtesy, knowing the Americans were sailing in the wake of the *Wyatt Earp*. "Radio masts OK but tremendous pressure shows in front of Ver-Sur-Mer [inlet]* making it impassable for dog teams. [*Wyatt Earp*] docked twelve miles from Little America. No sign of thawing this summer."[5]

The awkward task of hauling the *Polar Star* twelve miles to Little America was considered unnecessary. All the crew needed to do was to get the plane unloaded, attach the wings, get Ellsworth and Balchen airborne, let them make the twenty-hour flight to the Weddell Sea and back, then pack up and get the hell out of there.

The fuselage was lifted from the hold of the *Wyatt Earp*, followed by each wing, and the crew began the tricky job of assembly. Attaching the wings meant threading hundreds of tiny metal bolts, then attaching nuts, which was impossible using gloves. To stop their hands freezing, the crew rigged a canvas cover over the plane and warmed the air with four blow-lamps. The task still consumed two days. Then Balchen and mechanic Chris Braathen took the *Polar Star* up for two short test flights. Everything worked perfectly. Next, Balchen took Ellsworth up for thirty minutes and Ellsworth was thrilled to realize his great flight of discovery was about to begin. Olsen observed Ellsworth was "like a little boy in his excitement."[6] Even the weather for the following day promised to be clear.

But as the sea pounded the ice shelf, small sections near the edge began to crack and break off. Alarmed at the sight of the shelf breaking, Balchen took some of the crew and moved the plane about a mile farther from the edge. Wilkins questioned whether it was far enough but, as Ellsworth remembered, "Balchen said it would be better to take if back farther, but it would be safe for the night. Everyone was tired."[7] Ellsworth turned in, delighted the flight would take place the next day.

But his dream of polar immortality was rudely awakened at 4:00 A.M. by men shouting in Norwegian and the clamor of running feet. Ellsworth scrambled out of his bunk and rushed on deck to see the normally stable shelf buckling and cracking, as slabs of ice the size of football fields rose and fell, smashing each other at the edges. To Olsen, watching the

---

* On his previous expedition, Byrd had named a small inlet in the Bay of Whales the Ver-Sur-Mer Inlet. It was named for the village in Normandy where Byrd landed following his 1927 transatlantic flight.

phenomenon, it sounded like, "the tuning up of a mighty orchestra . . . as if the whole universe had begun to vibrate."[8] Gaps appeared between the slabs of ice. Even with the *Polar Star* a mile away, sitting alone under its canvas cover, Ellsworth could see the cracks snaking dangerously close to his precious plane. Nine crew members climbed over the side of the *Wyatt Earp* and, balancing on the heaving ice slabs, hurried toward the *Polar Star.*

When, after an hour, the men reached the *Polar Star,* an extraordinary sight greeted them. A crack in the ice ran directly beneath the plane. The *Polar Star* had dropped neatly into it and was only saved from plunging to the bottom of the sea by its wings, which spread across the ice on either side. The plane was too heavy to lift manually, so their only hope was to somehow get the *Wyatt Earp* close enough to hoist it on board before the crack widened.

After hours of delicate maneuvering, Captain Holth managed to penetrate the floes, some of which had the courtesy to drift away, to within about three hundred feet of the stranded plane. A cable was run out and for the next four hours the *Polar Star* was reeled in, inch by inch, to where it could be lifted on board. There was a deathly silence as the plane was hoisted clear of the ice. As it dangled from the derrick the damage was clear. The undercarriage was completely stoved in. There would be no flying this season.

Ellsworth was shattered. It was plain bad luck, and Ellsworth and Wilkins both seemed to attract it. The news got worse. In the urgency to thread its way as close to the *Polar Star* as possible, the *Wyatt Earp* had become trapped. After everyone had rested, Wilkins gathered the crew together and told them they were not to be upset over "that thing on the deck with the broken legs."[9] Glasses of champagne were circulated and Wilkins explained their present imprisonment in the ice was not serious.

By this time, having spent six weeks with Ellsworth, most of the crew had come to, at best, ignore him and, at worst, detest him. Magnus Olsen (who was in the camp that chose to ignore him), wrote of the misfortune:

> Sir Hubert's own calm and indomitable spirit had saved the situation . . . his whole attitude to everything had so cheered us that, along with the afterglow of the champagne, we were at

last impelled to tell our versions of the great drama which had
been enacted on the previous day. It was a tremendous honor
to serve under such a great explorer.[10]

After they had rested, the crew started the laborious task of blasting
their way free of the ice. First, holes ten feet deep were drilled by hand in
the ice. Then, sticks of dynamite taped to the ends of bamboo poles were
lowered into the holes. Caps on the top of the dynamite were set off with
an electrical charge, usually from a distance of about one hundred feet. The
results were unspectacular. The ice would simply rupture, lift fractionally
and fall back into place. Undeterred, the crew kept repeating the process,
until the *Wyatt Earp* was surrounded by cracks and small channels. By
that time, however, the engine could not be started because the propeller
and rudder were frozen in a solid block of ice. Explosives could not be
used, for fear of damage. So, for five days, the crew dynamited forward of
the bow and used a hand saw to produce cracks, then, walking on the ice,
man-hauled the *Wyatt Earp* toward open water. Once they were partially
free, they used an old Norwegian sailors' trick to warm the ice surrounding
the propeller and rudder. They slung hessian bags containing lumps of
carbide and rock salt over the side, so when the seawater soaked into the
bags, heat was generated and the ice melted.

Finally, after an exhausting week, the *Wyatt Earp* reached the open sea.

12

ALONE

JANUARY 1934–AUGUST 1934

On January 28, 1934, less than eight weeks after it had departed, the *Wyatt Earp* crept back to Dunedin, where the already despondent Ellsworth learned that Mary Louise and her mother had returned to America without bothering to wait for him. Ellsworth dithered, undecided about whether or not to repair the *Polar Star* and try again, or abandon the idea of crossing Antarctica. He was equally undecided about how to proceed with his marriage. Wilkins observed:

> I think he is not really keen to get back [to the U.S.]. Mary Louise wants him to open up Lenzburg [Castle] and stay there this European spring and summer, but he does not want to do that, so he sent a message to her today that she could go to Lenzburg and he would stay on the West Coast of America, or in the Grand Canyon, roaming about with a pack horse. She replied, "What do you mean by suggesting that I should go to Europe and you stay in America? What is it all about? You must come back and see me about this."[1]

Ellsworth suffered two weeks in New Zealand, before the SS *Mariposa* took him to San Francisco. On his arrival, Mary Louise and her mother bundled him onto a train for New York, where they all boarded another ship and sailed to Europe, where Ellsworth did, in fact, spend the next five months at Lenzburg Castle.

Wilkins was left in New Zealand to sort out the *Wyatt Earp* and the damaged *Polar Star*. "Each message from Lincoln sounds sadder and sadder and I doubt that he will make another attempt," Wilkins wrote to his wife:

> But one can never tell. He will probably say that he won't and then at the last minute change his mind. In any case I don't want to go on with the expedition again and will feel that if I get the boat ready, and see them start off, they can take care of themselves.[2]

By a stroke of good fortune a Texaco oil tanker was in port—Texaco provided petroleum products to the expedition in exchange for publicity—and was preparing to leave for California. The captain agreed to take the plane. The crew members who lived in America: Balchen, mechanic Braathen, and radio operator Lanz accompanied it. Wilkins put the *Wyatt Earp* into dry dock at Port Chalmers, where the hull could be examined after its encounter with the ice, and the engine could be overhauled.

Then, while he waited on Ellsworth's decision, he began to evaluate his employer, and just what he had got himself into, writing to his wife:

> [Ellsworth's] position is really pathetic. Without initiative, ability, or power, he can't really do anything. Fortunately, he knows it and what he wants is someone to do everything for him and see that he gets the credit. Of course, there are many people in the same position and who become famous because of other peoples' work, but they have to at least put up a front and poor old Lincoln can't manage to put up the front.
>
> He is still quite a puzzle—even to himself. He told me that he tried his best not to get married, but had to give in in the end and now has to keep both his wife and her Ma. I think they

both want to do what they can to make Lincoln happy but they, not any more than anyone else, know just what to do about it.[3]

Having summarized his thoughts on Ellsworth, Wilkins concluded his letter by adding some thoughts on Balchen:

> Balchen is, I think, sincere, but he has been accustomed to having everything perfect and does not want to take a chance on anything and I am not sure that I blame him, for he knows that Lincoln can afford to keep on. Perhaps it is best that they did not take a chance and try to repair the [plane] down there. To have done it and finished the flight this year would—if Lincoln decides to go on—have saved him about $75,000, for it will cost that to continue for another year. But then it is just as well for Balchen to spend Lincoln's money as to have Mary Louise and her mother spend it. And Lincoln anyway has no one else dependant upon him. Well that's enough about expedition affairs.[4]

In Antarctica, on his second trip south, Richard Byrd wanted to winter alone, in the heart of the continent, to achieve the greatest polar coup and eclipse any explorer who had been to either polar region. It was in his chain of command that Byrd blundered badly. In order to manipulate support, Byrd was prone to making promises he later broke. As his expedition neared Antarctica, more than one crew member believed he would have the honor of being second-in-command, and therefore in charge of Little America while Byrd was heroically battling the elements in the hut on the plateau. It was a decision Byrd should have announced earlier but, as the ice came into view, he offered the position to Tom Poulter, a member of the scientific staff. At first Poulter declined the appointment because it was his first trip south. Other, more experienced men, such as Harold June, had been to Antarctica with Byrd on his previous expedition. Poulter argued that one of those men should be promoted first. In fact June, who was the senior pilot, expected the position. Byrd pointed out that June drank heavily (there had been many wild drinking bouts on Byrd's first Antarctic expedition) and, after some persuading, Poulter agreed to accept the position. That made

June openly angry and he expressed his displeasure to Byrd. June pointed out that he had been with Byrd since the Arctic in 1926. Was this, June wanted to know, how Byrd repaid loyalty?

Byrd responded to this confrontation by making an unforgivable mistake, especially for a naval officer indoctrinated in the importance of discipline and clear lines of command. Having appointed Poulter second-in-command, Byrd then appointed June the "head of expedition staff." According to Byrd, June could, with a two-thirds majority vote of expedition members, overrule any order of any officer at Little America. That meant that if the men didn't like what they were being told to do, they could simply have a discussion and decide not to do it. It was a potentially unworkable arrangement from the outset.

To compound this folly, Byrd then put many men offside by leaving them to do the exhausting work of hauling the supplies across the ice to Little America (a route the men called Misery Trail), while he sailed east in the *Bear* to explore the coast. The men felt they were being left to do the heavy lifting while the star of the show went on a cruise. Nevertheless, from January to March 1934, Little America underwent a substantial redevelopment as Byrd's crew laboriously unloaded equipment and prepared for the winter ahead. New buildings were erected beside the ones that had been vacated four years earlier. Hangars, machine shops, a medical facility, bunkhouses, and a barn for the cows were built. Little America more than doubled in size.

The discontent among the men was alleviated by the fact they had stocked up on alcohol in New Zealand. During Byrd's cruise aboard the *Bear*, Poulter watched the men, led by June, smuggle their supplies into the abandoned buildings of the first Little America. The potential for alcohol abuse was increased by the expedition's physician, Dr. Guy Shirley, himself an alcoholic, who had brought huge quantities of whisky for "medicinal purposes." When Byrd returned from his brief trip to explore the coast, he witnessed Shirley being continually drunk and ordered him back to New Zealand on the *Bear*.* Fortunately for June and his cronies, Shirley donated his considerable supply of alcohol to them before he left.

---

* Shirley was replaced with a New Zealand doctor, Louis Potaka, who became the first Maori to travel to Antarctica.

By the middle of March, Byrd was sending parties south to lay supply depots for his Advance Base hut. But it was already late in the summer season and traveling, either with dogs or tractors, was becoming increasingly difficult. Byrd's stop at New Zealand, and his attempts to make a transcontinental flight from the Pacific Quadrant, had seriously delayed the rebuilding of Little America. That delay forced him to modify his plans.

Originally Byrd had wanted to winter high on the Antarctic Plateau. As he came to realize it was too late to transport the hut and supplies that far, he decided to set up Advance Base at the foot of the Queen Maud Mountains, six hundred miles away. But by March even that was out of the question. Byrd's Advance Base would ultimately be established just 123 miles south of Little America on the ice shelf. From a scientific point of view—taking weather observations and the like—there was no point. But Advance Base was not about science; it was all about Byrd, who freely admitted:

> . . . I had no important purpose. There was nothing of that sort. Nothing whatever, except one man's desire to know that kind of experience to the full, to be by himself for a while and to taste peace and quiet and solitude long enough to find out how good they really are.[5]

Byrd left Little America on March 22, and was flown to Advance Base. The lateness of the season and the difficulty in transporting the prefabricated hut over the ice meant the men had erected it hurriedly. It had been designed so the roof should sit flush with the surface of the ice, allowing snowdrifts to blow across it unhindered. But it had not been dug in deep enough and the roof protruded twelve inches, causing snowdrifts to accumulate and block the chimney and the trapdoor entrance. Another problem was that the hut leaked air through the hastily constructed joints. It was much colder inside than anticipated, making it difficult for the small kerosene-burning stove to warm the interior.

After Byrd had spent a week at Advance Base, the men who had erected it sledded back to Little America, leaving him alone. His adventure had begun.

◆

In New Zealand, Captain Holth and the Norwegian crew members of the *Wyatt Earp* were instructed to stay with the ship and wait until they received word as to if, or when, Ellsworth's next expedition might take place. The Norwegians soon learned there were small expatriate Norwegian communities in New Zealand, mainly consisting of ex-whalers. Embraced by these communities and receiving their wages from Ellsworth, they relaxed and enjoyed themselves.

Wilkins tried to make sense of his life and plan what he should do next. He had no money and was living on the small salary that Ellsworth was paying him to take care of the *Wyatt Earp*. He felt that his debt—moral or financial—had been repaid. He had organized the expedition and got everything successfully to the Ross Ice Shelf, until circumstances beyond his control had brought the whole affair to a premature end. He was alone and lonely; famous for a failed submarine expedition to the North Pole, while living in hotels at the bottom of the world, touring country towns and showing his films for a little extra cash. And waiting for the wealthy Ellsworth to make up his mind about what he wanted to do.

On the personal front, Wilkins had not seen his wife in two years and was conscious that she was dating other men. He had married Suzanne Bennett, an Australian-born chorus girl working in New York, shortly after he was knighted. It was a whirlwind romance, consummated at a heady time in Wilkins's life. It was soon apparent to Wilkins that Suzanne's main motivation in attaching herself to the famous explorer was to gain the title Lady Wilkins, then put it to use to elevate her career from chorus girl to movie star. (A strategy that was spectacularly unsuccessful.) Wilkins constantly wrote Suzanne long letters expressing his love, but she rarely replied, and when she did it was usually only to taunt him about his lack of success, his age, or the fact he was going bald.

In Dunedin, in early 1934, exhausted and undecided about his future, he sought guidance from, and refuge in, the metaphysical world. On February 15, after visiting a spiritualist show, he wrote excitedly to Suzanne:

> . . . there was a woman on the stage answering questions.
> She . . . told me the name on a visiting card in my pocket—I

being in the second row of the stalls and she being on the stage and blindfolded. The card was not mine, but that of Captain Nelson of the ship *Discovery*[II].* He had slipped the card into my pocket that morning and even I did not know the full name on it before the thought reader told me.[6]

For a person supposedly dedicated to promoting the scientific study of the powers of the mind, Wilkins ignored the obvious explanation that a card, so easily slipped into his pocket, could just as easily be lifted and read by a pickpocket working the lobby of the theater, then the information passed to the "thought reader."

But Wilkins did not have to spend long trying to ascertain his future from spiritualists because, in April, Ellsworth decided it for him by announcing he would make another attempt to cross Antarctica. Perhaps his decision was influenced by the knowledge that Byrd's hut was little more than one hundred miles south of Little America and therefore not providing an extraordinary show or unlocking the secrets of the interior of Antarctica as Byrd had originally hoped. Or perhaps it was the sense of stifling helplessness Ellsworth felt in the castle now being run by his wife and mother-in-law. Whatever the reason, or combinations thereof, Ellsworth instructed Wilkins to organize another trans-Antarctic flight for him.

Wilkins responded, saying that he would, at least, prepare the *Wyatt Earp*. Then he immediately sailed to London in the hope of convincing the British to give him a submarine to explore the Arctic. A legitimate opportunity to go north was an excuse to avoid going south, Wilkins reasoned. But the Royal Navy had no submarines available and no money to offer him, so Wilkins sailed back to New Zealand, stopping at Australia on the way. By August he was back in Dunedin, still hoping to meet his obligation to Ellsworth by simply arranging the ship and crew, but not going south himself. He would ensure everything was loaded on the *Wyatt Earp*, then wave it off. As he explained to Ellsworth by telegram:

---

* The British exploration ship *Discovery II*, captained by Andrew Nelson, was berthed in Dunedin at the time.

Gladly supervise preparation but think after departure you,
Balchen, Holth could manage everything including writing
[press releases]. I prefer not go south. Should supervise building
submarine but if you insist would not lecture [or] write [about]
your expedition.[7]

Ellsworth never bothered to respond and Wilkins, waiting in Dunedin
with the *Wyatt Earp*, turned again to a local spiritualist church to seek
guidance as to what to do. He explained another mystical encounter to
the indifferent Suzanne.

The medium said she could see a sparkling cross above my head
and a blazing square about me. Many spirits were standing near,
all willing and eager to help . . . urging me to go ahead more
firmly with my work and plans and assuring me of tremendous
success, which the medium said would be sure to be mine.

She also described one man, more or less like [Ben] Eielson,[*]
whom she said placed his hand on my shoulder and encouraged
me to go on . . . my mother, she said, was also there, and said
that while [my mother] knew I was not following the work she
planned—she wanted me to be a minister—she realized that
I could do more good if I went earnestly ahead and did what I
was trying to do.[8]

Wilkins was forever convincing himself to go forward with his vision
for the future of mankind. But while the spirits in the metaphysical world
were urging him to continue with his efforts to take a submarine under the
ice in the north, economic factors in the physical world were conspiring to
keep him in the south.

Meanwhile, in Antarctica, Richard Byrd was close to death.

---

[*] Ben Eielson, Wilkins's friend and pilot from the 1928 flight across the Arctic
Ocean, and the 1928 expedition to Antarctica, had died in a plane crash in the Arctic
in November 1929.

13

THE STARS FORECAST STRANGE THINGS

APRIL 1934–SEPTEMBER 1934

At Advance Base, everything worked reasonably well for the first two months. The gasoline that powered the generator for the radio gave off fumes and Byrd learned to store the generator in a food tunnel, only bringing it into the hut when he needed to use it. The protruding roof soon accumulated snow, making the trapdoor difficult to open, so Byrd dug another escape tunnel. He also found he was without a recipe book and, not knowing how to cook, had to continually radio Little America for instructions. Otherwise, things went to plan.

The same could not be said for life at Little America, where Tom Poulter, who was a nondrinker, had been left in charge of a boozy group of men who had no respect for his authority. There was also a sense among the men that their leader had forsaken them, and that Byrd's idea of wintering alone was only designed to glorify him. We are "tools for the Admiral's ambition,"[1] one man wrote in his diary.

While Harold June and the construction party had been erecting Advance Base, Poulter had attempted to rein in the drinking at Little America by confiscating some of the alcohol and hiding it. He had also buried what was left of Dr. Shirley's stash in the snow. After the construction team returned from Advance Base on April 1, Poulter relaxed the rules and let the men drink alcohol from their remaining supplies. Some got exceedingly drunk, fell in the snow, and almost froze to death. Rather than ordering the remaining alcohol to be dumped out, Poulter let the men keep drinking in the hope that their supply would soon be exhausted.

Fearing that Poulter might soon instigate total prohibition, June started gathering support among expedition members to overrule Poulter's command. Poulter reacted by attempting to form an executive committee to forestall June. All the while, the drunken binges continued. Knowing that Poulter had hidden Dr. Shirley's cases of whisky, the men would stagger around in the snow, probing with long metal rods, trying to locate it. Next, Poulter tried to calm the men by occasionally handing over a few bottles, but the peace offering did not produce the desired effect. The men immediately got drunk and those that didn't stumble around in the snow became increasingly antagonistic. Poulter reacted to the aggression by secretly pouring twenty cases of rye and bourbon into the snow, but not knowing the mother lode had been destroyed, the men continued to search for it.

At the same time, some of the men were directing their hostility toward Byrd, who on the previous expedition had been a willing participant in the drinking sessions. He had actually encouraged them. Now many men were annoyed that he had not only deserted them, but had left a nondrinker in charge. One expedition member wrote in his diary of the pathetic struggling of a group of men "to satisfy an already satiated leader's publicity complex." Another hung a sign around the neck of a dog that had frozen that read, "I died for Byrd. Why don't you?"[2]

Alone at Advance Base during April and May, Byrd enjoyed himself. "Indeed I look forward to the rest of my sojourn with pleasure," he wrote. The simple unhurried routine, combined with the lack of human contact, gave him ample time to reflect on his life, which he did:

> Yes, solitude is greater than I anticipated. My sense of values
> is changing, and many things which before were in solution in
> my mind, now seem to be crystallizing. I am better able to tell

what in the world is wheat for me and what is chaff. In fact, my definition of success itself is changing.[3]

In the stillness, a tiny helpless dot in a vast landscape of whiteness and purity, Byrd also began to sense, like many others who share a similar experience, a presence of God:

> The universe is not dead. Therefore, there is an Intelligence there, and it is all pervading. At least one purpose, possibly the major purpose, of that Intelligence is the achievement of universal harmony . . . The human race is therefore not alone in the universe. Though I am cut off from human beings, I am not alone.
>
> For untold ages man had felt an awareness of that Intelligence. Belief in it is the one point where all religions agree. It has been called many names. Many call it God.[4]

But while Byrd explored his consciousness and spirituality, he was slowly being poisoned. History offers two theories as to what poisoned him.* One points to the gasoline engine that ran the generator to power the radio. Byrd would crawl into the narrow tunnel daily and start the engine for his radio transmissions, but the fumes in the tunnel made him nauseous. The other theory points to the kerosene stove that Byrd used to heat the hut and cook his food. He needed to keep the stove burning to avoid freezing to death. The original stove had given off such strong fumes that the men setting up the hut had replaced it with a smaller coal-burning stove, which had been hastily converted for kerosene. That makeshift device was attached to an ill-fitting flue, which leaked. Slowly, as the weeks passed, Byrd's condition, as a result of the gasoline engine or the stove, or both, worsened.

By early June, Byrd realized he was sick but was unsure what to do about it. He desperately needed what little heat he could get from the kerosene

---

* A third possibility is that Byrd was suffering from alcohol poisoning, but this has never been investigated by Byrd historians. There is no record of how much alcohol Byrd took to Advance Base.

stove, because a few feet above him, the temperature was -60°F (-51°C). And he needed to keep crawling into the radio tunnel to send his messages. If he stopped, he feared his men would attempt to rescue him. A sledging journey across the shelf in the dead of winter would be almost suicidal. Byrd had to keep up the appearance that everything was fine at Advance Base while, in fact, he knew he was being poisoned.

At Little America however, Byrd's erratic signals were worrying Poulter. On June 14, Byrd asked if moisture would help reduce carbon monoxide, and asked Poulter to make exhaustive recommendations for keeping down carbon monoxide fumes. Poulter knew his leader was in trouble. He consulted Charles Murphy, who was Byrd's public relations man and one of the few men who was not part of June's drinking group. Should they attempt to reach Byrd in the dark of winter, with temperatures at -60°F and unseen crevices crossing their path?

At the same time, keeping Byrd's worsening condition a secret was impossible at Little America. Despite orders forbidding private radios, some had been smuggled in, and various men were eavesdropping on Byrd's communications with Poulter and Murphy, then relaying information to the United States. By late June, Byrd's condition was so well known that even the *New York Times* was speculating that he might need to be rescued. Byrd, meanwhile, was still torn between wanting to be rescued and not wanting his men to risk their lives. He issued instructions clearly stating that no attempt should be made to come and get him until the light was sufficient and men could make the trip without undue risk.

Poulter, whose scientific disciplines included astronomy, tactfully asked if he could be allowed to make a trip thirty miles from Little America, along the trail to Advance Base, to observe a meteor shower. Byrd gave his consent. On June 26, Poulter and three others went out on the trail with one of the tractors. Although an ordeal, the trip proved something of a success because, using torches, the men were able to follow the trail of flags that led to Advance Base. A week later Poulter posted a notice on the bulletin board announcing that a tractor party would be sent to rescue Byrd. He stated that he felt it would be safe to leave on such a trip in the last two weeks of July.

Harold June immediately called a meeting of the "executive staff," which rejected the idea as too dangerous. Poulter called another meeting, which supporters of both camps attended. When June announced that he wanted no responsibility for what might happen to the rescue party, Poulter took it as a sign that he would not veto the idea. Remarkably, that was the first of many meetings. The debate continued as expedition members moved motions, offered opinions, called more meetings, and objected to proposals. The bureaucratic squabbling at Little America continued for so long that the sun began to return before anything could be resolved.

On July 14, a faint glow appeared on the horizon. A week later, Poulter and four others left in a tractor, but they only got about thirty miles before a blizzard forced them to return. Byrd, by then, had given up all pretensions of not wanting to be rescued. In his feeble, pain-wracked state he radioed asking where the tractor was.

Poulter made a second dash for Advance Base on August 4, this time with only two companions: Pete Demas and "Bud" Waite. Both were loyal "Byrd men." After thirty-six hours they had only traveled twenty miles. The tractor's clutch began to slip and the trio turned back. Partway back to Little America the tractor stopped altogether and was abandoned. The three men staggered the final miles, half frozen. Poulter had another tractor prepared and a day later the trio departed again. For two days they made their way cautiously across the ice. Byrd, who had been at Advance Base for more than four months, would periodically open the trapdoor to stare across the ice in the dark of the perpetual night:

> At 6 o'clock I was again at the trapdoor. And this time I really saw something. Dead in the north a beam of light lifted itself from the Barrier, swept to the vertical, and fell; then it rose again, touched a star, and went out. This was unmistakably Poulter's searchlight, and my first guess was that it wasn't more than ten miles away.[5]

Poulter, Waite, and Demas arrived safely. They remained at Advance Base for two months, nursing Byrd back to health. Remarkably, they suffered no ill effects from either the kerosene stove or the gasoline engine. What caused Byrd's poisoning has been a subject of speculation ever since. Leaving Advance Base for the final time, he wrote:

I climbed the hatch and never looked back. Part of me remained forever at latitude 80.08 South: what survived of my youth, my vanity, perhaps, and certainly my scepticism. On the other hand, I did take away something that I had not fully possessed before: appreciation of the sheer beauty and miracle of being alive, and a humble set of values.[6]

Byrd may have been endowed with a humble set of values, but with Lincoln Ellsworth about to make another attempt to cross Antarctica, he still needed to ensure that he remained, in the eyes of the American public, his country's greatest polar hero. His manipulative mind studied ways he could turn his failure and near-death experience at Advance Base into a success that would surpass anything Ellsworth might do.

While Byrd recuperated at Advance Base, Wilkins waited in Dunedin for Ellsworth to arrive. On September 2, Wilkins explained to Suzanne:

[Ellsworth] is on the boat between here and Honolulu now. He must have been on a "bender" last night because he sent me a wireless saying that, as it was raining on the boat, he did not want to stay at the hotel in New Zealand and that, as he would not have anything to do with Byrd, he asked me to arrange a code by which we could communicate. But then he ended up asking if I didn't think it was possible for me to arrange with Byrd's ships to carry some of our supplies and finally said to cancel arrangements I had made here for him, and about which he had previously sent four or five cables to be sure that I had made.[7]

Ellsworth may have indeed been on a bender. On his second trip to New Zealand he was free of the watchful glare of Mary Louise and had found a boyfriend in Hawaii; a Hawaiian guitar player, name unknown. "I don't know if he is bringing his Hawaiian with him or not," Wilkins wrote, then added sarcastically, "if he doesn't he won't get the same tune played to him by yours truly."[8]

Despite his previous reluctance, Wilkins had convinced himself to go south again. With no other option, he was forced to take out his maps and study the problem of crossing Antarctica yet again. Various factors pointed to changing the original plan and starting from the opposite side of the continent. Chief among those was that Byrd was at Little America on the Ross Ice Shelf. A one-way crossing of the continent, starting from Graham Land and ending at Little America, would dramatically shorten the distance of the flight. Wilkins could sail the *Wyatt Earp* across the Southern Ocean to Graham Land, from where Balchen and Ellsworth could take off, then fly over the continent to the Ross Ice Shelf. Safely landed, they could enjoy Byrd's hospitality, while the *Wyatt Earp* sailed back across the Southern Ocean to collect them.

There was also the weather to consider. The best months for flying in the Antarctic were November and December, after the ferocious winter winds, yet before the summer fogs set in. Wilkins had made his long flight from Deception Island to Hearst Land during December. Byrd had flown to the South Pole in late November. The logical plan seemed to be to start from somewhere in Graham Land, in November, and fly to Little America. Deception Island was a possible starting point. If the bay was frozen the *Polar Star* could easily get airborne from there. If the ice in the bay was not frozen, it might be possible to take off using the newly tested pontoons. The new plan was fundamentally the same as what Wilkins had attempted in 1928 and 1929, when Byrd had been at Little America the first time.

During the northern summer, the *Polar Star* had been repaired and Balchen had test flown it across America. After that, he, mechanic Braathen, and radio operator Lanz had returned to New Zealand with the repaired plane aboard the SS *Monterey*. Ellsworth had sailed on the more luxurious SS *Mariposa*.

Wanting an extra crew member, Wilkins advertised in a local paper, and received more than four hundred responses. A twenty-year-old Dunedin lad, Alastair Duthie, who explained he had skiing and mountaineering experience, joined the *Wyatt Earp*.

"I have a presentiment that there is some rather strenuous work ahead of me before we get through with this year's efforts," Wilkins wrote to his wife after complaining, as usual, that she never wrote to him. Then he added,

"Goodness knows what will happen and the stars forecast strange things for me."[9] But a day before he sailed, Wilkins finally received an unexpected letter from Suzanne. He read it to learn that the wife he had not seen for more than two years was preparing to have a child. His reaction, which he expressed to her in a letter the following day, reveals something of the personality of one of the most enigmatic characters in polar history:

> So you are preparing to have a baby. Ah hah. So that's it. Well I have with me four books about the habits and complaints of women—thought I had better put in some of my time studying such things so as to be able to take care of you. When I come back I will be a regular women's doctor—so your man had better be careful what he's about because you will have to tell me all the treatments and I will tell you if it is the right thing to have done.[10]

The *Wyatt Earp*, with Ellsworth, Wilkins, Balchen, and fourteen crew members, left Dunedin on September 19, 1934, bound for Antarctica a second time.

As the *Wyatt Earp* sailed, another Antarctic expedition was nearing Graham Land. When Wilkins had flown along the east coast of Graham Land and Palmer Land in 1928, he had reported a series of channels and straits presumably reaching the Bellingshausen Sea. The largest of these, and the nearest to Hearst Land, he named Stefansson Strait. In 1934, the British Graham Land Expedition intended to sail down the west coast of Graham Land and Palmer Land to locate the western end of Stefansson Strait (if it existed) and see if it was possible to sail through it to reach the eastern side, as seen by Wilkins. The expedition was led by John Rymill who, like Wilkins, was a South Australian. Rymill had purchased an old three-masted schooner, which he renamed *Penola*, and his nine-man expedition was intending to establish a winter headquarters at Marguerite Bay, on the west side of Graham Land.

14

THE THIRD MAN

OCTOBER 1934–JANUARY 1935

have never known a drearier voyage," Ellsworth wrote of the monthlong trip from Dunedin to Deception Island, off the west coast of Graham Land. "We rolled and wallowed at seven knots across the most desolate stretch of water on Earth. During the entire twenty-six days, we did not meet one vessel. No whale's gleaming back broke for a moment the tortured monotony of the sea."[1]

Deception Island is an active volcano that, with the exception of the caldera, sits below water. The horseshoe-shaped rim forms a natural harbor, which opens to the sea through a narrow channel. In the 19th century, Norwegian whalers discovered the island offered shelter from storms and regularly sought refuge there. Frequent visits saw the island evolve into a base for the whalers' factory ships and, by 1914, they had established shore-based facilities to boil down whale carcasses, extract the oil, and store it in steel tanks. Falling prices for whale oil, as a result of the Depression, forced the closure of the whaling station in 1931. Today the island is a popular destination for Antarctic cruise ships, bringing tourists to photograph the rusting remains of the whaling station, or to enjoy the unique experience of bathing in the warm water that bubbles up from the volcano below, while surrounded by snow fields.

Early on the morning of October 14, 1934, the most violent weather of the voyage greeted the *Wyatt Earp* as it approached its destination. Captain Holth, who had been to Deception Island previously, identified a landmark as Castle Rock. He continued cautiously to reach a flat slab of stone, Sail Rock, rising one hundred feet above the sea then, as *Wyatt Earp* pitched and rolled, he inched between the cliffs that guarded the entrance to the harbor. The ship squeezed in. Wilkins and Ellsworth eagerly scanned Whalers Bay and were disappointed. They observed only open water. Wilkins remembered that in 1920 the ice had been six feet thick. In 1928 it had been two feet thick. Now there was no harbor ice, and consequently, no runway for the *Polar Star*. Their thoughts turned to the snow cover ashore, hopeful that it might provide a flat area suitable for their purpose.

The *Wyatt Earp* tied up at the whaling jetty. Balchen donned his skis and soon located a relatively flat area, covered with snow, from which he believed he could get the fully laden *Polar Star* airborne. He also understood the rising summer temperature meant the snowfield would only last a few weeks. There was no time to waste if they were to get Ellsworth into the air and on his way to Little America.

But even within the protection of the volcano's crater the winds blew with such ferocity that five frustrating days passed before the crew could unload the plane. Eventually, with the *Wyatt Earp* huddled beside the tiny jetty, the crew struggled to lift the *Polar Star*, without its wings, from the hold of the ship, then hauled it to higher ground. Again, the men went through the frozen-finger process of attaching the wings to the fuselage by means of hundreds of tiny nuts and bolts. Finally, on October 29, the propeller was ceremoniously lifted onto the engine shaft. The *Polar Star* was ready for a test flight and, unlike nine months earlier, this time it was safely resting on solid ground.

On the opposite side of the continent, the recovering Byrd was shrewd enough to understand that, publicly, he had to appear to be enthusiastically supporting Ellsworth's trans-Antarctic flight. He wrote in a diary intended for publication:

We are all following, with utmost sympathy and interest, Ellsworth's efforts to complete his transcontinental flight. We are now furnishing him with daily and sometimes twice daily weather reports. Ellsworth and Balchen face a long and difficult flight. Their probable track and what they are likely to find on the way are a lively topic of conversation here.[2]

Byrd instructed his meteorologist, Bill Haines, to radio weather reports to the *Wyatt Earp* and, on October 29, Haines reported the weather was clear at his end. All Ellsworth needed was clear weather on his side and he could fly into the history books. But that evening, after a day of sunshine, snow squalls and the inevitable frustration, set in.

To keep Ellsworth motivated, and ensure everything was in readiness, Wilkins suggested they run the engine briefly. Everyone thought that was a good idea. Without further discussion, the hand-cranked starter mechanism was slotted in beneath the engine cowling and mechanic Chris Braathen gave it a hefty turn. Rather than the engine bursting into raucous life, there was a sharp bang, like a pistol shot, and the propeller flopped lifeless after half a turn. Something was seriously amiss. The Pratt & Whitney air-cooled radial engine was hurriedly pulled down to reveal a connecting rod (con-rod) between a piston and the crankshaft had broken. To protect the engine from corrosion during the long sea voyage, the cylinders had been filled with oil, which Braathen had forgotten to drain before the hasty attempt to test the engine. And the news got worse. A search through the many boxes of parts revealed there were no spare con-rods.

A conference was held and Wilkins suggested a radio message be sent to the Pratt & Whitney factory in Connecticut, to have the necessary part flown to the southernmost port of Chile: Magallanes,* nine hundred miles to the north. It would mean sailing the *Wyatt Earp* across one of the stormiest oceans in the world to pick up a package that may or may not be delivered successfully, but with no alternative it was certainly worth a try.

---

* Magallanes is also known as Punta Arenas. It was officially named Magallanes in 1927, then reverted to Punta Arenas in 1938.

"I am determined to carry on until I succeed or see that there is no hope left to make the flight across Antarctica,"[3] Ellsworth reported bravely to the *New York Times*, when the delay was explained. Two days after the disastrous attempt to start the engine, Wilkins and the crew began the voyage to Chile.

Ellsworth and Balchen, along with Braathen, meteorologist Jorgen Holmboe, and Dr. Dana Coman,* chose to wait at Deception Island. During their enforced time together, Ellsworth had the opportunity to get to know the man he expected to pilot the *Polar Star*. "Balchen was moody and temperamental . . . subject to sudden fits of temper," he wrote. "Once, just as we were sitting down at table, Dr. Coman let one of the cats** into the dining room of the whaling station cottage. Balchen picked up the animal and threw it against the wall."[4]

The *Wyatt Earp* reached Magallanes on November 9, where Wilkins immediately hired a car and drove twelve hours to the Argentinean city of Rio de Gallegos. He enjoyed a hot bath, ate a hearty meal, wrote a letter to his wife, and collected the con-rods, which had already arrived. Twenty-four hours later he was back on board and the ship was plying its way south again. The *Wyatt Earp* returned to Deception Island after a sixteen-day round trip. It was still early enough in the season to make the flight.

Byrd, meanwhile, had ground parties with dog teams fanning out from Little America to scout for the best possible landing areas. The teams were instructed to stay out on the ice, listen via radio for the flight, and be prepared to lay bright orange sheets on the ground to form patterns, such as "T" (suitable for landing), "Y" (fair landing field), or "+" (unsuitable for landing), along with various other signals for indicating the direction of Little America. Byrd also radioed:

> I suggest that you advise me the width of your skis so that if
> any landing has to be made over sastrugi it can be levelled off
> to ski width. When you are ready for weather reports from field
> parties let me know.[5]

---

*   Coman, an American, had replaced the Norwegian doctor from the first voyage.
**   Feral cats, left by the whalers, had bred and thrived at Deception Island.

Ellsworth just needed the right weather.

During the period the *Wyatt Earp* was absent fetching the con-rods, Balchen, in turn, had the opportunity to assess Ellsworth's capabilities. He had come to the conclusion that Ellsworth was incompetent in most things. In particular, Balchen harbored serious doubts about Ellsworth's ability to navigate. Balchen's uncle, Leif Dietrichson, may have told him this previously. (Dietrichson had been Ellsworth's pilot in the Dornier Wal flying boats in 1925 and had later refused to share navigating responsibilities with him on the airship *Norge*.) In any case, after the return of the *Wyatt Earp*, Balchen argued that they needed to carry a third man in the *Polar Star*. He wanted someone who could navigate. It would be difficult and uncomfortable for the third man to squeeze in the narrow, two-seater plane, but Balchen insisted. Ellsworth, naturally, was totally opposed to the idea, later writing:

> A third man could only be taken at the sacrifice of fuel or of camp and travel equipment on which our lives might depend, if the plane was damaged in landing. This proposal was so violently at variance with my whole scheme and theory of the crossing that I could not believe that Balchen really meant it.[6]

Balchen's reluctance to trust Ellsworth wasn't the only issue. The delay in getting airborne, caused by the broken con-rod, meant the nearby snow had begun to melt. Patches of black volcanic rock dotted Balchen's proposed runway, and with each passing day the ground revealed more black and less white. It took ten days to repair the engine and, by that time, the snow had melted sufficiently to ensure the plan to take off from Deception Island had to be abandoned.

Wilkins faced the same problem he had faced previously on the two Wilkins-Hearst Antarctic Expeditions: Where could he find a suitable flat runway from which to get a fully fueled plane airborne? Previously, he had tried grading a runway from the rocky ground at Deception Island, but the basalt had stubbornly resisted that idea. He had explored the west side of Graham Land and not found a flat island. There was only one area left to consider: the notorious Weddell Sea.

Today we know that on each side of Antarctica there is a huge bight. On the side facing the Pacific Ocean it is the Ross Sea, while facing the Atlantic Ocean it is the Weddell Sea. Currents, which are driven forcibly from the oceans to the north, flow into these great bights to scoop up millions of tons of ice that have descended from the Antarctic Plateau and, in a swirling clockwise motion, sweep it out to sea. In the Ross Sea where, at the western extremity Victoria Land does not extend north, the piled pack ice easily reaches open water. At the western end of the Weddell Sea, however, the Antarctic Peninsula extends north. Here the ice cannot escape so freely. Trapped, it becomes deadly as it is caught, crushed, jumbled, and tumbled over itself. And small rocky islands jut from the water and conspire with the ice to crush any ship foolish enough to venture into the area. The northwest corner of the Weddell Sea is the most dangerous coastal area in the Antarctic.

In February 1902, Swedish explorer Otto Nordenskjöld and a small party were landed on Snow Hill Island at the edge of the Weddell Sea. Returning in December, their relief ship found it impossible to reach them and had to move away from shore. Returning again in February 1903, the ship was caught and smashed by the ice, marooning the relief party on nearby Paulet Island. Nordenskjöld's group, which had already built a hut, spent a second winter in Antarctica, while the relief group survived in a small stone shelter, before all the men were eventually rescued. Nordenskjöld claimed the area had "a desolation and wildness, which perhaps no other place on earth could show."[7]

Another person to risk entering the Weddell Sea was Sir Ernest Shackleton, who ignored the advice of the whalers and based his decision on his two trips to the more benign Ross Sea. When he attempted to unload the team that planned to walk across Antarctica, his ship *Endurance* was famously caught and crushed. In the twenty years since the *Endurance*, no one had tried to navigate the Weddell Sea. In fact, in more than thirty years, no one had returned to visit Nordenskjöld's hut.

But Wilkins's previous experience told him there was no other possibility of finding a flat runway. Venturing into the infamous Weddell Sea was their only hope.

The *Wyatt Earp* left Deception Island and, after a short trip north, nosed its way through the Antarctic Sound, where the expedition members stared in awe at the sheer ice walls of glaciers that towered three hundred feet over their ship. Once through, they were greeted by a labyrinth of tiny islands. Cockburn Island "proved to be only an incongruous reddish brown mountain rising abruptly 2,000 feet."[8] It was kept ice-free by volcanic warming. Seymour Island reminded Ellsworth of the Badlands of the Dakotas; barren and desolate when silhouetted against the snow and glaciers of the larger James Ross Island. Before they could get a view of Snow Hill Island, a fog set in and they sailed past it, unable to see from one side of the *Wyatt Earp* to the other. They groped their way through the thick white mist to bump into the Weddell Sea ice shelf. Instead of finding flat ice, suitable for getting the *Polar Star* up to takeoff speed, they found "a mild season had pitted its surface with loose refrozen crystals on which a heavy plane could not ski."[9]

They decided to wait and inspect Snow Hill Island when the fog lifted. Wilkins knew that Nordenskjöld's hut was on the west side, facing James Ross Island, which lay across a narrow strait. He proposed that they sail into the strait to look for a runway on the protected side. But the *Wyatt Earp* found too many shoals and was unable to navigate the water, so Captain Holth was forced to take the ship to the exposed east side of Snow Hill Island, drop anchor, and wait for the weather to clear. After an exhausting trip from Deception Island, the tired crew sagged into their bunks. The next morning, when everyone awoke, the fog had lifted and the gale had subsided. Ellsworth came on deck to be greeted by a glorious panorama:

> The twenty-five-mile length of Snow Hill Island lay clear before our eyes—the most theatrical island of the archipelago. The northern tongue of it—a low coastal plain perhaps twenty miles square in area—was brown, stony, and barren. Behind that the island had a turtle-back formation, rising on gentle slopes to a height of 900 feet; and this whole flattened dome was clothed in a glacier which, being white, had given the morsel of land its name.[10]

Wilkins, Ellsworth, Balchen, and Second Mate Lauritz Liavaag walked to the plateau. There, about a mile inland, they found the ideal runway for which Wilkins had searched unsuccessfully on his two trips with the Lockheed Vegas. Ellsworth, who had been close to abandoning the whole enterprise, noted "my spirits, which had been lower than the barometer, now rose to a keen pitch of anticipation."[11]

The glacier from the plateau was only ten feet high where it met the water, providing a natural wharf for the *Wyatt Earp* to tie up. The *Polar Star*, which had been lashed on the deck with its wings still attached, was unloaded and easily taxied up the glacier to the plateau. Then the crew set about the more laborious work of hauling drums of fuel and crates of supplies up to the plateau as well. Ellsworth left the hired hands to do the heavy lifting and hiked across the island on snow shoes to visit Nordenskjöld's hut. He found it just as it had been when it was vacated thirty years earlier:

> The evidences of the hurried departure were as plain as though the thing had happened yesterday. The skeletons of three white sled dogs lay in front, just where they had fallen when shot. Near them was a pair of rusty ice-skates and a pair of shoe-trees, dropped in flight. Piled against the cabin were several cases of canned sardines, pepper and mustard, and cakes of chocolate. The chocolate tasted as good as new . . . Inside were the same evidences of flight.[12]

Ellsworth collected some clothing, boots, equipment, a gramophone, and some cylindrical wax records, which he later donated to the American Museum of Natural History.

When he returned to the *Wyatt Earp*, he found everyone optimistic about the chances of a successful flight. The *Polar Star* was ready and Wilkins and Balchen had even taken it up for a test flight.

But on Ellsworth's return to the ship, Balchen again raised objections to flying, saying he wanted a third man in the plane. He continued to argue Ellsworth could not be relied upon to navigate accurately. Wilkins, Balchen, and Ellsworth tried to resolve the issue, but as they negotiated back and forth, a gale blew in and resolved it for them. Extra person or not, there would be no flying until the weather cleared. Then, to add to Ellsworth's frustration, the glacier began to calve, so the *Wyatt Earp* was moved, while Captain Holth waited for the massive slab of ice to float away.

On the opposite side of the continent, Byrd summarized the problems they faced:

> [Meteorologist] Bill Haines was talking about it today. This late in the season, Bill says, the chances against the right conditions for the flight are about 100 to 1. Weather, of course; the same sort of thing we're up against, but on a much larger scale. Where we need a clear stretch of only 400 miles or so, they need clear weather between two hemispheres. The weather experts and pilots here seem to think that Ellsworth's only hope this season is to ignore weather at his end and seize the first stable weather at Little America, gambling on the chance of breaking through and finding good weather for landing here. [13]

The primary concern with taking off in poor weather and chancing their luck, Byrd pointed out in his public diary, was that Balchen and Ellsworth would cut off their chance to retreat if they did not break through into clear weather, and that flying in poor weather limited observation and made the flight, ostensibly for exploration, pointless.

Two weeks went by before finally, on December 18, the wind dropped and Balchen declared the weather suitable for flying. The *Polar Star*, having been left on the island, was now covered in snow, so that only the top of its engine was visible. The crew trudged up to the plateau and, with shovels, dug out the plane before starting and warming the engine.

After a late supper, Balchen agreed to take Ellsworth up for a test flight. They took off successfully, flew south along the coast, and returned two hours later. The repaired engine worked perfectly and they had been in radio contact with the *Wyatt Earp* the entire time. Yet again, it seemed everything was set. Even Balchen, perhaps sensing the mounting annoyance of both Wilkins and Ellsworth with his reluctance to pilot the plane, had agreed to make the flight relying on his own and Ellsworth's navigation.* In fact, Wilkins was so confident (or so eager to get them away) that he sent a radio message to the *New York Times* announcing the flight was about to take place.

Still the weather had other ideas. It changed again and they were forced to wait. Everyone watched nervously as the sea ice slowly closed around the *Wyatt Earp*, threatening to cut off their escape. Only the fact that the wind was blowing from the west meant that the ice was not forcing the ship against the coast. If the wind turned, the *Wyatt Earp* would be trapped. They knew they could not stay long.

As they waited, Ellsworth remained in his cabin, depression settling on him like a fog. When he did emerge, it was usually to complain the men were not working quickly enough, or to question why everything was taking so long. He began to speak of canceling the expedition. To alleviate his darkening mood, Balchen and Wilkins proposed an alternate plan. Perhaps a short flight over some nearby unexplored area would satisfy his ambition. But Ellsworth was adamant. He had come south to fly across Antarctica. It was the long flight or nothing. As each day passed it seemed more likely it would be nothing. "At last I was facing the bitter thought that the flight might be impossible this year,"[14] Ellsworth wrote.

During this prolonged stagnation, Wilkins, Magnus Olsen, and some Norwegian members of the crew took the opportunity to escape Ellsworth's despair and the confines of the *Wyatt Earp*, and camp on Snow Hill Island. They set up a tent, and Olsen recalled:

> Sir Hubert Wilkins was an extremely taciturn man, and there-fore on the rare occasions when he did talk, it was always worth listening to. As we lay resting in the tent that night for the first time, he mentioned the submarine *Nautilus*, which he had

---

* Wilkins prepared navigational instructions for the flight from Snow Hill Island to the Bay of Whales. The instructions are undated, but it is likely Wilkins prepared them during the two weeks they waited at Snow Hill Island for the weather to clear, and they were enough to convince Balchen to make the flight without a third person. The instructions are reproduced as an Appendix.

bought for a dollar from the United States Navy, and of his attempt to pierce the ice cap in the Arctic. Although he had to abandon the venture, he regarded the attempt he had made as having been worthwhile, and told us that sometime, someone else, with financial backing, would succeed in carrying out the project. His philosophy was that every person had ideas which appeared crazy to others, and while they might be laughed at and brushed aside at the time, someone else was sure to bring it forth as his own idea, and be given a chance to carry it out.

Before he bade us good night and dropped off to sleep, he gave me a piece of advice that should be followed by all aspiring explorers. "Remember, Magnus, you will never gain anything without personal wealth, or government backing."[15]

Wilkins had devoted years of his life to repay his debt and now, for the second time, the expedition appeared to be over. Ellsworth declared it was time to load the *Polar Star* back on board and leave, so Wilkins investigated whether he could make the flight. Balchen could fly the plane and Wilkins could certainly navigate. On December 29, Wilkins sent a secret message to Isaiah Bowman of the American Geographical Society, asking for money to take over the expedition and make the flight himself:

> Confidential: Ellsworth tired waiting, is packing to return tomorrow. Have not yet proposed anything to him and not sure he would agree to any proposal, also apart from what I might personally subscribe would need about $20,000 to carry on another year or $10,000 for rest of this season.[16]

But before Bowman had a chance to respond, the weather cleared. Jorgen Holmboe issued his meteorological report suggesting that they would have clear weather. Byrd radioed that the weather was clear on the Ross Sea side. Ellsworth emerged from his cabin, excited the flight was back on. The crew dug the *Polar Star* out of the snowdrift again and began preparing it, but the task of shoveling the snow took a full day and Ellsworth grumbled that they were not working fast enough. "With a little more speed in preparing the *Polar Star* we might have taken off that day,"[17] he wrote.

By the time the plane was ready (January 1, 1935) fog had shrouded Snow Hill Island and visibility was reduced to a few meters. The flight was off again. Everyone felt they had chanced their luck with the Weddell Sea pack ice long enough. It was time to go home. A disheartened Ellsworth admitted that the expedition, his second to Antarctica, was over.

15

A HIGHER TYPE OF COURAGE

JANUARY 1935–APRIL 1935

A t Snow Hill Island the crew waited three days for the fog to lift before
they could begin the strenuous task of hauling the still-full drums of
fuel down from the plateau. As they toiled through the morning, up
and down the glacier, the weather unexpectedly began to clear. It stopped
snowing and the wind dropped. Byrd sent the weather report from Little
America, confirming it was clear at both ends of the route. On an impulse
Ellsworth suggested to Balchen that they attempt the flight. Balchen,
surprisingly, agreed. The crew scurried about to check the plane and start
the engine. Wilkins, also hopeful the flight would finally be done, radioed
a prepared statement from Ellsworth to the *New York Times*:

> The great adventure, so long awaited, is at hand. The motor is
> warming up, and soon its roar will be breaking the silence that
> veils the Earth's last great unknown, as Balchen and I wing our
> way across Antarctica, with the opportunity of all that pertains to
> the opening of a continent for the last time in human history.[1]

Then Ellsworth made one of his stranger decisions and sent a radio message to Byrd. He asked if, once he arrived at Little America, he could remain there for the winter, after Byrd had abandoned the base and returned north. Furthermore, Ellsworth also enquired if "one of your pilots and a mechanic [would] care to join me in place of Balchen and Braathen."[2] Even if he successfully crossed the continent, Ellsworth was in no hurry to return home, apparently. He had previously suggested to Mary Louise that he may wish to stay in Antarctica. Now he seemed to be seriously considering it. At Little America, Byrd quickly circulated the word among his crew and, remarkably, five men volunteered to spend another winter in Antarctica. Byrd relayed the news to Ellsworth.

Balchen and Ellsworth shook hands, posed for Wilkins's movie camera, then climbed aboard the *Polar Star*. The weeks of blizzards had altered the flat runway so that it now sloped downhill, becoming a series of gentle undulations. Those undulations, combined with the fact that the wind was blowing from the higher end, meant Balchen would need to taxi the fully laden plane uphill to get airborne. The crew watched as the *Polar Star* moved into position before Balchen opened the throttle. But the combination of the uphill slope, the undulations, and the heavy load proved too much for the *Polar Star*. Balchen taxied back and forth for thirty minutes, growing increasingly impatient. Finally, unable to contain his frustration, Balchen turned the plane around and steered it off the runway and onto the glacier flowing down to the water where the *Wyatt Earp* was moored. Wilkins and the ship's crew watched in horror as Balchen opened the throttle to maximum revs and the plane, with a tailwind, sped toward them. At the edge of the ice the *Polar Star* would either lift into the air or plunge into the water. In the seat behind Balchen, Ellsworth clung on, scarcely daring to open his eyes. The plane shot from the ice like a bullet from a barrel, skimmed the water for half a mile and then gradually began to gain altitude. Balchen brought the *Polar Star* around in a wide circle, flew over the cheering crew of the *Wyatt Earp*, then took it to three thousand feet and headed southwest.

Wilkins radioed another preprepared statement to the *New York Times*. It began by declaring the great flight was underway and ended by quoting Ellsworth's favorite poem, "Who Has Known Heights," by Mary Brent

Whiteside. As the *Polar Star* became a speck on the horizon, Wilkins was concluding the exultant radio message with the words, "Who once has trodden stars seeks peace no more."

Ellsworth was finally on his journey to join the stars of world exploration.

Balchen followed the coast of Graham Land. Ellsworth busily made observations of the landscape in his notebook. He saw that, because everything was so choked and buried under the ice, it was difficult to distinguish land from sea. In fact he became so engrossed in his notebook he did not notice Balchen bank the *Polar Star* to starboard and turn around. Moments later, Ellsworth looked up to see the peaks of the mountainous spine of the peninsula, which he had previously observed on his starboard side, could now be seen out of his port window. He shouted at Balchen, whose laconic response was the weather was too bad to continue.

Ellsworth stared in disbelief at what he described as "a wisp of a squall" with "the sun showing on both sides of it." Surely it was not enough to give up? But Balchen was flying north, back to the *Wyatt Earp*. It finally dawned on Ellsworth:

> So at last I began to realize the truth. Balchen was not going through with this flight unless he found absolutely perfect flying conditions, and they were something we might have to wait years to find. Two years of planning and work were going by the board. I knew that Balchen was a good judge of weather and that by turning back we might be escaping a storm—yet next day we had ideal weather at the *Wyatt Earp*. I shall always believe we could have gone through.[3]

Two and a half hours after taking off, the *Polar Star* returned to Snow Hill Island. Wilkins grabbed his camera when he heard the approaching plane and was on hand to film the landing. The grainy images show Ellsworth climbing from the plane, ignoring the camera, and stomping off without speaking. Wilkins stopped filming. Unsure what had happened, he approached Balchen who responded, "Ellsworth can commit suicide if he likes, but he can't take me with him."[4]

Perhaps, in Balchen's judgement, the weather was so poor that the flight was impossible. Perhaps he felt he could not rely on Ellsworth to navigate accurately, or assist them to get airborne should they be forced down. Or perhaps he genuinely believed the depressed Ellsworth had some sort of death wish. Friends had feared he might take his life ever since his sister, Clare, had died. Whatever the case, Balchen said little on the subject, other than that he had attempted the flight, found the weather bad, and turned around. According to Ellsworth:

> Balchen had his side of the story. He told Wilkins afterward that in the camp on Deception Island, when the five of us were waiting for the *Wyatt Earp*'s return from Chile, he had made up his mind that he could not rely on a single man for sufficient assistance in the event of a forced landing. That was when he began asking for a third man in the plane. He had decided he would not attempt the flight with me alone, unless conditions were such that we could make it nonstop.[5]

At Little America, hearing that the flight was abandoned, Byrd sent a consoling message. Ellsworth had previously made a vague insinuation that Byrd's radio operator, Charlie Murphy, was feeding Balchen false weather reports giving Balchen a reason not to make the flight so, after expressing his sympathy, Byrd pointed out:

> I do however congratulate you indeed for using your good judgement in not taking chances in spite of the weather that probably would have resulted in disaster. It often takes a higher type of courage not to do a dangerous thing than it does to do it. During the latter days the weather over here was uncertain as it always is at this time of year but in spite of my concern I did not give you any suggestions because I was afraid it would be misunderstood. We did our best to keep you informed of the weather.[6]

Ellsworth, however, still had simmering doubts about Byrd's motives.

Any flying for the year was finished, but not the expedition. The wind had turned and was blowing from the east. They had stayed in the Weddell Sea too long and the *Wyatt Earp* was in danger of being crushed. Gales buffeted the ship as it heaved itself against the edge of the glacier. It was four days before the wind allowed the men to load the *Polar Star* hastily on the deck and lash it down. The ship pushed north, to where it was held fast by encroaching ice for five days. At times the crew would try to dynamite their way through, but it was futile. After a week, they were still only sixty miles from Snow Hill Island. A shift in the wind broke up the ice and they returned to the island, this time sheltering in the strait on the west side. The crew took the opportunity to visit Nordenskjöld's hut. For another five days the pack forced them to anchor near the hut.

The *Wyatt Earp* had enough provisions to spend the winter, but there was no guarantee they would be released from the ice in spring. Wilkins radioed the British research vessel *Discovery II*, asking its movements. Might it be possible, he wondered, to fly some men to Deception Island, from where the *Discovery II* could take them to South Georgia and they could return north? In fact, Wilkins nominated the three men who most wished to escape a winter in Antarctica. Ellsworth, who a few weeks earlier was considering wintering at Little America, was at the head of the list, followed by:

> Braathen, airplane mechanic, who must go to hospital for stomach operation although he is not yet a bed case, and a third man, [Jorgen] Holmboe, [a] Norwegian government man whose leave so long since expired that if delayed longer he doubtless will lose his position.[7]

While Holmboe and Braathen had legitimate reasons for not wintering there, the rest of the crew was aware that Ellsworth simply did not want to spend any more time on his ship than he absolutely had to. Captain Andrew Nelson of the *Discovery II* (the man who had slipped his business card into Wilkins's pocket ten months earlier) responded with a qualified offer of assistance, pointing out that he was not entirely a free agent and could not afford to be delayed. But if the men were at Deception Island when he was there, he would take them. Luckily, before the negotiations needed to continue, the ice made a channel and the *Wyatt Earp* sailed back through the Antarctic Sound to Deception Island.

Most of the Norwegian crew was exhausted and, after almost two years of faithful service, they were openly saying they had had enough of the expedition and Ellsworth's dark moods, arrogance, and ingratitude. Arriving back at Deception Island they received the final insult.

In their seven-week absence, members of John Rymill's British Graham Land Expedition, which was trying to locate and confirm Stefansson Strait, had visited the abandoned Norwegian whaling station and vandalized the place. Doors, windows, furniture, and even the piano were smashed. Broken crockery was strewn about and every drawer and cupboard had been ransacked. Wilkins reported, 'There was human excrement on the floor of the mess room of the whaling company's barracks and also less than six feet away from the pathways to other buildings."[8]

Horrified at the wanton and needless destruction, Magnus Olsen immediately skied to the nearby cemetery, fearing the Norwegian graves would be desecrated, but was relieved to see that "the marauders had not found the old, isolated graveyard . . . The stones were as we had left them."[9]

Wilkins had always enjoyed the support and hospitality of the Norwegian whalers at Deception Island. In his report to the owners, the Hector Whaling Company, he pointed out that on his previous visits, and while the *Wyatt Earp* used the facilities to repair the *Polar Star*'s engine, any supplies taken had been replaced and the station left in good order. He concluded:

> About the material removed, I mention only in passing. It is the dirty, wrecked condition in which the place was left that I wish to comment on, particularly because the company owning the buildings at Deception Island have so generously and courteously assisted several polar expeditions and would doubtless continue to do so if they felt they could receive ordinary consideration in return.[10] *

---

* Wilkins also wrote to John Rymill, the leader of the British Graham Land Expedition, to express his disgust at the vandalization of Deception Island. Rymill did not appreciate the criticism and in his book on his expedition enjoyed pointing out that Wilkins's Stefansson Strait did not exist.

If the Norwegians, who had agreed to crew a Norwegian ship in an attempt to help an American cross Antarctica, needed any more reason to quit the expedition, they found it when they walked among the trashed buildings and human feces of their countrymen's former home.

The long voyage back across the Pacific to New Zealand was out of the question. On January 21, 1935, they headed, instead, for the closer port of Montevideo, Uruguay. On the trip north a plague of rats, which had found its way on board at Deception Island, swarmed over the ship eating everything in their path. They even ate the ship's cat. Miss Piggy survived.

On the return voyage Ellsworth mostly stayed in his cabin. He continued to ignore the crew and issued his orders through Wilkins. After two voyages and months of close confinement, he still did not know many of their names. About a week before the *Wyatt Earp* arrived in Montevideo, Wilkins addressed the men, asking how many would be willing to return for a third trip if required. The question was met with stony silence, so Wilkins quickly added, "Don't make your mind up now, but think about it and let me know before we drop anchor."[11]

At Montevideo, Ellsworth immediately left the ship, crossed the River Plate to Buenos Aires, and flew back to the United States. Some time before he left the *Wyatt Earp*—possibly while the ship was still in Antarctica—he had scribbled an undated note and handed it to Wilkins. It read:

> I will continue my effort to cross Antarctica only under the following conditions. Namely that:
>
> 1. Both Sir Hubert Wilkins and Bernt Balchen accompany the expedition.
> 2. Only two men fly in the plane.
> 3. Opportunities of weather conditions to fly are taken that were <u>not</u> [Ellsworth's underline] considered this year with agreement to landing if necessary.
> 4. No meteorologist accompanies the expedition except one who will be available for weather reports at that [Ross Ice Shelf] end.
> 5. No more flying considered after January 1.

6. Balchen agrees to go on a salary of $4,500 per month after reaching Valparaíso or Buenos Aires where the ship will winter [and] the plane will be left until its departure October 20 for Deception Island.[12]

If Ellsworth was going to make another attempt he wanted everything to be the same as his second expedition, except he had to start the flight on time, not have any of the nonsense about a third person in the plane, nor any of the nonsense about delaying the flight or turning back because of poor weather.

From Montevideo, Bernt Balchen sailed to America, writing to his wife shortly before he left:

> [Ellsworth] will probably go down again this fall, but I am definitely not going again. Both he and Wilkins have been a big disappointment during the difficult times. They both like to take all the credit they can get, but they are weaklings when things are going against them. They have made several attempts, in the most delusive way, to blame me for there being no flying this year. I have cleared out my [things] and don't give a damn about them.[13]

An exhausted Wilkins was left to sort out the ship and the crew. He began by sacking most of them. The men, Wilkins pointed out to Suzanne in a letter sent soon after the ship reached port, were more than willing to leave the ship because, "when they saw [Ellsworth's] behavior in general they all got disgusted and now with the exception of two or three they would all like to be clear of the expedition, as in fact I would too if that were possible."[14] Wilkins never made clear whether he was talking about the crew's disgust at rumors that Ellsworth was gay, or the fact that Ellsworth was always the last to board and the first to leave and only did minimal work.

Meanwhile, in New York, Mary Louise was confiding to her friends that Ellsworth was gay, and when that news reached Suzanne, she was pleased to have something new with which to taunt Wilkins. In a letter that has not survived she told Wilkins of the gossip, and mocked him for being employed by a gay man. Wilkins replied in the same matter-of-fact manner as he did to Suzanne's "pregnancy":*

> I am not the least bit concerned as to what people say. He may be a sissy for all I know, but I do know that I gave my word that I would do the job of putting him in a position for doing the flight he has made up his mind to do and that is that. One does not argue or ask to get out of a contract by word of honor. However Lincoln may volunteer to release me and you can bet that I would be mighty glad of the chance to be free.[15]

Although he was indicating that his reason for staying with the expedition was because he had given his word, Wilkins was also conscious that he had few opportunities to earn money while America was gripped by the Great Depression. He had written to various contacts in New York and learned, "It is more difficult for one in my position to earn one hundred dollars now than it was to earn one thousand three years ago."[16] Even the possibility of touring and showing his films in theaters seemed unlikely because, as he explained to a Paramount News executive:

> There is little of interest to the movie public. There has been very little action and what did take place was either always at midnight or when the weather was unsuitable for filming. The crowd on this expedition have no interest in the films and will not do anything especially in the interest of pictures, so I am afraid that there is very little of use in the negatives despatched, except a plain record of what happened, e.g. nothing.[17]

First Mate Magnus Olsen, Second Mate Lauritz Liavaag, Engineer Harald Holmboe, and the cabin boy Bjarne Larsen, stayed with the *Wyatt Earp*. The rest of the crew sailed for Norway. The *Wyatt Earp* was taken to sea, and the skeleton crew set about ridding it of rats. More than one hundred were forced overboard before it returned to Montevideo, and Wilkins checked into a hotel

---

* Apparently, nothing came of Suzanne's "pregnancy."

to oversee storage of the *Polar Star* in a local warehouse. The four remaining Norwegians settled down to spend the winter in Montevideo, with Ellsworth paying their wages, and await his decision. Olsen had the unenviable task of presenting Miss Piggy to a local butcher and commented after the event, "not one of us ate a pork chop as long as the ship remained in harbor."[18]

Ellsworth bypassed the gossiping tongues of New York and headed straight for the castle without Mary Louise, who was finding she preferred his Italian villa.*

Alone again, Ellsworth pondered his future. He was, he felt, a laughing-stock. He had spent a decade trying to write his name into history books and he was still only a footnote. While he tried to decide what he should do, the normally reclusive Ellsworth granted an interview to a *New York Times* journalist who penned a telling portrait of both the man and his environment:

> In Switzerland there is no more picturesque castle outside or inside than the Ellsworth home. The first thing that strikes one on entering the living room is the ticking of several ancient clocks in different notes. One finds several of these ancient clocks in every room one enters. It excites your curiosity to find out that each one is running and telling a different hour.
>
> Mr. Ellsworth explains that there are seventy-two clocks in the castle.
>
> "My father collected them," he says.
>
> In the ancient Gothic fireplace a cedar fire crackles in the cool evening on an extraordinarily high pile of wood ashes.
>
> "Those are ashes of all the fires that have ever burned in that fireplace in twenty-four years," Mr. Ellsworth says. "My father would never let them be disturbed and I have carried on."[19]

Perhaps driven by the past more than drawn to the future, Ellsworth felt he had to carry on. He had commenced a task in the name of his father and, despite his disappointment and detractors, he could no more stop now than he could clean the fireplace or sell the clocks.

---

* Ellsworth had also inherited the Villa Palmieri, in Fiesole, overlooking Florence.

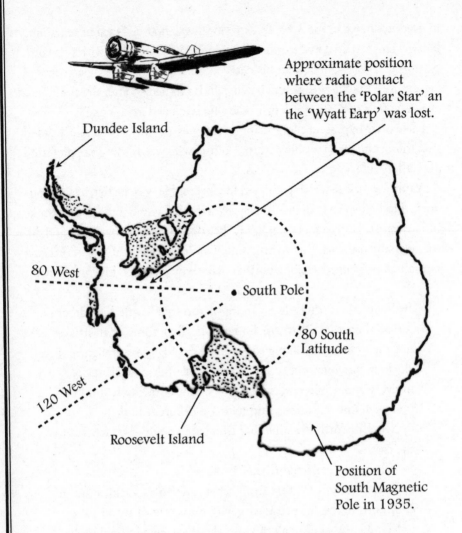

Dundee Island

Approximate position
where radio contact
between the 'Polar Star' an
the 'Wyatt Earp' was lost.

80 West

South Pole

80 South
Latitude

120 West

Roosevelt Island

Position of
South Magnetic
Pole in 1935.

Ellsworth's Flight

Ellsworth hoped to fly south from Dundee Island until he reached
80 degrees south latitude (shown as a circle). From there he
expected to fly a great circle route west to reach Roosevelt Island in
the Ross Sea. The abandoned base at Little America was to the north
of Roosevelt Island. Between 80 and 120 west longitude was
unexplored and unclaimed. Ellsworth's magnetic compass pointed
toward the South Magnetic Pole.

PART III
THE HEART OF THE ANTARCTIC

Who has known heights and depths shall not again
Know peace—not as the calm heart knows
Low, ivied walls; a garden close;
And though he tread the humble ways of men
He shall not speak the common tongue again.

Who has known heights shall bear forevermore
An incommunicable thing
That hurts his heart, as if a wing
Beat at the portal, challenging;
And yet—lured by the gleam his vision wore—
Who once has trodden stars seeks peace no more.

—Mary Brent Whiteside

ABOVE LEFT: Lincoln Ellsworth. Desperately lonely, and still trying to win his father's approval, he decided to become a polar explorer at the age of forty-four. ABOVE RIGHT: James W. Ellsworth, who used his enormous wealth to collect works of art. He is photographed with his second wife, Julia, at the Lenzburg Castle about 1915. BELOW: Lincoln Ellsworth (right) and Roald Amundsen. Ellsworth wanted to emulate Amundsen's great feats of polar exploration.

ABOVE LEFT: Stranded on the Arctic ice in 1925. Ellsworth, Amundsen and the crew of the *N25* struggle to build a runway for their flying boat. ABOVE RIGHT: The Italian-built airship *Norge* leaving its hangar at Kings Bay, Spitsbergen. BELOW: Umberto Nobile, the commander of the airship *Norge*. Nobile insulted Ellsworth by publicly declaring he was incompetent and merely a passenger on the North Pole flight.

ABOVE: Richard E. Byrd, the U.S. Navy reservist. After beating Ellsworth to the North Pole, Byrd also became determined to beat him across Antarctica. BELOW: Sir Hubert Wilkins (center) with Lady Wilkins and Ellsworth at Lenzburg Castle in 1929. Wilkins had travelled to Switzerland hoping to get Ellsworth to sponsor a submarine expedition in the Arctic.

ABOVE: The Arctic submarine *Nautilus*. The Wilkins-Ellsworth Trans-Arctic Submarine Expedition was plagued with problems from the outset. BELOW: Western frontier marshal Wyatt Earp pictured later in his life. Ellsworth considered Earp the bravest man who ever lived and purchased some of Earp's possessions from his widow, Josephine.

ABOVE: Mary Louise Ulmer (left) taking flying lessons in Switzerland, at the time she met Ellsworth. Her mother is pictured at right, while the man with them is unknown. BELOW: Ellsworth's original Antarctic pilot, Bernt Balchen (left). He is pictured with the *Polar Star*'s mechanic Chris Braathen.

ABOVE: The converted Norwegian fishing boat, which Ellsworth renamed *Wyatt Earp*. It was hoped its hull would be strong enough to withstand the Antarctic ice packs. BELOW: Sir Hubert Wilkins, who had twice attempted to fly across Antarctica, and who would organize and manage Ellsworth's four expeditions.

ABOVE: The *Polar Star* narrowly escaped being lost when the Ross Ice Shelf broke up and cracks appeared beneath the plane. BELOW: After almost being lost on the Ross Ice Shelf, the *Polar Star* was lifted back on board the *Wyatt Earp*. The damage to the undercarriage is clearly visible.

ABOVE: The *Polar Star*, without its wings, is unloaded at the abandoned whaling station at Deception Island on Ellsworth's second expedition to Antarctica. BELOW: Mechanic Chris Braathen fitting the replacement con-rod to the *Polar Star* at Deception Island.

ABOVE: Ellsworth visiting Nordenskjöld's hut on the west side of Snow Hill Island. Ellsworth was the first to visit the hut in more than thirty years. BELOW: Ellsworth poses with the flags he will carry on his trans-Antarctic flight. Pilot Hollick-Kenyon can be seen, smoking his pipe, leaning on the fuselage of the *Polar Star*.

The *Wyatt Earp* trapped in shelf ice on the east side of Snow Hill Island. It was feared the ship would be crushed and the crew stranded for the winter.

ABOVE: Ellsworth (left) and Hollick-Kenyon pose for photographs shortly before departing Dundee Island in 1935. BELOW: In a posed photograph Ellsworth demonstrates the polar sled he will use should he need to complete his journey on foot.

ABOVE: The *Polar Star* on the plateau at Dundee Island that will be used as a runway. BELOW: A previously unseen mountain range appears from ice, high on the Antarctic plateau. The photograph was taken by Ellsworth a few hours into his trans-Antarctic flight.

ABOVE: Camp III, high on the Antarctic Plateau. At the time, Ellsworth and Hollick-Kenyon were the only two men on the continent. BELOW: Digging out the *Polar Star* at Camp III. Constant snowdrifts would bury the plane before Ellsworth and Hollick-Kenyon could get airborne.

ABOVE: Camp III, high on the Antarctic Plateau. Ellsworth wrote in his diary that he had no idea where he was. BELOW: The *Wyatt Earp*, with the *Texaco 20* on its deck, arrives at the Bay of Whales, hoping to find Ellsworth and Hollick-Kenyon.

ABOVE: Pilot Bernt Balchen (left) and Sir Hubert Wilkins with the *Polar Star* in Norway.
BELOW: The last frontier on Earth. A photograph, taken by Ellsworth as the *Polar Star* wings
its way across Antarctica.

TOP: Two Northrop Gammas in Antarctica. The *Texaco 20* (left) is pictured on the Ross Ice Shelf, after the crew of the *Wyatt Earp* (seen in background) recovered the abandoned *Polar Star*. CENTER: Crew members from the British research vessel, *Discovery II*, dig down to the abandoned huts at Little America, hoping to find Ellsworth. BOTTOM: The *Polar Star* today. After it was recovered it was donated to the Smithsonian National Air and Space Museum, Washington, D.C.

16

THE GREAT UNKNOWN

APRIL 1935–NOVEMBER 1935

Once Ellsworth found the quiet determination to go on, in the face of the setbacks and the sniggering, he penned his own press release then had his publicist, Harry Bruno, send it to the newspapers:

> The far horizon! [Ellsworth wrote] How infinitely distant it really proves to be. What a lure to lead the traveler on into regions unknown in a quest for new knowledge concerning the planet upon which we dwell. Out of man's yearning for light and still more light, has come the civilization we live in. And the call of the wild, thank God, is still in the blood, for so long as the human ear loves to hear the pound of the deep sea surf upon lonely coastlines and the human eye watch the play of the Northern Lights across desolate snow-fields—so long then will the great unknown lure him on till the whole of it vanishes.[1]

Preparing to seek, once again, refuge in the great unknown, Ellsworth went hiking by himself in the Swiss Alps and instructed Wilkins to organize the third Ellsworth Trans-Antarctic Expedition.

"I am doing my best to persuade Lincoln not to go on,"[2] Wilkins had informed his wife from Montevideo a month earlier, but in truth he, like Ellsworth, had no other options. No wife promising a contented family life calling him home. No other horizon with unknown land on the far side, ready to offer up its secrets to the explorer. Only Antarctica was left. The thing had to be done now.

For the weary Wilkins, the plan would remain unchanged from the second expedition. He would load the *Polar Star* on the *Wyatt Earp*, sail down to Graham Land, get Ellsworth and a pilot airborne and heading toward Little America, then sail the ship around to the Ross Ice Shelf to pick them up.

Wilkins asked Balchen if he would be willing to make a third attempt and the answer was an emphatic "no." After the second expedition Balchen had collected his wife and child and sailed to Norway for a vacation. Wilkins rued Balchen's decision because, as he pointed out, "there is no man more capable of doing it if he sets out."[3] Wilkins's other consideration was that Little America was now abandoned. Byrd's expedition had packed up and returned home during the southern summer. There would be no one to send weather reports from the other side of the continent and no one to lay markers on the ground indicating safe landing places. Additionally, if they managed to reach Little America and land safely, Ellsworth and his yet-to-be-found pilot would need to survive alone in the abandoned base, while the *Wyatt Earp* came to collect them. Allowing for the voyage across the Southern Ocean and negotiating the pack ice extending from the Ross Ice Shelf, Wilkins estimated the fliers would need to survive at Little America for a minimum of six weeks.

Because of that, Wilkins needed to know exactly what, in terms of fuel and food, was still at Little America. He wrote to Byrd, who was busy touring and speaking about his recent near-death experience at Advance Base. Byrd generously volunteered particulars, pointing out that, "as the information you may get from other sources in regard to what is at Little America may be inaccurate, I thought it would be of value to you to know just what is there." Then one of Byrd's crew, Alan Innes Taylor, added a detailed map of Little America, describing where drums of fuel, food, and other supplies were located. Innes Taylor concluded his accompanying letter by saying:

In the tunnels of the main section of the camp you will find some food. The radio hut and the hut just south of it, in which I lived, you will probably find in the best condition. The others, I fear, will be caved in by the time you get there.[4]

The *Wyatt Earp* spent the southern winter at Montevideo. Of the four members of the original crew, Magnus Olsen was promoted to captain, Lauritz Liavaag was promoted to first mate, while engineer Harald Holmboe and cabin boy Bjarne Larsen kept their positions. Wilkins sought replacements for the others.

He also turned his attention to the issue of a pilot. Ellsworth wanted two men capable of flying the *Polar Star* on this trip. If one refused to fly, or turned back as Balchen had done, he wanted another ready to climb into the cockpit. Wilkins sought advice from his old Arctic mentor, Vilhjalmur Stefansson, who recommended he advertise among the pilots of Canadian Airways. Of the applicants, Wilkins selected Herbert Hollick-Kenyon and James (Joe) Lymburner.

Hollick-Kenyon was born in England in 1897. He was a big, barrel-chested, pipe-smoking pilot who had learned to fly during World War I and had emigrated to Canada afterward. He had over six thousand flying hours in a variety of planes, a liking for scotch whisky, and a reputation for not suffering fools. He had limited navigation experience, but wrote on his application that he had read the theory of the bubble sextant and didn't think that using one would present any difficulty.

Joe Lymburner, a thin laconic Canadian, had fewer flying hours (1,600), but he was a competent mechanic. As Chris Braathen would not be returning this year, Lymburner could act as the reserve pilot and also be in charge of the *Polar Star*'s engine.

Hollick-Kenyon and Lymburner arrived in Montevideo. Wilkins proposed they each fly the plane to familiarize themselves with its capabilities, pointing out, "It is a lot of trouble and expense, but safer to have the pilots fly it here than smash it up down there [in Antarctica]."[5]

Unfortunately, during the first test flight the engine cut out and Hollick-Kenyon landed heavily, tearing a hole in the underside of the starboard wing. The repairs took two weeks and used up any time available for further test flights. Consequently, the pilots would have to sail to Antarctica unfamiliar with the *Polar Star* and relying on Balchen's description of its speed and fuel consumption.

At the end of his stay at the castle, Ellsworth took the *Graf Zeppelin*, which had begun making regular passenger flights between Germany and Brazil, to Rio de Janeiro. On arrival, he learned the *Polar Star* was being repaired and rather than wait, he went tiger hunting in the jungles of Brazil. He emerged from the hunt a week later and sailed to Montevideo, where he met his pilots and new crew members. Radio operator Walter Lanz was the only American to return from the previous expedition. He was joined by three fellow Americans and four new Norwegians. With Ellsworth, Wilkins and the two pilots, the *Wyatt Earp* had a complement of sixteen. Captain Magnus Olsen noted that the multinational crew meant "there was much less camaraderie than we had enjoyed during the previous two years." He also noted it was agreed:

> . . . we Norwegians would be entirely responsible for the ship, but would assist where necessary in taking equipment ashore. Regarding the plane, our responsibility would be confined to hoisting it from the hold and onto the barrier, thereafter it was to be handed over to Mr. Hollick-Kenyon and his companions.[6]

Still not wanting to spend any more time onboard the *Wyatt Earp* than was absolutely necessary, Ellsworth instructed Wilkins to sail it to Magallanes because, having completed his tiger hunt, he now wanted to go mountain climbing in Mendoza, 730 miles inland. The *Wyatt Earp* left Montevideo, without Ellsworth, on October 17, 1935.

Ellsworth returned from his climbing and, while waiting for a passenger ship to take him to Magallanes, took it upon himself to send a telegram to Byrd asking about the supplies at Little America. Despite the pressures of his schedule, Byrd replied immediately with a letter dated October 20, but, for reasons unknown, it was not posted until October 26. In the letter Byrd again explained the location of the drums of fuel and other supplies, as Innes Taylor had previously explained to Wilkins. Quite justifiably, Byrd added:

Since I am lecturing, twice a day, in a different city every day, I am greatly handicapped and will have to ask my supply officer where the other supplies are. I will have to radio you the disposition of the other supplies.[7]

When he did not receive the response immediately, Ellsworth grumpily told the press that despite a personal request, Byrd had not been forthcoming with information about the supplies at Little America and that Byrd's unhelpfulness was seriously jeopardizing his safety. After further bad-mouthing Byrd, Ellsworth sailed to Magallanes, where he was reunited with his expedition, yet still unaware that Wilkins already had the information regarding supplies at Little America. "We picked up the last letters that could reach us before we emerged from the Antarctic," Ellsworth complained in a local newspaper. "Still no word from Byrd."[8]

The *Wyatt Earp* sailed on October 28, and Byrd's repetitious letter arrived at Magallanes two days later.

The trip south to Deception Island took five days. There the expedition found the harbor blocked by heavy pack ice, blown together by a westerly gale, so it was another two days before they could break through to the abandoned whaling station, where the *Polar Star* was assembled. With thin harbor ice, and the rocky ground already exposed, Wilkins decided not to waste time. On November 11, they sailed for the Weddell Sea.

On their previous trip they had sailed past Dundee Island, which was farther north. Unlike Snow Hill Island, which was surrounded by the treacherous Weddell Sea ice pack, Dundee Island was enclosed by a half-mile hem of shelf ice that was solid to the shore, effectively offering the *Wyatt Earp* somewhere to tie up. Wilkins and Ellsworth disembarked and found the ideal flying base. There were long, sweeping flat sections of hard snow. (Neither Wilkins nor Ellsworth offered any explanation as to why they did not consider the island the previous year.)

The expedition set up a base at the northwestern end of Dundee Island. Here the lack of camaraderie among the crew, which Olsen had noted, brought the expedition to a temporary halt. The Norwegians lifted the fuselage and wings onto the ice, then dragged them to solid ground. The American crew took over, hauling the components to a location where the *Polar Star* could be assembled for the flight. Later that morning Olsen, with some of the other Norwegians, skied to the base camp to find:

> To our utter astonishment . . . instead of witnessing a scene of activity, we saw the three plane mechanics cowering under tarpaulins, heating themselves with two of the blowers that were intended to heat the engine of the plane. It was not our business to interfere, and we Norwegians returned to the ship.[9]

The Americans, who according to Olsen had "given priority to maintaining a smart appearance," and therefore were not properly dressed for "the cruel conditions of the Antarctic,"[10] refused to do any further work until the Norwegians assisted. The Norwegians, in turn, refused to extend their responsibilities beyond the immediate vicinity of the ship. Olsen recalled that work came to a stop and a meeting of all parties was called. The upshot was that the Norwegians would agree to help the shore party but they would do so only on the condition that:

> Our instructions were to come from Sir Hubert himself and from no one else. Sir Hubert gave his word on that, and called the base crew to the ship to explain everything to them in our presence.[11]

To what extent Ellsworth was involved in the discussions, or had been a cause of the disagreement, is unclear. In the two chapters of Olsen's book that describe the voyage of the *Wyatt Earp* to Dundee Island and the preparation of the *Polar Star*, Ellsworth is not mentioned, while Wilkins is constantly referred to as the "leader" of the expedition.

With the *Polar Star* eventually assembled, the motor was carefully checked and Hollick-Kenyon took the plane for a successful test flight. The weather remained clear. Everything appeared ready for the flight across the continent.

17

CHASING THE SUN

NOVEMBER 19–23 1935

E llsworth and Hollick-Kenyon had to fly 2,200 miles, more than half of
which was over an unexplored area of the Earth's surface. That unexplored area, lying roughly in the middle of their flight, could be flat
ice shelf, towering mountains ranges, or a series of islands. They would be
taking off from a point north of the Antarctic Circle (63°5' South, 55°9'
West), flying to within six hundred miles of the South Pole, and through
more than one hundred degrees of longitude (over a quarter of the way
around the globe) to an ice shelf the size of France, on which they needed
to locate a buried base, only indicated by radio aerials protruding from the
snow. It would take no mean feat of navigation.

Bernt Balchen had learned to fly in Norway, where whiteouts and
areas of featureless landscape meant pilots flew on instruments. In the
1920s, while pilots in America were flying from one state to another by
following railway lines and swooping low to read the name on railway
stations, Balchen was flying with a compass and a stopwatch. He was
proficient in using air speed indicators, drift indicators, and bubble

sextants.* For navigators such as Balchen, a key to knowing where they were was knowing the plane's speed. They worked out their direction with a compass and how far they had traveled by speed and elapsed time: a method of navigation known as "dead reckoning." On arrival, they sometimes checked their location by taking sights with a sextant.

Balchen was proficient at dead reckoning navigation. So was Wilkins. Importantly, Balchen and Wilkins knew that a key to dead reckoning was knowing the plane's flying speed, and the only way to accurately measure that was to time a flight from point A to point B. Balchen had flown the *Polar Star* and claimed its top speed was 220 mph and that it cruised at 150 mph. But Balchen had made that test flight in America, when wheels were fitted. In the Antarctic, when skis were fitted, he had only made short flights and not taken the opportunity to measure to what extent the wide flat skis added air drag and slowed the plane. Hollick-Kenyon had not had the opportunity to make a long flight, with either skis or wheels, to verify the plane's speed. His one flight at Montevideo had ended prematurely in a crash landing.

Wilkins was not confident Ellsworth could navigate with any competency. Ellsworth could follow a magnetic compass course and he could tell the time, but he had never demonstrated any further abilities. He was not proficient at using a sextant, which involved measuring the elevation of the sun and consulting an almanac. As a consequence, Wilkins believed that to get Ellsworth and Hollick-Kenyon across Antarctica with even a vague hope of locating Little America, he needed a plan simple enough for Ellsworth to understand. That is exactly what he devised.**

According to Wilkins's plan, for the first four hours, Hollick-Kenyon and Ellsworth would follow the coast almost directly south. After four hours, they should have covered six hundred miles, passed the "Stefansson

---

* Appendix A gives a fuller explanation of the instruments and problems of polar navigation.
** Wilkins's plan, quoted here and reproduced as an appendix, had been worked out eleven months previously for Ellsworth and Balchen to fly from Snow Hill Island. Either the newer plan for taking off from Dundee Island has been lost, or Wilkins could not be bothered reworking his complicated calculations for the third expedition, and Ellsworth carried the previous year's plan.

Strait," and be over Hearst Land, close to 80° South latitude. They would then turn and follow their compass bearing west, along the 80° South meridian (known as a great circle route because one is circling the Earth at a constant latitude). If Ellsworth and Hollick-Kenyon could stay on their great circle route, they should reach the Ross Ice Shelf. Once they reached the shelf they should be able to identify Roosevelt Island, the snow-covered landmass predicted by Amundsen and discovered and named by Byrd, that stabilized the shelf south of the Bay of Whales. After flying beyond Roosevelt Island, they needed to visually locate the Bay of Whales and the radio aerials sticking up from Little America, which was 78°39' South.

Ellsworth and Hollick-Kenyon had identifiable landmarks for the first and last six hundred miles of their flight. For the first six hundred they were following the coast to Stefansson Strait and Hearst Land, while for the last six hundred they had the known mountain ranges that bordered the Ross Ice Shelf, Roosevelt Island, and the Bay of Whales. It was the one thousand miles in the middle where they needed to stay on course using their instruments.

Wilkins had an idea to assist them here as well. He would have them start the flight at 8:00 A.M. Greenwich Mean Time (0800 GMT), four hours before it was noon on their meridian of longitude. After flying south for four hours (or the first six hundred miles), when they turned to follow their great circle route west, it would be their noon—the sun would be at the highest point in the sky, off their right, or starboard, wing. If Ellsworth was to take an elevation of the sun at noon, he should be able to take repeated elevations and verify their progress keeping the sun off, or forward of, their starboard wing, as they chased it across the sky. Hopefully, keeping the sun on their right side, Ellsworth should be able to locate the five-hundred-mile-wide Ross Ice Shelf.

Most importantly, the plan was so simple that Ellsworth could not only understand it, but he could take credit for it. He declared in a press release prepared by Wilkins:

> I have decided now to fly a great circle course from here to the Bay of Whales, Ross Sea, and to maintain a constant ground speed of 150 statute miles an hour. This should easily be possible

since the *Polar Star* has a possible speed of 220 mph by opening up the engine, or throttling down, depending on the force and direction of the winds we meet, we expect to maintain a constant speed which will greatly facilitate our navigation.[1]

Ellsworth and Hollick-Kenyon also needed a plan if anything went wrong. Again, Wilkins wrote detailed instructions on what to do, depending on where they were forced down. If they landed, or had difficulties during the first four hours, they would attempt to return to the *Wyatt Earp*. If they landed and were unable to return, they would attempt to cross the mountains to the west coast of the peninsula and wait for the *Wyatt Earp* to reach them. (The Weddell Sea to the east was impenetrable by ship.)

Beyond the first six hundred miles, when they turned west to follow their great circle route, they would be initially flying over Hearst Land. Wilkins and Ben Eielson had discovered Hearst Land in 1928. No one had seen it since. Wilkins had described it as, "What appeared to be truly a part of the Antarctic Continent . . . this land extended as far as we could see, beyond a shoreline spreading roughly east and west."[2]

Once they were above Hearst Land, Ellsworth and Hollick-Kenyon would be in unknown territory. For the next five hundred miles, should they be forced down, the plan was not to walk back to the west side of the peninsula (at the time still believed to be a series of large islands), but if possible, to walk north to Charcot Island in the Bellingshausen Sea. Various whalers and explorers had seen the island and Wilkins had flown over it in 1929. The island was connected to the continent of Antarctica by an ice bridge.* After entering Hearst Land, and flying over unmapped territory for five hundred miles, they still had another five hundred miles before they reached the Queen Maude Mountains to descend to the Ross Ice Shelf. If they were forced down during this stage of the flight it would be too far to turn back to Charcot Island. They would have passed halfway, and would need to keep going to make for Mount Mabelle Sidley, a peak seen by Byrd in Marie Byrd Land. Here Ellsworth's instructions explained he would:

---

*   Later named the Wilkins Ice Shelf—it collapsed as a result of global warming in 2009.

. . . leave a message and look for a depot and possibly remain there with the expectation of being relieved. However, if . . . we have food sufficient to reach Mt Grace McKinley, I might decide to leave a note at Mt Mabelle Sidley and proceed to Mt Grace McKinley.[3]

Should they be forced down once they had passed between the Queen Maud Mountains and Marie Byrd Land they would continue on foot, across the Ross Ice Shelf, to Little America. The most dangerous part of the flight was the one thousand miles in the middle. Should anything happen once they had flown too far to return to the *Wyatt Earp*, yet not far enough to be able to walk to Little America, they would have little chance of survival.

The *Polar Star* would carry a disassembled fourteen-foot sled and provisions for the two men for five weeks. Wilkins estimated that, under optimum conditions, Ellsworth and Hollick-Kenyon could travel fifteen miles a day, hauling the sled. Five week's rations might allow them to travel about five hundred miles and reach one of the predetermined rendezvous points, depending on where they came down. It was an extremely optimistic proposition, considering that neither man had any experience man-hauling a sled in the harshest environment on Earth. The greatest polar explorers in history had not managed anything like it.

A key part of the plan was the radios. Ellsworth and Hollick-Kenyon could only expect to be rescued if they could communicate where they were, or where they were heading. Two radio sets would be carried. The main one, with a one-hundred-watt output, was powered either by a portable generator or the plane's engine. The second was a smaller trail radio with a fifteen-watt output. It was powered by furiously cranking a small handle to turn a generator.

For the historic flight, Ellsworth had brought along his personal mascots, flags, and good-luck charms. These included a Mickey Mouse doll given to him by his wife, an ox shoe he had found in Death Valley, an American flag sewn by his niece, Clare, along with five flags belonging to various scholastic or scientific organizations. With the exception of the American flag, which he intended to drop to claim undiscovered land for America, Ellsworth planned to return the flags to their owners at the end of the expedition. He also carried his most precious possession—Wyatt Earp's ammunition belt.

The first attempt to get airborne was a failure. On November 19, 1935, with Hollick-Kenyon at the controls, the *Polar Star* failed to lift off from the thawing snow.

They tried again the next morning and the *Polar Star* got airborne with less than half a mile of runway. Ellsworth was thrilled, believing years of effort were about to pay off. The thrill was short-lived. An hour into the flight Hollick-Kenyon noticed the fuel gauge had cracked and was in danger of rupturing. Should it break, fuel would spurt into the cockpit. He passed a note to Ellsworth, explaining what was happening, and turned the plane around. They were back at Dundee Island three hours after leaving and the faulty fuel gauge was replaced.

The good weather continued to hold and the next day everything was made ready again. The air was still and cloudless. Hollick-Kenyon warmed the engines and Ellsworth shook hands with everyone, hopeful that this time nothing would go wrong. Hollick-Kenyon taxied the *Polar Star* along the runway and minutes later they were soaring over the island. Three and a half hours after takeoff, Ellsworth looked ahead to see what Wilkins, in 1928, had named Stefansson Strait. He observed it was much narrower than Wilkins had described.

Four hours into the flight, and with favorable winds, they were nearing Hearst Land, about to enter unknown territory. Unsure of what lay ahead, Hollick-Kenyon put the plane into a climb, leveling out at 7,000 feet and passing Wilkins's previous southernmost point. Soon mountain peaks appeared ahead. An undiscovered mountain range confronted them, crossing their path diagonally. Ellsworth was overjoyed:

> This was the greatest hour of my life. Obviously here was a mountain system of major importance, and our eyes were the first to behold it. They had been here almost since mundane time began, for I could plainly see what I thought was stratification, and therefore placed them as of sedimentary origin. At once the true name of these mountains came to me, and I wrote it down in my diary—the Eternity Range.[4]

Hollick-Kenyon continued to climb as the *Polar Star* entered cloud. Through a break in the clouds, they saw rocks only a few hundred feet below. The mountains were getting higher. The *Polar Star* climbed to twelve thousand feet and into clear sunshine. Ellsworth was busy with his camera and notebook when he saw more clouds ahead: "Nevertheless, since everything was functioning perfectly . . . I assumed that we could fly through it, according to plan."[5]

Ellsworth assumed wrong. Five hours after they had lifted off he looked up from his notebook to realize that Hollick-Kenyon was turning the plane around. Ellsworth couldn't believe it. Was this Bernt Balchen all over again? Surely, he wondered, they weren't going back.

"What are you doing?" he yelled at Hollick-Kenyon above the roar of the engine. The curt Hollick-Kenyon simply shook his head, offering no explanation, and continued to bank the plane to the left. Ellsworth could not understand it. Then he noticed Hollick-Kenyon wasn't retracing their route, but actually heading east, toward the Weddell Sea. Perhaps he intended to land there and wait for the weather to blow over. But an hour later, they had passed Hearst Land and Hollick-Kenyon headed north, keeping doggedly on toward Dundee Island.

Ellsworth was furious. They had repeatedly discussed that if they met bad weather, they would land and let it pass before continuing. It was one of the conditions of the flight he had specified after Balchen had turned around the previous season. But Hollick-Kenyon was ignoring him. Ellsworth saw Hollick-Kenyon calmly eating a biscuit. When he casually passed a note back saying, "I've just had lunch. Have you?"[6] Ellsworth was too upset to answer. Neither man spoke or passed any notes for the remainder of the journey.

The *Polar Star* landed at Dundee Island and Ellsworth scrambled out and stormed toward the *Wyatt Earp*. Wilkins asked what had happened, but Ellsworth ignored him. Wilkins conferred with Hollick-Kenyon, who simply explained they had been flying into headwinds, traveling slower than expected, and using excessive fuel. They had also burned extra fuel gaining twelve thousand feet to cross the previously unknown mountain range. Flying into a brewing storm, not knowing what was ahead or whether or not they would have enough fuel was, in his opinion, unwise. So, without consulting Ellsworth, he had turned the plane around and flown back.

Wilkins went on board the *Wyatt Earp* to speak to Ellsworth who, still upset, said, "Tomorrow I am trying again, but I don't want Hollick-Kenyon. I'm going to take Lymburner."[7] Wilkins asked him to reconsider. Hollick-Kenyon was the better pilot and knew the route, while Lymburner was tired from having worked long hours to prepare the plane, but Ellsworth refused to listen. A short while later Hollick-Kenyon went to Ellsworth's cabin and said, matter-of-factly, "I understand you would prefer Lymburner on the next flight. That's quite all right by me."[8] Then he turned and walked out.

Sitting alone in his cabin, his grand plans for polar glory having evaporated yet again, Ellsworth began to calm down and weigh the facts:

> In returning to Dundee Island [Hollick-Kenyon] had, after all, only used his pilot's judgement. True, it was our agreement to land in bad weather, but to have attempted a landing in fogged mountains would have been sheer suicide. Then, the plane had burned so much fuel over Hearst Land fighting the headwind, it was doubtful if we had enough to make it to the Ross Sea.[9]

Ellsworth would try again, with Hollick-Kenyon as pilot and, he announced, "Next time we won't turn back."[10]

Two days later, at 1:00 A.M., Bjarne Larsen roused Ellsworth in his cabin and told him everything was ready. The weather appeared fine. Ellsworth dressed hurriedly. On his feet he wore a pair of camel-hair socks, followed by woollen socks, moose-hide moccasins, then finally waterproof canvas boots. The moccasins were a curious choice for a man who might be faced with a five-hundred-mile trek in the Antarctic, but Ellsworth had found them comfortable on his monthlong trips in the Grand Canyon, and advised:

> Moccasins, which the Westerners wear, are much better [than boots]. After you ford a stream in moccasins, you can wring them out and put them on again fairly dry. Their disadvantages are that they flatten and callus the feet and that they wear out quickly . . . I used to carry a sackful of moccasins with me [in the Grand Canyon], wearing out a pair every three days.[11]

Over his shirt and woollen trousers he wore a Siberian squirrel parka that Amundsen had given him. Having dressed, Ellsworth went for breakfast, looking in on Hollick-Kenyon's cabin on the way:

> Hollick-Kenyon was the most fastidious man I ever knew on a polar expedition. He always shaved every morning, no matter how hard the circumstances; and every night before supper, if there was even a chance to melt snow, he always sponged down to his waist—in marked contrast to Balchen, who had a fine Viking scorn for soap and water.[12]

After a hearty breakfast of bacon, eggs, and coffee for Ellsworth (Hollick-Kenyon ate more sparingly) the two men left the *Wyatt Earp* and started the fourteen-hundred-foot climb to the plateau where the *Polar Star* was waiting. They walked slowly, so as not to build up sweat inside their parkas, which would later freeze as they sat immobile in the plane. Joe Lymburner had been at the plane since midnight, checking the engine and preparing it for the flight. Wilkins was also there, having spent hours going over each piece of equipment.

At the plane both Ellsworth and Hollick-Kenyon donned parachutes and posed for photographs. (The film of the departure shows them fitting the parachutes. No mention of them is made anywhere, nor are they shown anywhere else. Whether or not Ellsworth wore a parachute on his previous attempts is unknown.)

Ellsworth sensed "a finality about it all I had not experienced before."[13]

There is no written record of what was said at the departure. Wilkins's film shows the large frame of Hollick-Kenyon, made larger by his bulky furs, climb up the side of the *Polar Star* using the foot- and handholds. Then he pushes the cockpit canopy back to climb in. He pulls the canopy forward and Ellsworth climbs in behind him. Ellsworth gives a cheery wave to the camera before pulling his section of the canopy back over his head. The two men are cut off from everything, except their tiny plane and each other. The engine starts and the propeller spins ferociously, stirring clouds of snow and ice. Gracefully, the streamlined silver Northrop Gamma moves forward, its port wing almost touching the top of Wilkins's camera. Hollick-Kenyon taxies about a quarter of a mile into the distance, until, before the days of zoom lenses, the plane is a silhouette against the muted glow of the sky. Wilkins stops panning and lets the plane move from the left of the screen to the right, gathering momentum for takeoff. The *Polar Star* is airborne and flies out of the picture at 0804 GMT, November 23, 1935.

18

LOST

0800–2200 GMT, NOVEMBER 23, 1935

O nce the *Polar Star* was airborne, Hollick-Kenyon banked, then flew
back over the island and dipped his wings to acknowledge the men
below, who were cheering and waving wildly. Almost immediately,
Ellsworth starting using his 35mm Leica; keeping a photographic log,
recording when a frame of film was exposed and in which direction he
was pointing his camera when he exposed it. Hollick-Kenyon checked
his instruments and sent a test message to the *Wyatt Earp*. The radio was
working, and radio operator Lanz received it clearly. During the next hour,
Wilkins and the crewmembers who had assisted the takeoff hurried back
to the ship and crowded around the radio to listen to the messages as they
were received.

At 0830 GMT* Hollick-Kenyon reported they were still climbing and
were passing James Ross Island. The Pratt & Whitney radial engine was

---

* All times quoted for the flight are Greenwich Mean Time. Hollick-Kenyon used
twenty-four-hour (military) time in his logbook. Remarkably, Ellsworth used twelve-hour
times, often omitting to record A.M. or P.M.

turning at 1,720 rpm: its ideal cruising speed. Hollick-Kenyon also reported they were flying into a headwind with an estimated strength of around fifteen mph. Forty-five minutes after takeoff, he reported he was on a magnetic compass bearing of 180°, flying at 7,400 feet and the Indicated Air Speed (IAS) was 126 mph.

On the *Polar Star* the IAS was measured by an Air Speed Indicator on the left side of the fuselage. A small, wind-driven propeller turned a speedometer, which the pilot could then read. A headwind increased the revolutions of the propeller, thereby making the indicated speed faster then the actual ground speed. If, for example, the IAS was 125 mph and the strength of the headwind was 15 mph, then the plane's ground speed was possibly closer to 110 mph.

An hour later little had changed. The crew aboard the *Wyatt Earp* learned the *Polar Star* had leveled out at 7,000 feet and the IAS was still 126 mph. Hollick-Kenyon was steering a more westerly course on a compass bearing of 210°.* They were still flying into a headwind with an estimated strength of 15–20 mph. At 1015 GMT, Hollick-Kenyon radioed that the wind strength was increasing. He was now following a compass bearing between 180° and 190° and flying at 7,400 feet.

At 1046 GMT, Hollick-Kenyon noted in his logbook that the right rear fuel tank was empty and that he had switched to the left front wing tank. He also made a calculation in pencil. In two hours and forty-six minutes he had consumed 67 gallons of fuel at a rate of 24.5 gallons per hour. Wilkins's carefully detailed flight plan was based on the *Polar Star* flying at 150 mph. At that speed, it would cross Antarctica in less than fifteen hours. Flying at 120 mph it would take almost eighteen and a half hours and if its actual ground speed was 110 mph, it would take twenty hours to reach Little America. The *Polar Star*'s capacity was 466 gallons. Consuming fuel at a rate of 24.5 gallons per hour meant it had a total flying time of 19 hours.

It was going to be a close call.

---

* In 1935 the South Magnetic Pole lay beyond Little America in Victoria Land. While their magnetic compass bearing indicates they were flying south, they were, in fact, flying in a westerly direction. The difference between True North and Magnetic North (Magnetic Variation) for the various stages of the flight is given in the Appendix.

At 1115, Hollick-Kenyon radioed that he was over the barrier ice. "We too far east. Going to make compass course 190." Then a few minutes later he radioed, "compass 190." Curiously, it was Hollick-Kenyon who was realizing they had drifted east. Ellsworth's diary/log for the period only reveals he was taking photographs.

At 1123 Hollick-Kenyon informed the *Wyatt Earp* he had taken the *Polar Star* to 11,000 feet and could see Cape Eielson dead ahead. Cape Eielson was the eastern extremity of "Stefansson Strait" and, if it was eighty to one hundred miles ahead (Hollick-Kenyon's possible range of sight), they were not only still too far east but, after less than four hours of flying, they were almost an hour behind schedule. Hollick-Kenyon informed his listeners he was changing the compass course to 210° "to bring us west of Cape Eielson." He also radioed ominously, "IAS 110. Very slow."[1] **

At 1241 Hollick-Kenyon explained he was at thirteen thousand feet and still climbing. He noted the fifty-two-gallon left front wing tank was empty, so the *Polar Star* was now using twenty-seven gallons per hour. The higher consumption was probably due to gaining the altitude. At 1255, almost five hours into the flight, the listeners on board the *Wyatt Earp* heard the fliers had passed Stefansson Strait and were nearing the mountains seen in the distance on their flight three days earlier. This time the sky was clear and, despite the headwind slowing their progress, they had no intention of turning back. For the next hour they flew above the mountains that Ellsworth had already named the Eternity Range.

Six hours into their flight, and almost two hours behind schedule, they had crossed the Eternity Range and commenced their great circle route. The next known landmarks were one thousand miles ahead. They were the mountains that bordered the Ross Ice Shelf on the other side of the continent. The nearer, the Queen Maude Range, discovered and named by Amundsen, would be on their left, while Marie Byrd Land

---

*   All radio messages were taken from the Hollick-Kenyon and Ellsworth diaries, along with notes between pilot and navigator, quoted from the manuscripts in the Michael Ross Collection.

**   Cape Eielson is found on modern maps as Eielson Peninsula. It is located at 70°35' South and 61°45' West. It was named by Wilkins in 1928 for his pilot Ben Eielson.

with the Rockefeller Mountains, discovered and named by Byrd, would be on their right.

Writing a report for the newspapers on Ellsworth's behalf, Wilkins had previously explained the two mountain ranges would be the signposts to the Ross Ice Shelf. The fliers had to locate them and fly between them.

> If no indication of land has been seen by the time we are halfway across, we might swing more southerly to come within sight of the extension of the Queen Maude Mountains. In any case, the southeastern end of the range, as reported by Amundsen and Byrd, should be located between the eleventh and twelfth hour out, if our course and speed have been maintained. About thirteen hours out the Rockefeller Mountains should be seen to the northward of our course.[2]

At 1350, perhaps noticing that Ellsworth was not taking sightings, Hollick-Kenyon passed him a note saying, "It is opening up nicely ahead. Better keep that camera and sextant busy, eh." Ellsworth took his first elevation of the sun, but did not record the angle or his computations.[3]

Cramped in the narrow cockpit, his broad shoulders and barrel chest squeezed on all sides, Hollick-Kenyon flew on relentlessly. Behind him, Ellsworth peered over Hollick-Kenyon's shoulder to glimpse the white plain that was appearing before them, or he stared to either side, often lifting his camera to snap a photograph of an ice sheet that had waited more than thirty-five million years to greet human beings.

Having crossed the Eternity Range, which had spread to their left and right, the peaks piercing the snow became less frequent. Hollick-Kenyon brought the plane down to 10,000 feet. Flying conditions were ideal.*

Beyond the mountains they were greeted by a vast polar plateau. Hollick-Kenyon recorded his IAS as 120 mph and was pleased to radio to the *Wyatt Earp*, "Getting better all the time. Not much wind. Lots of places where one could land."[4]

---

* Altitude figures quoted are approximate, based on Ellsworth's barometer.

Hollick-Kenyon was steering a compass course of 185° and recorded that the altitude of the ground was between 6,000 and 7,000 feet. They were flying lower. "Seems to be end of mountains," he noted.[5]

At 1455 the normally reticent Hollick-Kenyon passed Ellsworth a note reading, "Well, so this is the Antarctic. How do you like it?' Ellsworth responded, "Yes. 100%."[6]

Ellsworth was anxious to know when they had passed 80° West. The area of Antarctica to the east of this meridian of longitude (20° West to 80° West—over which they had just flown) was the United Kingdom's Falkland Dependency Claim.* From 80° West, continuing ahead of the fliers to 120° West, mostly comprising the unexplored Pacific Quadrant, was unseen and unclaimed. As the first person to reach the area, tradition dictated that Ellsworth had the right to name any land discovered and claim it for his country.

Ellsworth knew that 80° West was approximately one thousand miles from Dundee Island and, had they been flying at 150 mph, the *Polar Star* would have reached the area in seven hours. But they were flying slower than anticipated. It would be nearer to nine hours before they could be certain they had crossed 80° West.

After flying for seven hours, the navigator asked the pilot where they were, by handing him a note reading, "How far from 80?" Hollick-Kenyon scribbled a note and passed it back, "I estimate about along 70 now, roughly two hours to 80—but unless we land and take a sight I would wait three— to make certain."[7] At least Hollick-Kenyon understood they were two hours, or more, behind schedule.

The pair flew on. An hour later Hollick-Kenyon sent a radio message, which was received by the *Wyatt Earp*. Lanz wrote it down as:

> I estimate that we are at sevent . . . one . . . erabouts . . . my guess
> is . . . at . . . pect still clear . . . to s . . . ight dull . . . little no wind.[8]

Aboard the *Polar Star* Hollick-Kenyon did not receive a reply and began to suspect that he had lost contact with the *Wyatt Earp*. He passed a note to Ellsworth:

---

*   Argentina had a counterclaim on a section of it.

Aircraft transmitter appears to have gone out of action. Casing hot and no reception of our signal in receiver. Only thing to do is go on. We have another [radio] for land use.[9]

Hollick-Kenyon had told Ellsworth to wait until they had been flying ten hours to make certain they were over unclaimed territory before claiming it for America. Ellsworth was content with nine. At 1709, he slid the cockpit canopy forward and tossed out the American flag that had been sewn by his niece. In his diary he wrote simply, "What a thrill."[10] After years of attempts, he had discovered new land. He claimed it for the United States and named it, not for himself, but for his father: James W. Ellsworth Land.

Hollick-Kenyon recorded the IAS as 122 mph. The visibility was 150 miles in every direction. Except for a few odd peaks they could see nothing but snow plains. Beneath them spread a white featureless landscape. Puffs of snow blew up, so the fliers could judge the direction of the wind, but there was nothing against which to measure the drift of the plane or the ground speed. In his diary Ellsworth quickly wrote: "No landmarks visible. Only limitless expanse of white."[11]

Ten hours into the flight, far away to the north, toward where Byrd had taken his ship into the Devil's Graveyard in a fruitless search for land, Ellsworth saw mountains poking through the snow. He named them the Sentinel Range and the central peak Mount Mary Louise Ulmer, in honor of his wife.* They flew on.

At 1835, Hollick-Kenyon passed a note saying, "water sky dead ahead."[12] A water sky is the appearance of a dark blue sky, caused by reflection off water. It indicated they were nearing the sea. But how could that be, without having reached the mountains that edge the Ross Ice Shelf? Had they somehow veered north and were heading for open ocean instead of the ice shelf? If that was the case, why were they still flying at nearly ten thousand feet? And Hollick-Kenyon's magnetic compass bearing was 190°. They were flying west.

A bewildered Ellsworth took a sextant sighting, quickly did his calculations, and arrived at the surprising conclusion they were not north of

---

*   Modern maps show it as Mount Ulmer.

their route, near water, but close to the South Pole, much farther south than they expected to be. That did not make sense. An hour later the water sky vanished without explanation, and they were still above the plateau.

At 2035 they had been in the air for twelve and a half hours. Their flight plan told them that they should have been off the plateau and over the Ross Ice Shelf, but they were still flying at 8,000 feet. There was no sign of the Queen Maude Mountains to their left or the Rockefeller Mountains in Marie Byrd Land to their right.

Things got more confused. Hollick-Kenyon saw a water sky again. This time it was ahead and to their right. Far away to their left were mountains. But which mountains? Were they somehow skirting the coast to the north of the Rockefeller Mountains? If that was the case, then they were going to miss the Ross Ice Shelf altogether.

Ten minutes after seeing the water sky to his right, Hollick-Kenyon handed Ellsworth a note reading, "I really have no idea where we are."[13] Hollick-Kenyon knew that Ellsworth had no idea where they were either, but understood their only chance was to follow the compass course set by Wilkins and, hopefully, it would lead them to the Ross Ice Shelf. But if they had drifted off course, was it to the north, toward the ocean, as the water sky indicated, or to the south, nearer the Pole, as Ellsworth's calculations indicated? They were conscious they could not waste fuel by flying hundreds of miles searching for the Ross Ice Shelf.

Finally, they decided they had no option but to land and attempt to determine their position. It would be risky because the plateau was covered with a fine swirling mist and they could not see whether the surface underneath was packed hard or made up of soft snow that would trap the *Polar Star*. Still, there was no choice. It was attempt a landing or continue flying, not knowing where they were going, until they ran out of fuel.

At 2155 Hollick-Kenyon skillfully brought the plane down to land with a jolt on granular snow that was packed so hard that the skis made no impression.

After fourteen hours in the cramped cockpit, both men climbed stiffly out of the plane and looked around. Their elevation was 6,300 feet. They were on the plateau and the undulating white silence stretched to the horizon in every direction. "We stood in the heart of the only unclaimed land in the Antarctic—in the world,"[14] Ellsworth wrote.

But where were they? Near the South Pole, as Ellsworth's sight from the plane had indicated? Or near water, as the water sky had indicated? Nothing made sense.

19

THANK GOD YOU'RE DOWN THERE

NOVEMBER 23–28, 1935

On the ground (Ellsworth would later name it Camp I), Hollick-Kenyon drained the oil to stop it freezing in the engine, then inspected the plane and found small crumples between the wing and the fuselage, caused by the heavy landing.

They had been in the air a little less than fourteen hours. Hollick-Kenyon knew they had followed the coast south from Dundee Island, then had turned to follow their compass bearing along the 80° South latitude line of meridian. But following that great circle route, how far west had they flown? Based on their estimated speed and the time they had been in the air, Hollick-Kenyon believed they had reached 141° West.

Ellsworth took a sight with his sextant, made his calculation, and declared they were only at 104° West. That would put them more than four hundred miles from where Hollick-Kenyon's dead reckoning placed them.

Both men understood it was unlikely they had enough fuel to reach Little America, even if they could find it. And Hollick-Kenyon did not want to use fuel running the portable generator to power the large radio. Instead they attempted to send signals using the smaller, hand-cranked trail radio. But nothing was heard in response.

The weather became "hazy," preventing Ellsworth from taking a sun sighting, so the weary men set up the tent, crawled into their sleeping bags, and rested for ten hours. When they emerged, the sky was clear again. Ellsworth took another sighting which, incredibly, gave their position as 80°20' South and 85°50' West—more than six hundred miles from Hollick-Kenyon's dead reckoning position and almost one thousand miles from Little America. Could they still be so far from their destination after almost fourteen hours of flying? The two men discussed the situation and agreed they had no choice but to follow their compass course until their fuel ran out. Before leaving, Ellsworth honored his pilot by naming the area Hollick-Kenyon Plateau. The name is still used today.

Hollick-Kenyon got the *Polar Star* airborne and, with "weather thick ahead," he followed a magnetic compass course of 196°. But they were only in the air for thirty minutes when a whiteout forced them down again. Unable to see what was below him, Hollick-Kenyon expertly landed the plane in the fog.

The pair spent two days on the ground at Camp II. Ellsworth recorded nothing of his navigational observations in his diary. He did, however, say that he took two photographs and noted "November 25 and 26 in camp." He also commented:

> A certain amount of snow clung to our canvas boots. This melted
> in the tent . . . the leather moccasins I had unwisely worn began
> to shrink with dampness, impeding blood circulation in my feet.[1]

Ellsworth was a long way from the Grand Canyon.

Hollick-Kenyon was more liberal with his record keeping. He noted that Ellsworth took a sight of the sun at 1335 on November 25 to calculate their position as 80°58' South and, almost impossibly, only 90° West. Another sight at 1500 on November 26 had Ellsworth concluding they were farther north, at 77°42' South and farther west at 117°30' West.

Hollick-Kenyon, however, did not record his frustration with his navigator. He did note there were clouds around all day and some frosty haze, the visibility varied greatly, and the temperature was minus 20–25°F. He also attempted to contact the *Wyatt Earp* using the trail radio, but except for time signals out of Buenos Aires, he heard nothing.

At five minutes before midnight on November 26 the pair taxied the *Polar Star* before lifting off on the next attempt to locate the Ross Ice Shelf. They followed a magnetic compass course of 179°, with their IAS 118 mph.

Ellsworth was finally forced to put pencil to paper and wrote that they took off "in great uncertainty about the precise direction of Little America." They only flew for fifty minutes. They had begun the flight in a clear midnight sky. Less than an hour later they landed in fog, with a storm approaching, having only flown approximately ninety miles. They were still at 6,200 feet. Watching the approaching storm, and fearing the strong wind would pick up the *Polar Star* and fling it to oblivion, they hurriedly dug trenches for the skis and dragged the plane forward so that the wings sat flat on the snow. Then they set up their tent and crawled inside as the blizzard hit them like a wall.

Wilkins was in a predicament. The last radio contact from the *Polar Star* had been received at 1610 (November 23). Hollick-Kenyon had been able to communicate that they were still flying and still on course. But the fragmentary message was puzzling. Was he trying to communicate that he thought they were only at 71° West? That would mean they had only traveled about eight hundred miles in seven and a half hours. It was much slower than expected.

Wilkins knew Ellsworth and Hollick-Kenyon had passed the Eternity Range, so there was no possibility that they would be attempting to return to the *Wyatt Earp*. The plan, if Ellsworth and Hollick-Kenyon landed after passing the mountains and were not able to get airborne, was for them to load their supplies on their sled then walk north, to the edge of the landfast ice and from there eastward to Mount Monique, Charcot Island.

Had they come down shortly after 71° West? If so, were they trying to walk to Charcot Island? Or were they were still flying when radio contact was lost? In many respects, 1610 was the worst possible time to lose radio contact—less than half way into their flight. Wilkins had to decide whether to head for Charcot Island or for the Bay of Whales. It was a decision complicated by the fact that the *Wyatt Earp* had become trapped at Dundee Island, held fast by the westerly drift of the ice.

It was also time for the uncomfortable task of informing Mary Louise that radio contact with her husband had been lost while the *Wyatt Earp* was trapped in the corner of the Weddell Sea. Wilkins radioed the news.

Mary Louise, waiting in New York, reacted calmly. First, she contacted the family lawyers, Morris & McVeigh, and informed Charles McVeigh that his wealthy client was missing, somewhere in Antarctica. McVeigh sent a radiogram to Wilkins saying, "Thank God you're down there,"[2] and authorizing him to do whatever he thought necessary to instigate a search. If that involved purchasing or hiring another airplane, then Wilkins had the authority to do it.

Next, Mary Louise contacted Richard Byrd, who was lecturing and still smarting from the criticism that he had purposely denied Ellsworth assistance. Mary Louise wanted to know what could be done to locate her husband. Byrd explained patiently that there was not a lot that he could do from the United States, but perhaps someone in Australia or New Zealand could be convinced to sail to the Bay of Whales, to see if Ellsworth was there. Byrd then went on to point out that he considered the Australian explorer Sir Douglas Mawson the most qualified man in the Southern Hemisphere to mount a search. On behalf of Mary Louise, Byrd contacted Mawson and asked if Australia would consider searching for Ellsworth.

Meanwhile, three days after the *Polar Star* had left Dundee Island, the wind turned, releasing the *Wyatt Earp*. Freed from the viselike grip of the ice, the little ship escaped and took shelter on the west side of Snow Hill Island, again standing off from Nordenskjöld's hut. Amid the stream of concerned radiograms from Charles McVeigh, Mary Louise, and Ellsworth's brother-in-law, Bernon Prentice, Wilkins decided his best course of action was to get another airplane, so he could search the Antarctic coast or even, if Ellsworth and Hollick-Kenyon were not found, follow their flight across the continent. He asked McVeigh if he could locate another Northrop Gamma and, if he did, could it be flown to Magallanes?

Wilkins then waited for the ice pack to disperse. Before leaving Snow Hill Island he left a note at Nordenskjöld's hut in case the *Wyatt Earp* did not complete the return journey. The note concluded:

The MS *Wyatt Earp* proceeded on November 26 to Deception Island, there to await information from the representatives in New York with reference to the relief airplane. The flights to lay depots will be made if Ellsworth and Kenyon are not heard from, or if they are not found at the Bay of Whales. (Signed) Hubert Wilkins.[3]

Two days later the *Wyatt Earp* reached Deception Island, where Wilkins received a radio message from Bernon Prentice. A Northrop Gamma plane was on its way to Magallanes. The *Wyatt Earp* sailed north to meet it.

20

MAYBE IT'S ALL TO TRY US

NOVEMBER 28, 1935–DECEMBER 5, 1935

A t their third landing place, Ellsworth and Hollick-Kenyon huddled in their tent, waiting for the blizzard to abate. Ellsworth's diary for November 28, 1935, simply records, "Lay all day in our sleeping bags with drift and gale reaching 40 mph." The following day he wrote, "Our sleeping bags are cold. Grease and dirt is the order of the day in camp. Our small primus [stove] leaks, so use the fire pot."

The strong wind continued and the pair understood they were going nowhere soon. When they peered out of their tent, they could see the *Polar Star* was still where they had left it, but it was beginning to be covered with snowdrift. They also understood that when the blizzard finally passed it would be a laborious task to dig it out.

Despite knowing it was unlikely they had enough fuel to reach Little America, they still felt it was worth using some of the precious liquid to run the portable motor and generator to send a signal from their 100-watt radio, which they usually only operated during flight. They strung antenna wires from bamboo poles and brought the motor and generator inside the tent, so that they could warm them sufficiently. After spending hours getting the small motor started, during which time the exhaust soot turned the interior of the tent a filthy gray-black, the appointed time for their scheduled radio contact arrived. Hollick-Kenyon flashed their estimated position, then switched on the receiver to listen. At that moment, the magneto in the generator burned out and the radio went dead. Ellsworth noted in his diary that at least Hollick-Kenyon:

> . . . did succeed in getting out a message of our whereabouts to the *Wyatt Earp* if [radio operator] Lanz ever did receive them and to say that we had been blizzard bound for three days and were waiting for weather.[1]*

Henceforth, any broadcasts from the larger radio could only be made while the engine of the *Polar Star* was running. Ellsworth and Hollick-Kenyon turned in desperation to their weaker trail radio, but when they tried to generate enough electricity by quickly turning the hand-operated generator, they stripped the teeth off one of the gears.

Confined to their tent, and with nothing to do and nothing to talk about, Hollick-Kenyon, who had studied the theory of navigation, was still puzzled over Ellsworth's inability to take observations and draw conclusions that did not vary wildly. Something was clearly amiss. Sometime during their second day at Camp III, Hollick-Kenyon decided to inspect Ellsworth's sextant to see if he could determine where they were, or at least why Ellsworth seemed unable to do so. Hollick-Kenyon only had the sextant in his hands for a few moments before he noticed something that Ellsworth had missed. The index mirror was out of alignment.

A sextant's function is to accurately measure the angle between horizontal and an object in the sky. In Ellsworth's case, the sun. Ellsworth carried a Bausch & Lomb bubble sextant. It determined horizontal, not by looking at the horizon as sailors did, but by looking at a bubble, not unlike a carpenter's level. With the sextant held perfectly horizontal, the sun was

---

*   The message was not received by the *Wyatt Earp*.

sighted and its image reflected through an index mirror to read the angle. Once the angle of the sun was accurately measured, the navigator looked up the date and time of the sighting in an almanac, then found the corresponding angle to determine position. Sextants are delicate instruments and navigators carefully protect them from knocks and bumps. The index mirror, so critical for an accurate reading, is usually set by the manufacturer and locked in place.

How long the index mirror on Ellsworth's sextant had been out of alignment, Hollick-Kenyon had no idea. Perhaps the mirror had been jolted by the heavy landing at Camp I. Perhaps Ellsworth had knocked or mishandled the sextant during the flight. Or maybe it had been that way from the beginning. But Ellsworth's sextant was out of alignment and he had not realized until Hollick-Kenyon had inspected it.

It must have been a disappointing time for Ellsworth, whose one job on the flight had been to navigate. Until that time his diary entries had been brief, but on his third day at Camp III, he summarized his worries:

> November 30: One trouble after another now. First the airplane transformer burns out. 2: Cooking primus leaks. 3: The trail [radio] set slips a gear thus leaving us with no communication with the *Wyatt Earp*. Suppose she is already starting to lay bases for us along the coast, knowing nothing of where we are. 4: The sextant is out of order. What next? The snow still drifts and the next thing to do is dig out the camp and the plane and try and reach Little America. Probably not enough gas to get there. The speed on skis isn't what we thought for we are certainly behind schedule. We have gotten three time ticks from Buenos Aires. Kenyon and I both agreed it was best to get on to Little America instead of trying to fix up the radio here.[2]

Having noticed the problem with the sextant, even more remarkably, it was Hollick-Kenyon who worked out how to fix it. Sextants can be checked quickly in the field by setting the index arm to zero. One imagines the sun is sitting on the horizon, so the angle is zero, and sets the sextant accordingly. Ellsworth wrote it was Hollick-Kenyon who:

. . . happened upon the simple expedient of putting the bubble on the snow horizon, then setting the index at zero and locking it there. We both of us instantly realized that this would give us a roughly correct set [of observations].[3]

On their fourth day, the wind dropped and the two men emerged from the tent to see the sun for the first time since they had landed at Camp III, and to find the *Polar Star* half buried under drift snow. They immediately cut blocks of ice and built a wall to protect their tent, lest the wind pick up again.

Then, with the reset sextant, Ellsworth took elevations of the sun and calculated they were at 80° South and approximately 114° West. They were, in fact, on course, but still had over six hundred miles to travel before they reached Little America. Their position also meant they had to be near the western end of the polar plateau and, if they could get in the air, hopefully they would find themselves descending to the ice shelf. Whether or not they had enough fuel was another matter.

The *Polar Star* was packed with snow, so Ellsworth spent the day crawling inside to scrape it out. The broad-shouldered Hollick-Kenyon found he could not wriggle very far into the narrow fuselage, so the laborious chore was left to Ellsworth, who used his tin drinking mug as a scoop and described his experience as "One of the worst days I have ever spent." Referring to flattening an airfield for the Dornier Wal flying boat, when he, Amundsen, and the others were stranded on the ice in the Arctic, Ellsworth noted tersely in his diary, "Even a worse job than [19]25."[4]

Ellsworth's unwise choice of moccasins for his feet was also taking its toll. He had completely lost sensation in his left foot.

Hollick-Kenyon appears more philosophical about their trials, because Ellsworth also noted in his diary, "Kenyon says, 'maybe it's all to try us.'"[5]

After an exhausting twelve hours scraping away at the snow inside the *Polar Star*, Ellsworth collapsed in his sleeping bag, warmed by a nip of the grain alcohol that Wilkins had included in their food box.

The following day (December 2) Hollick-Kenyon climbed into the cockpit of the plane and spent the day clearing fine snow from his instruments. That evening, he and Ellsworth agreed that whatever happened, they would get airborne in the morning and fly west. On the morning of December 3, they emerged from the tent to see that it had snowed over-night and they needed to dig out around the plane again. They attacked the job with a desperate enthusiasm, and by midday had cleared the area. Now they needed to get the skis out of the trenches, which they had dug to allow the wings to sit flat. They unloaded everything from the *Polar Star* to lighten it and, after covering the engine with a canvas hood, lighting a stove under it, then heating the engine for forty-five minutes, they tried to start it. That involved cranking the engine over a couple of times, then using the battery-powered starter motor. After five attempts the *Polar Star* burst into life.

Hollick-Kenyon taxied the plane forward, lifting the skis out of the trenches, and they began the hasty job of loading everything on board. But before they could strike the tent, a storm front swept in from the southeast, bringing high winds and snow. They had no choice but to secure the plane and pitch their tent again.

In his diary Ellsworth revealed his growing pessimism, writing the snow-brick wall they had built to protect them from the wind, "would be our mausoleum," then added:

> Looks as though we [are] 650 [miles] from Bay of Whales with
> no hope of getting there. God forbid this airplane stuff anyway.
> One is so helpless when something goes wrong.[6]

On the morning of December 4, the wind had dropped again and they repeated the process of digging the snowdrift away from the *Polar Star*. Then they heated the engine and got it started before quickly loading everything on board. With "the sky not too promising,"[7] they were airborne at 1920 and bid farewell to Camp III, which had been their home for a week.

Hollick-Kenyon steered a magnetic compass course of 190°, until Ellsworth measured the drift and put it at five degrees. Hollick-Kenyon altered his bearing to 195°. An hour after they had taken off, he noted they were flying at 4,700 feet. The Indicated Air Speed was 125 mph, thanks to the easterly wind at their backs, which would carry them farther before they inevitably ran out of fuel. At 2235, more than three hours after leaving Camp III, Hollick-Kenyon brought the plane lower to estimate the elevation of the surface. He recorded it in his log as one thousand feet. His compass course was 185°. Ellsworth wrote in his diary at 2303, "Came down to get a sight. A beautiful calm night. The boundless snowfield sparkling like diamonds."[8]

They were flying over the Ross Ice Shelf.

But where on the shelf? Their only signpost to the Bay of Whales now was Roosevelt Island, a snow-covered hump, eighty miles long and forty miles wide. It was almost impossible to distinguish from a distance. Hollick-Kenyon and Ellsworth understood they could not waste fuel flying around in circles trying to locate the island.

At 2310 Hollick-Kenyon brought the plane down for a fourth successful landing and, with new confidence in their sextant, they reckoned their position to be 79°29' South, 153°27' West.

They had crossed Antarctica with extraordinary accuracy.

After ten hours on the ground, they took off again at 0900 on December 5 and flew in the direction they hoped would lead them to Roosevelt Island and Little America. They were only in the air fifty minutes when the saw the white hump. As they flew over it, they looked forward to see a water sky, then beyond the island the slate gray water of the Ross Sea.

They had barely seen the water when the Pratt & Whitney engine, after twenty hours and fifteen minutes of faithful performance since Dundee Island, began to falter. In an instant, the last fuel tank was dry. The propeller jerked to a standstill in front of their eyes and Hollick-Kenyon again demonstrated his skill by landing the powerless plane.

In his log, the pragmatic Hollick-Kenyon recorded:

> 1005 Landed. All tanks consumed. Camp Roosevelt. Approx position two miles NW Roosevelt Island. Fine Calm. Snow soft and lightly drifted. Antennas erected but could not start motor generator for 1200 SKED [scheduled 1200 broadcast]. Unable to rig flying antenna in time to transmit on flight. Open sea visible before landing. Estimated position about four miles east of camp at Little America.

Estimated ground speed of entire flight 101 mph. Average consumption 22.81 gallons per hour. Total flying time 20 hours 15 minutes.[9]

In his diary, Ellsworth wrote: "Came to Roosevelt Island. Beyond stretched the ice free waters of the Ross Sea. The goal of four years of dreaming."[10]

21

A FRIENDLY GESTURE

O n the same day that the *Polar Star* flopped to a stop just north of Roosevelt Island, Sir Douglas Mawson in Australia was explaining that he was not eager to search for the missing fliers. Mary Louise's request for assistance from Byrd had been forwarded to Mawson, who put the responsibility back on Wilkins. Mawson, who never had a high regard for Wilkins, informed Australia's federal treasurer, Richard Casey:

> Wilkins's position on the expedition has, I believe, been an unimportant one but there was a provision that, should the present emergency arise, Wilkins should be in full charge and empowered to make a search. Wilkins has looked forward to this moment. There is obviously now a chance for him to do something and reap the reward for his three years devoted to the expedition in a very junior capacity.
>
> Provided Wilkins is in the field to complete Ellsworth's wishes regarding search etc. I would not feel disposed to enter

the arena myself unless, of course, there was something I could do that Wilkins could not.[1]

Casey was interested in Australia's Antarctic territorial claims and knew Mawson and Wilkins personally.* After listening to Mawson's argument against searching, Casey sought a second opinion from John King Davis, the experienced ship's captain who had been to Antarctica with both Mawson and Shackleton. Davis showed more enthusiasm and pointed out that if Ellsworth and Hollick-Kenyon had gone down in the first half of their flight, then it was unlikely they would have survived. He explained his reasoning to Casey:

> When one realizes that an attempt to reach Charcot Island would mean traversing an unknown range of mountains of considerable height to reach the seaboard, where they could not rely with any certainty on obtaining provisions, or of being rescued, I think this must be rejected in favor of a probable attempt to travel the greater distance to the Bay of Whales, where they know food supplies are available and where rescue would only be a matter of time.[2]

The fliers, Davis believed, would be either dead or at Little America. Casey agreed with him and, at a time when the Australian Government was keen to impress America, the experienced politician suggested that it would be a friendly gesture toward America if Australia were to make some attempt to rescue the fliers.

But what, exactly, could Australia do? Mawson and Davis had spent a decade trying to convince the government to set up bases in Antarctica, both to reinforce its territorial claim and as permanent weather stations, but the country still did not have a ship suitable for Antarctic waters.

Fortunately however, the British ship *Discovery II*, which a year earlier had been stalking the waters around South Georgia to scare off the

---

* Australia's three permanent Antarctic bases are named Mawson for Sir Douglas Mawson, Davis for John King Davis, and Casey for R. G. Casey.

Argentineans, was now conducting oceanographic research in the Indian Ocean. Perhaps Australia could borrow that. Casey sent a cable, via the Australian High Commissioner in London, to the Discovery Committee, asking if it might temporarily suspend its scientific research to place the ship at the disposal of the Australian Government. Always happy to demonstrate its rightful dominance in Antarctica, the Discovery Committee promptly gave its consent.

When Davis informed Wilkins of the decision, he replied indignantly that the offer of assistance was unnecessary, at least in the immediate future: "Unless delays experienced Ellsworth's Expedition's own plans meet all requirements until mid January, after which would be time [to] despatch *Discovery* to Bay of Whales."[3] But Wilkins's attempt to refuse help was ignored. Excitement for an Australian expedition to Antarctica was already gathering momentum in public and political circles. A Yank and a Brit were lost in Antarctica and Australia was going to rescue them.

The fully provisioned *Discovery II* was south of Fremantle, Western Australia, when Commander Leonard Hill (who had recently replaced Captain Andrew Nelson) received orders to proceed to Melbourne and collect two planes, pilots, and additional crew members. F. D. (Francis) Ommanney, a British naturalist traveling on board, recalled:

> But we still knew nothing of the reason for our summons to Melbourne except that it had to do with Lincoln Ellsworth, the American aviator, who, we believed, was to make this summer his third attempt to fly across the Antarctic Continent. One evening I was reading in my cabin, supporting myself against the rolling of the ship. Deacon and Marr came in. "We're to take on two airplanes in Melbourne," they said, "and two pilots. We are to take in stores for four months and go down to the Bay of Whales. That's all we know."[4]

Here at last, the excited Ommanney realized, was the chance to visit Antarctica.

When the *Discovery II* arrived at the small port of Williamstown, a suburb of Melbourne, the British crew realized they had sailed into a national fervor. In the two weeks it took to remove the samson post on the afterdeck and build a platform to hold a plane, people flocked to Williamstown to see the ship that was going to rescue Ellsworth. Ommanney wrote:

> In spite of the fact that we were called the "Good Will ship" and "Australia's Gesture," we found that people quite genuinely meant it when they said to us in clubs, in pubs, or in the street, "Good on yer, *Discovery*! Hope you find him!" And when young men and girls, lean, bronzed, superb, sailed across the harbor in their skiffs to "see the *Discovery*" . . . they had caught the sense of the gesture their stripling race was making.[5]

The Ross Ice Shelf, December 5, 1935:

Ellsworth and Hollick-Kenyon sat silently in the *Polar Star*. The flight they had expected to make in fourteen hours had taken twelve days. But despite getting lost, the failure of the radios, and being trapped on the ground by blizzards, Lincoln Ellsworth and Herbert Hollick-Kenyon had crossed Antarctica. They had seen, and stood in, the heart of the last unexplored continent in the world. Now all they had to do was locate Little America so they could survive to tell their tale. They climbed out of the *Polar Star*, dug trenches for the skis, and hauled the plane forward so its wings sat flat on the snow. Then they spent the next forty-eight hours resting. After they had rested, Hollick-Kenyon scavenged fuel sloshing in the corners of the plane's tanks and attempted to repair the portable generator. Ellsworth recorded their daily routine in his diary:

> Continued S.E. wind and snow squalls. Still in our [sleeping] bags. We eat twice daily. Morning oatmeal with bacon boiled in it and evening a mug of pemmican. I like Coman's pemmican flavored with spice best. It was more tasty than the Danish. The temp here hangs on the freezing mark. Quite different from the -5 degrees Fah[renheit] on the 6,000 feet plateau. Every evening at 2200 GMT we try to get contact with the *Wyatt Earp* using our 100 watt portable generator. Whether or not they hear we

do not know. But hope they are not laying bases [near Charcot Island]. Ye Gods. A 300 mile walk to the sea.[6]

By December 8 the weather had cleared. Ellsworth and Hollick-Kenyon stood on the plane and scanned the horizon for the radio masts they knew protruded from Little America. (They had not brought binoculars.) To the northwest they saw irregular ice hummocks which they suspected were snow-covered buildings. Hollick-Kenyon also thought he could make out an ice-covered tower. They were uncertain whether it was Little America, but seeing nothing else, they strapped on snow shoes and, without taking additional supplies, set off in that direction. After walking for two hours the "buildings" appeared no closer, so they returned to the plane and rested.

The following day they assembled their sled, packed it with ten days' worth of rations, and set off again. Expecting to soon reach Little America, they left their tent erected beside the *Polar Star*. The going was slow. The soft wet snow made hauling the sled difficult but, after a draining nine miles, they reached the hummocks only to discover the "tower" was merely an ice pinnacle and the "buildings" were snowdrifts.

Their disappointment was aggravated by the realization they had left the sextant in the plane and were unable to check their position, or attempt to determine in which direction Little America might lie. With no shelter, they left the sled where it was and hurried back to the *Polar Star*, where they rested, grabbed the sextant, packed the tent, and then made another nine-mile slog back to the loaded sled. It was, Ellsworth wrote in his diary, "awful going. Our feet sinking into the snow and soaking wet."

They returned to the sled at 0300 on December 10. In twenty-four hours they had hiked an exhausting twenty-seven miles. Hollick-Kenyon was "pretty well done in." They set up the tent, ate a small meal of mixed nuts, and rested for seven hours, after which Ellsworth took sightings and estimated they were twelve miles south of Little America.

On December 11 they set out again. After the previous heavy hauling in the soft snow they agreed they would only travel at night, when the snow hardened. Plodding on, with Hollick-Kenyon exhausted and Ellsworth stumping along on a left foot he could not feel, Ellsworth suddenly shouted that he could see water. Hollick-Kenyon looked and agreed. It had to be the Bay of Whales. They must have been traveling too far to the west.

The tired men felt they could reach their salvation after a rest, so they pitched their tent again, then varied their diet by treating themselves to bacon and boiled powdered milk. Ellsworth, believing he would be safely in a dry hut within hours, took off his left moccasin to examine his foot for the first time since leaving Camp III at 6,000 feet. The foot was covered with large blisters.

After resting for most of the night, Ellsworth got his blistered foot covered and the pair set off in the direction of the water they had seen. But after walking for six hours, a devastated Ellsworth's wrote in his diary:

A snare and a delusion. The Bay of Whales. Where? We traveled twelve miles today at two miles per hour, but where was the water we saw yesterday. No more. The second no wind [day] on our trip and the weather misty with no visibility except toward the west of our route of travel. So tomorrow we head in that direction. One little bird dropping in the snow. No other sign of life. Down to our last quart of fuel now.[7]

Later the same day he recorded they had walked another ten miles toward a water sky, and that it was:

Like walking on a fog bank. Can't see any irregularities under foot. Sometimes ahead it looks as though we were going into a depression. At other times, as though we were going up. But always the flat monotonous barrier surface. No desert was ever more monotonous. Objects that appear near are miles ahead. We approached a ridge and thought to get an extended view.[8]

As they struggled to the top of a ridge, hoping to get a better view, the two men heard the lapping of waves. They stumbled quickly forward and stared down, almost in disbelief. Below them, salt water splashed against the ice. It was the open water of the Ross Sea they had seen from the *Polar Star*. But where was Little America?

Again they pitched their tent, ate and rested. On December 13, Ellsworth recorded:

> The 13th is both my lucky and unlucky day. It was this day two years ago that the plane went through the ice. It is astonishing to think that Kenyon and I are the only two humans on this continent of 5,000,000 square miles. [9]

Perhaps Ellsworth was becoming disoriented. The *Polar Star* had been damaged, almost two years earlier, in January. He was making his diary entry in December.

By December 14 their search had become aimless. They had reached the edge of the barrier and stared down into the sea, but in whichever direction they looked, they could not see Little America.

On December 15, ten days after the *Polar Star* had run out of fuel, Ellsworth was out of ideas. The two men decided they had no choice but to walk in whatever direction they chose until they could walk no longer. They had enough fuel to prepare one, or at the most two, hot meals. With the same fatalistic determination, focused by a lack of options, with which they had climbed aboard the *Polar Star* at Camp III, they now packed the sled and stumbled on their way.

Fifteen miles later they found two abandoned tractors. They had reached the small inlet that Byrd had named Ver-Sur-Mer and had used to unload his ships. This was one end of the Misery Trail that led to Little America. With new energy, they followed the edge of the inlet east until Ellsworth recorded, "Topping a rise we looked down on the most desolate remains of past habitation I have ever witnessed. I have seen deserted mining camps in the west but nothing to equal this. Only a lot of masts and the stove pipes of buildings sticking out of the snow." [10]

They scrambled toward their beacons of salvation and found two glass skylights that were relatively free of snow. They smashed one and lowered themselves down to the room below. It was Byrd's radio shack. Next, they lowered the supplies from their sled and set about making the room habitable. The radio shack at Little America consisted of two rooms. The first, where Ellsworth and Hollick-Kenyon had entered through the skylight, had once housed radio equipment. In this room Byrd's failing voice had crackled through from Advance Base as the poison slowly unhinged his mind. The second room was lined with bunks and was where the staff had slept. Ellsworth and Hollick-Kenyon were delighted to find a small stove and a sack of coal.

On his three expeditions, Ellsworth had carried a bottle of brandy, given to him by Mary Louise before the first. He opened it, and he and Hollick-Kenyon took a celebratory drink. Then, finding themselves in darkness for the first time in three weeks, they slept for twenty-four hours.

After they woke, Ellsworth wrote in his diary:

> We dug a tunnel and made steps down to the door of our shack. Found three sacks of coal for our stove in the snow including a sack of hard tack, also a drum of gasoline for our primus. In the shack was a tin of strawberry jam and some marmalade. A can of G.W. coffee and numerous bottles of malted milk tablets. We can get all our snow for water without putting our head out. Cleaned everything up including our dishes. Shaved and took our first wash in three weeks and settled down to await the arrival of the *Wyatt Earp*. When she will arrive we don't know for it is a 3,000-mile voyage from Dundee Island to the Bay of Whales. Anyway, we have made the crossing and that's something so we can afford to be patient, dreary as it is here.[11]

22

A SILENCE THAT COULD BE FELT

DECEMBER 15, 1935–JANUARY 26, 1936

O n December 15, 1935, the day Ellsworth and Hollick-Kenyon lowered themselves into the sanctuary of the radio shack at Little America, the *Wyatt Earp* was still in Magallanes, Chile. Wilkins was waiting to get the plane promised by Charles McVeigh and Bernon Prentice. He was also still planning to search Charcot Island and the unmapped coast in the Pacific Quadrant, but he held little hope of finding the fliers there. If the *Polar Star* had landed, or crashed, when the radio contact was lost, the chances of the two men being alive were extremely remote. And if they did reach the coast somewhere farther west than Charcot Island, the likelihood of the *Wyatt Earp* negotiating the ice pack that had stopped Byrd in 1933 was equally remote. Nevertheless, Wilkins had to cross it off his list before he could proceed to the Ross Ice Shelf. "Expect to find Lincoln at Little America," Wilkins wrote to his wife from Magallanes. "In any case we will have done all we can and be back [in New York] by the end of March."[1]

Anxious to get on with it, Wilkins received word that the pilot bringing the relief plane from California refused to fly to Magallanes, where there was no landing field. The nearest airstrip was at Rio de Gallegos, Argentina. Frustrated, Wilkins and Joe Lymburner loaded the pontoons for the *Polar Star*, which were carried on the *Wyatt Earp*, onto a truck and drove 130 miles to the airfield, where they fitted the pontoons to the new plane before Lymburner flew it back to the Magallanes and landed in the harbor.

The relief plane was also a Northrop Gamma, with the exception that it was a single-seater. The *Polar Star* had been especially built with the twin cockpit to accommodate Ellsworth. On the sides of the relief plane was emblazoned the name *Texaco 20*, to acknowledge the generosity of the company that had loaned it. Once the *Texaco 20* was securely lashed to the deck of the *Wyatt Earp*, Wilkins was ready to depart. Before leaving he wrote to his wife:

> I suppose you have heard that the Australian Government will send two planes on the SS *Discovery [II]* to look for Ellsworth. I know there are two fellows [Mawson and Davis] out there who would jump at any chance to get to the Antarctic and no doubt they are working this opportunity. I suppose they are saying also that at last they have caught me napping and have to come to my rescue. However I have wired to the government out there saying that the sending of two planes is not necessary as yet and will not be unless something happens to the *Wyatt Earp*, which is not likely. Anyway, if they do get down and pick up Ellsworth it means that we will be home all the sooner and we can't be home soon enough for me.[2]

In Melbourne, the *Discovery II* was ready to sail by December 23. Crowds lined the jetty at Williamstown to cheer its departure. A year earlier, Australian aviator Charles Ulm had disappeared on a flight from California to Hawaii and the U.S. Navy had mounted an extensive, yet unsuccessful, search. Now Australians felt they were repaying a debt by supporting a search for an American, and local papers reported people shouting to the crew, "Do it for Charlie! Find him for Charlie!" Women waved, or threw flowers and kisses.

On board the *Discovery II* were two planes; a Gipsy Moth 60X and a Westland Wapiti. Added to the crew were two Royal Australian Air Force (RAAF) pilots, along with five Australians.

On December 25, 1935, Ellsworth wrote in his diary:

Christmas Day. We have already celebrated a day too early. Wouldn't have known it except when walking down to Ver-Sur-Mer the clouds cleared and there was the sun with a great bight in it and we remembered that on the 25th there was a total eclipse. With the white snows beneath it was a unique sight to behold. Yesterday, our Christmas, we found a small home made plum pudding tucked away on the top shelf in our cabin and it made a real Christmas for us, what with the remains of the small bottle of cognac given me by my wife and carried for three years on the *Wyatt Earp*.

All yesterday morning I spent digging out the drifted snow from the shaft entrance to our home. We are on our last sack of coal and only light the stove in the evenings now. It is cosy with the stove even if it does melt the snow around the stove pipe and skylight with a continuous dripping of water on the floor. Every day I walk six miles down the bay to where the tractors are, where we have put up our tent with two yellow streamers and a note that we are at Little America so the *Wyatt Earp* will know where we are. The wait here is trying indeed, knowing nothing of the whereabouts of the ship. The Bay of Whales has not started to open yet, although the number of seals increases daily on the ice. I suppose it is a sign that open water is coming soon and I hope also the *Wyatt Earp*. Longingly I scan the horizon for her.

Our daily routine is as follows. Supper around 9:00 P.M. In our sleeping bags until 3:00 or perhaps 4:00 P.M., the next day. A light meal of perhaps oatmeal with raisins and tea. Clean up our cabin perhaps wash the dishes depending on how clean they are from the last meal. Melt snow for the evening meal.

Then I take a walk on snow shoes to the tractors, look out to sea for the *Wyatt Earp*, and return home generally to find that Kenyon has broken in the skylight of another cabin and found another sack of coal or some more bottles of Worcestershire sauce, cans of tobacco, magazines, or marmalade. Kenyon makes bannocks [flat bread] of self raising flour we found and Maxwell House coffee, also rummaged, that can't be beat for flavor and after a stew of bully beef rich with chilli sauce, we settle down in our bunks for a quiet smoke until bed time. Our routine saves both food and fuel for we don't know how long we may have to stay here. Found two and a half more sacks of coal. We were down to our last half sack. Thank heavens there is half a drum of fuel left.[3]

On December 28, five days after the *Discovery II* had left Melbourne, the *Wyatt Earp* reached the heavy ice surrounding Charcot Island. The sea was rough, and Wilkins decided against trying to get the *Texaco 20* airborne. After three days of waiting for calmer seas, which didn't materialize, Wilkins headed straight for the Ross Sea. The *Discovery II* and the *Wyatt Earp* were now in a race to reach the Bay of Whales first.

For the following two weeks, Ellsworth's diary entries are brief. (The entries in Hollick-Kenyon's pilot's log ceased when the plane landed north of Roosevelt Island.) Ellsworth's jottings mainly noted changes in the weather. He did record, on January 11, that they had lost half a day somewhere, probably by sleeping through it, then took the time to record his frustration again on January 14:

Continuous foggy weather ever since the 6th. Today it is snowing again. Still warm. Will the *Wyatt Earp* never come for us? Wilkins said five or six weeks to come the 3,000 miles from Dundee Island and here it is almost seven. One can't sleep all the time and it is awful not to be able to read. My glasses are in the plane, along with all my flags and souvenirs. The thing I care most about is the Wyatt Earp cartridge belt. Fear the plane is doomed to remain there forever, for though only sixteen miles away no one realizes how much sixteen miles is in this country.[4]

A day later Ellsworth made his final entry in his diary. "The first penguins this year in the Bay of Whales. One flopped on the skylight over my bunk as I lay writing. One month today since we arrived here."[5]

After reaching the Ross Sea on January 8, the *Discovery II* spent a week trapped in the pack ice, unable to find clear water through which it could sail to the Bay of Whales. The Gipsy Moth plane was lowered over the side of the ship and, in a small lead of open water, pilot Eric Douglas managed to get it airborne to look for a route by which the ship could escape. He found none. Commander Hill received a radio message from Wilkins explaining that the *Wyatt Earp* had reached the Ross Sea and was also attempting to negotiate the pack. Ommanney, swept up in the spirit of the competition, recalled:

> [*Wyatt Earp*] gained on us that day and we began to think that all our labor and the Captain's anxiety had been in vain. Very early the next morning the floes thinned out and, in a little over seventy-three degrees south, we left them and came into another world . . . we had won.[6]

The *Discovery II* was through the pack ice on January 15, while the *Wyatt Earp* was still struggling to get free. The British ship, named to honor Scott's original *Discovery*, cruised the edge of the shelf until, like Scott, it found the Bay of Whales.

At 8:20 P.M., the ship's officer broadcast an excited message. He could distinguish two orange flags fluttering from poles at the top of the ice. Someone was at Little America. Or at least had been recently. The crew fired signal flares and waited for a response. None came. Assuming the transcontinental aviators were either dead or at Little America, the Gipsy Moth was lowered onto the water and Eric Douglas, along with Flying Officer Alister Murdoch, took off. They circled once, then followed the bay south. Eager to participate in the climax of the *Discovery II*'s Antarctic adventure, a ground party assembled their new sledging equipment, scrambled onto the ice, and hurried after them.

Shortly after getting airborne, Douglas and Murdoch recognized radio masts, and what appeared to be the roof of a hut. Douglas circled the biplane again and flew lower to notice orange-colored strips near the poles. Then a man crawled out of the roof, stood straight and waved his arms frantically at the plane. According to Douglas:

> This caused great excitement between us as we realized it must be either Ellsworth or Kenyon. I continued to circle and after a few minutes we threw overboard a small bag attached to a letter from the Captain of the *Discovery [II]* congratulating Ellsworth and Kenyon on their achievement and asking them that, if they were well enough, to start out on the seven-mile hike to the Barrier face where they would be met by a land party from the *Discovery [II]*. We observed the figure pick up the parachute and wave.[7]

On the ice, it was Hollick-Kenyon who retrieved the parachute and package, read the note, then he scrambled back down and relayed the good news to Ellsworth, whose feet, by this time, had become so painful that he had difficulty walking. Hollick-Kenyon read the note to Ellsworth, who was still without his reading glasses. It was signed by Commander Hill and directed the men to start for the edge of the shelf to meet the ground party coming their way. Next the two men opened the accompanying package to discover chocolate, raisins, and sweetened concentrated orange syrup. Ellsworth's foot was so painful he suggested that Hollick-Kenyon go and meet the ground party, then bring them back to collect him. The pilot didn't need any further urging to escape the confines of the radio shack and, after grabbing his few personal possessions, he left Ellsworth with a promise he would be back in no more than three hours. Then Hollick-Kenyon climbed fifteen feet into an overcast night sky and never looked back.

Less than halfway to the coast, Hollick-Kenyon greeted the ground party and, rather than despatch them to collect Ellsworth, persuaded them the American was fine where he was and they should return to the ship.

Hollick-Kenyon arrived at the *Discovery II* a little after midnight. The onboard crew eagerly pressed against the railings to witness the rescue of the Antarctic adventurer. Would the heroic explorer be carried aboard, barely conscious after his ordeal? Would his emaciated face be covered with frost and his hoarse voice barely audible? Ommanney watched the ground party return:

> . . . as he climbed aboard up the rope ladder we lined the rail and cheered him. He was shaved, washed and spruce and exuded an air of well-being which, we had to confess, was something of a disappointment to us. We had conjured up in our imaginations thin features, covered by a matted growth of beard and wasted by weeks of starvation diet in a twilight cell buried beneath the snow. But his cheeks shone from a recent shave and his stalwart frame in a check shirt showed no signs of anything but abundant health and vitality. He sat down, slowly filled and lighted a pipe and said:
>
> "Well, well! The *Discovery* eh? This is an affair. But, I say, it's awfully decent of you fellows to drop in on us like this. Thanks, I'll have a whisky and soda."[8]

Commander Hill explained that he was, "prepared to go out then and bring Mr. Ellsworth in, but Mr. Kenyon assured me that there was really no need for such haste." Ellsworth was fine and had plenty of food, Hollick-Kenyon, told them. He would be happy to wait another day in the radio shack. Hollick-Kenyon followed his drink with a hot bath, fresh clothes, and another drink. Then the reticent Englishman, who had rarely spoken to Ellsworth during their eight weeks together alone in Antarctica, opened a floodgate of conversation and kept the crew up most of the night regaling them with stories of his adventures.

In the morning a second relief party, which included Ommanney, set off to collect Ellsworth and, more importantly, see Little America for themselves. The six-man party reached the radio shack and descended, where Ommanney saw the depressed Ellsworth, "lying on a wooden bunk amid a silence that could be felt."[9]

Having trudged seven grueling miles, the relief team told Ellsworth they wanted to rest in the bunks for a while and asked him if he had any food for them. "Hollick-Kenyon said you had," they insisted. Ellsworth recalled:

> I invited them to help themselves. They cleaned up everything, especially praising tea made with snow water, the first any of them had ever tasted. They said it was the best tea they had ever drunk, though I could tell no difference between snow-water tea and any other.
>
> After that they stripped the shack of everything they could find for souvenirs—calendars, strainers, anything.[10]

After packing their booty on their sled, the ground party added Ellsworth and headed back to the ship. They only stopped once on the way to rest and eat more chocolate. Listening to Ellsworth talk during the sled trip, Ommanney observed he was, "rather a naïf and childlike old boy who hadn't much idea why he was flying across the Antarctic or what he hoped to achieve by the feat."[11]

Ellsworth followed Hollick-Kenyon's sterling example of a hot bath, a stiff drink, and fresh clothes. Then a pair of glasses was borrowed that suited him well enough for reading and the ship's doctor attended to his feet.

Three days after Ellsworth was lifted on board the *Discovery II*, the *Wyatt Earp* appeared as a small black dot on the otherwise white horizon, threading its way precariously through the ice pack. It took another week to safely clear the floes and it tied up against the shelf on January 25.

A motor launch from the *Discovery II* transported the refreshed Ellsworth and Hollick-Kenyon to their expedition ship, where they related the details of their flight across the continent. Then, having instructed Wilkins to retrieve Wyatt Earp's cartridge belt, Ellsworth and Hollick-Kenyon returned to the well-appointed *Discovery II*.

Wilkins and Lymburner led a small party across the ice to fetch the *Polar Star*. The journey was made in six and a half hours. Lymburner refueled the plane, spent two hours warming the engine, then got it started. Next the sled, which had been hauled across the ice, was roped behind the plane and, with Lymburner at the controls, the *Polar Star* was taxied to the edge of the shelf, while the remainder of the team rode on the sled. After four years of planning and two failed attempts, the transcontinental journey of the *Polar Star* and Wyatt Earp's cartridge belt was complete.

When the plane reached the edge of the ice shelf, Wilkins saw the launch from the *Discovery II* approaching again, with Ellsworth and Hollick-Kenyon waving from the bow. The *Wyatt Earp* crew might have been forgiven for thinking that Ellsworth was coming to express his gratitude for the years of work and devotion that helped him successfully cross Antarctica. They would have been mistaken. Without coming on board his ship, Ellsworth called out for his reading glasses, souvenirs, and cartridge belt, then announced he and Hollick-Kenyon would sail to Australia on the more comfortable *Discovery II*. Olsen lamented, "They did not seem to mind our being left behind to face once more the most dangerous sea journey in the world!"[12]

The leader of the expedition bade his crew goodbye and returned to the *Discovery II*, which cast off and was negotiating its escape from the pack while the wings were being unbolted from the *Polar Star*. It eventually took the *Wyatt Earp* six weeks to sail back past the Devil's Graveyard to Deception Island, before it commenced a ten-week journey to New York via Cape Horn and the east coast of South America.

23

CHUGGING ON

After the Australians had shown such enthusiasm for rescuing Ellsworth, he felt it only fair that he should reward them with his presence at a series of celebratory events held in his honor. In Melbourne, he made a special point of thanking Sir Douglas Mawson, who had traveled from Adelaide to welcome him, and John King Davis, who became his unofficial host for the visit. Ellsworth was shown the sights of Melbourne, then flown to Canberra to lunch with Prime Minister Joseph Lyons, who was moved to say during a speech:

> Mr. Ellsworth's life of adventure, risk and courage was an inspiration to all mankind . . . Mr. Ellsworth was one of the most intrepid of modern explorers. Whereas he might have led a life of ease, he had preferred a career of usefulness and service to his country and to the world.[1]

Swept up in the complimentary atmosphere, Flight Lieutenant Eric Douglas, who had flown over Little America and seen Hollick-Kenyon emerge from the radio room, paid special tribute to Ellsworth by naming his first-born son, Ian Ellsworth Douglas.

The British felt that the Australians, who had done little more than borrow their ship, had no right to be the sole dispenser of the accolades. On February 14, less than a week after Ellsworth arrived in Australia, Leonard Hill, the commander of the *Discovery II*, was awarded the Order of the British Empire (OBE) for his role in the rescue.

Ellsworth bravely endured the fuss made of him for a week before learning, to his delight, that his favorite steamer, the *Mariposa*, would shortly sail to America. He booked a passage home, where the congratulations continued. Even the U.S. Congress went so far as to honor him with the Silver Medal of Congress, presented by President Franklin Roosevelt.

The *Wyatt Earp* eventually reached New York. Wilkins, as contractually stipulated, was not on board for the carefully stage-managed return, but the *Polar Star* was assembled and lashed to the deck for all to see. Ellsworth donated the plane to the Smithsonian Institution.*

While Ellsworth basked, Wilkins drew maps and attempted to plot the course the *Polar Star* had flown. He was aware that Ellsworth's dead reckoning estimates and sun observations were hopelessly inaccurate and that Ellsworth had little idea of the locations of the mountain ranges he had discovered. If Ellsworth said they were in a certain place, and future explorers found them somewhere else (which they did), it might prove embarrassing. Working on his best estimates from Hollick-Kenyon's dead reckoning, Wilkins tried to locate the Eternity and Sentinel Ranges with known geography, then sent the maps to Ellsworth accompanied by detailed instructions:

> The sketched in mountains on the chart are approximately correct . . . determined by working back from your landings at which positions were fixed [with the adjusted sextant]. This working back is an important point to mention to anyone plotting your

---

* The *Polar Star* was later transferred to the National Air and Space Museum in Washington, DC, and remains there today.

route. Otherwise . . . the positions at stated times over the edge
. . . are not likely to be correct.[2]

Wilkins's estimates were later shown to be out by only eighty to one
hundred miles.

Next Harold Clark, Ellsworth's business manager, found someone to
ghost write Ellsworth's autobiography, and Wilkins attempted to patch
things up with Byrd, who was still upset with the criticism he had received
for supposedly denying Ellsworth information about the supplies at Little
America. "Far from trying to injure you, I have many times fought battles
for you when people come to me with tittle tattle,"[3] Wilkins wrote, alluding
to the rumors of Byrd's North Pole flight being faked. Byrd responded to
Wilkins's half-apology, half-accusation, in a conciliatory manner:

> I have been labouring under the impression that you desired to
> injure me . . . I did not deserve it and it would be very difficult
> for anyone to prove that I did because too many people know
> that I tried very hard to cooperate with Ellsworth. The radio
> [message] did not sound like you. If it had been published I
> would have been forced to say some disagreeable things. I have
> always felt, and said many times, that you were one of the few
> explorers who did not manage to arouse bitterness. Naturally,
> I was surprised at this unfair act on your part toward one who
> has always been your friend.[4]

But Lincoln Ellsworth still harbored resentment toward the man who
had beaten him to the North Pole a decade earlier, and he took another
swipe at Byrd in his autobiography, *Beyond Horizons*, claiming, "We had
not heard from Byrd, so there was a possibility that Little America had
been cleaned out when the Byrd expedition left."[5]

In *Beyond Horizons*, Ellsworth paid little acknowledgement to the many
people who had helped him cross Antarctica. He repeatedly claimed he
made all the decisions regarding the purchasing and fitting out of the *Wyatt
Earp*; he had personally selected the plane and had a hand in its design;
he studied the conditions in the Antarctic and solved the problems of its

navigation. Nowhere in the book was there a photograph of Wilkins, who received only brief mentions. The crew members of the *Wyatt Earp* were either ignored or described as "my cabin boy" or "my meteorologist." The reader was told that Ellsworth was in command of the ship the entire time it was at sea. Roald Amundsen, Ellsworth explained in *Beyond Horizons*, was the greatest polar explorer in history. After the flight of the *Norge*, Amundsen had passed the baton of exploration to Ellsworth, who not only accepted it, but gloriously and almost single-handedly, carried it across the frozen frontier in the south.

Six months after *Beyond Horizons* was published, Byrd managed to upstage Ellsworth again. Byrd published *Alone*, his personal account of his harrowing ordeal at Advance Base. Although claiming it was his diary of events, the book was, like most things Byrd did, a heavily edited, calculated attempt to glorify his heroics. *Alone* instantly became a bestseller. It has remained in print ever since and is considered a classic of polar literature. *Beyond Horizons* enjoyed only one print run and was soon forgotten.

By the time *Beyond Horizons* was published in 1937, fame's spotlight had already moved on and, finding himself in the shadows again, Ellsworth slipped back into depression. In an attempt to attract attention, he announced he would fly across Antarctica a second time, but like most of what Ellsworth said, no one took it seriously. He procrastinated while Mary Louise tried to cheer him up by presenting him with possible options for a permanent home. Mary Louise had resigned herself to the fact that she and Ellsworth would not have children of their own, so she tried to interest him in adoption, but Ellsworth repeatedly said that his own childhood was so miserable that he could never express affection and did not want children around him. The couple would remain childless. In many ways, the son had become the father.

Following his years of faithful service, Wilkins hoped that Ellsworth might let him use the *Wyatt Earp* for his own plans of establishing land-based weather stations in Antarctica. The area of Antarctica that interested him was the coast that lay directly south of Australia. That, he knew, would also interest the government, because Australia claimed sovereignty over what it called the Australian Quadrant. But, as had recently been demonstrated, Australia did not have a ship capable of reaching its territorial claim. Wilkins developed a strategy whereby he would convince Ellsworth to make a flight over the Australian Quadrant and claim the area for the United States. Then, with the Australian Government stung into action by the possible loss of its territory, Wilkins would present himself as the ideal candidate to establish and maintain weather stations in the area. The government could hire Wilkins and purchase the *Wyatt Earp* from Ellsworth. Ellsworth would get another trip to Antarctica and the chance, once again, to fly over previously unexplored land. The Australian Government would get a ready-made Antarctic program, including an experienced explorer and suitable vessel, while Wilkins could live in Australia and, hopefully, even convince his wife to join him. Everybody won.

Wilkins put the idea to Ellsworth, whose response was typically vague and lethargic. When he asked Wilkins to investigate suitable planes in case he did return to Antarctica, Wilkins suggested that Ellsworth visit the Northrop factory in California, which had built the *Polar Star*. After the visit, Jack Northrop confided in Wilkins:

> I thoroughly appreciate the difficulties you must experience in assisting Mr. Ellsworth to reach a decision as to what his activities are to be. He visited us for a short time early this spring, and it was very apparent at the time that he did not have the slightest idea what he wanted to do with regard to further polar exploration.[6]

Ellsworth wandered as far as Canada and Mexico, sometimes in the company of Mary Louise, looking for a potential permanent home.

While he waited for Ellsworth's answer, Wilkins took the *Wyatt Earp* to Norway to have it refitted in the hope that he would soon own it. Still, Ellsworth continued to talk about returning to Antarctica but was unable to make up his mind about another expedition. Wilkins was unrelenting. He flattered Ellsworth and appealed to his love of the outdoors, writing:

> I have recently talked to several people who have been in the Enderby Land area and one of them—one of the owners of the Norwegian whaling fleet—says that the mountains, a few miles

inland from the Enderby Land coast, excel the Graham Land Mountains in magnificence.[7]

Ellsworth was still undecided. Sounding disappointed that his time in the spotlight had been so brief, he wrote back:

> . . . it is only 50-50 whether or not I shall decide to go to Enderby Land. I wish my enthusiasm was more, but it isn't; it brings nothing afterward. The thing is I can find nothing else, so I just keep chugging on, hoping for better but it doesn't seem to come.[8]

After a year of chugging on, Ellsworth was more receptive to another expedition, so he asked Wilkins to investigate a flight from the Bellingshausen Sea, over the unexplored coast so that he could see James W. Ellsworth Land again. "Approximately how far from ship necessary to fly to find land off Ellsworth Land. How many flights necessary?"[9] Wilkins skillfully deflected this query, which was on the wrong side of the continent for him, warning that the Northrop Delta he was considering would not be suitable. Also, he pointed out, Ellsworth would need to fly over three hundred miles of broken pack ice, where a forced landing would be fatal. "There would not even be a chance,"[10] Wilkins told him. Ellsworth was convinced. Enderby Land in the Australian Quadrant it would be.

By August 1938 the *Wyatt Earp* was ready and manned with a new Norwegian crew. First Mate Lauritz Liavaag was the only exception. He had been on all previous voyages—the first when he had served as second mate.

Ellsworth instructed Wilkins to sail to Cape Town, where he could meet the expedition, then took the opportunity of his African visit to spend five weeks big game hunting in Nairobi. Finally, with Ellsworth, Wilkins, pilot Joe Lymburner, two new planes, and the new crew, the *Wyatt Earp* left Cape Town on October 29, 1938, and met the pack ice three weeks later. It spent five weeks finding a way through. On January 2, 1939, Lymburner and Wilkins went up in the Aeronca seaplane, scouting for an area from which the larger Northrop Delta could take off on skis. Unable to find a suitable runway, the expedition moved slowly east until, on January 7, a frozen area of flat ice between the coast and a small island was deemed suitable. Here at last was the opportunity to get the Northrop Delta unloaded, let Ellsworth make his short flight inland, and they could all go home.

Wilkins presented Ellsworth with a copper canister and a proclamation claiming the area on behalf of the United States of America. The coordinates for the farthest point south that Ellsworth would reach were left blank. It was Ellsworth's responsibility to fly south, work out where he was, fill in the coordinates, seal the proclamation in the canister, and throw it from the plane before he turned around. Ellsworth carried a copy of the proclamation and he was to also write the coordinates on that and bring it back with him. Wilkins could hardly have made it simpler.

During the late afternoon, the Northrop Delta (Ellsworth never named it) was put onto the ice and test flown. It was loaded with a sled and emergency rations for two men for five weeks. With Lymburner and Ellsworth the only men on board (the Northrop Delta was designed to carry eight passengers), it took off at 6:00 P.M. Two hours and forty minutes later Ellsworth and Lymburner returned. Lymburner would later relate:

> [We] flew into where Lincoln Ellsworth decided we were far enough toward the Pole to drop the cylinder, opened the window, flung out the cylinder . . . and then turned around and went back to the boat and that was the end of the flying trip.[11]

How far south did Ellsworth and Lymburner fly? Probably about two hundred miles. It is only possible to estimate the distance based on the cruising speed of the plane and the time it was airborne. Ellsworth, as usual, was not sure where he was. On the flight, he calculated his position and scribbled the figures on the typed proclamations, before tossing one out the window and bringing the other back. Wilkins immediately pointed out Ellsworth's coordinates were not geographically possible, later explaining in his report to the Australian Government:

> The actual figures on the record dropped, and which were inserted above the underlines, were written with a pencil by Ellsworth during the flight and are, due to error, quite different.

A copy of the record dropped was brought back and when I
pointed out the mistake in the figures, the penciled figures were
erased and ones similar to those written above [in Wilkins's
report] were inserted. This copy then corresponded with what
it had been Ellsworth's intention to drop, and it is this changed
copy which will eventually be submitted to the Department of
State, Washington, USA.[12]

Having erased Ellsworth's erroneous figures, Wilkins filled in his
original estimate: 72° South, 79° East. There is no record of Ellsworth's
erroneous figures.

Ellsworth having made his short, pointless flight, proudly announced,
"Eighty thousand [square] miles of country never seen before by human
eyes has today been added to the known area of the world's surface."[13]

A day later the Northrop Delta was safely stowed on deck and the ship
was prepared for its return north. While the loyal Liavaag was chipping
ice from a large floe to supplement the fresh water supply, his right knee
was crushed and needed surgery. The ship's doctor, H. T. Rhoads, decided
it was best to make straight for the nearest port, which would depend
on where the *Wyatt Earp* emerged from the pack ice. After a week of
negotiating the floes, the ship sailed for Hobart, Tasmania, reaching it
on February 4, 1939.

By the time the expedition reached Hobart, the Australian Government
had read Wilkins's radiograms and decided to purchase the *Wyatt Earp* and
Ellsworth's two planes. It appeared, initially at least, that Wilkins's clever
plan had worked. But unknown to Wilkins, the availability of the *Wyatt
Earp*, along with all the talk of establishing Antarctic bases, had only served
to inspire his old rival, Sir Douglas Mawson.

Mawson, Wilkins, and Ellsworth met in Sydney, at the Australia Club,
on February 9, 1939. (Remarkably, or perhaps as the result of a tip-off, a
Sydney Morning Herald photographer was at the club and photographed the
three famous explorers.) Mawson told Ellsworth that he was satisfied with
the ship and the airplanes, and that the Australian Government wanted
to buy them for an Antarctic program. When Wilkins raised his idea of
leading the program, Mawson explained he intended to lead it himself.

Ellsworth, having sold his ship and planes, had no further interest in the negotiations and returned to America shortly after the meeting. Wilkins remained in Australia and persisted in putting his submissions to the government. Finally, frustrated by Mawson's campaign to thwart his plans, Wilkins accepted the inevitable and sailed back to America.

Two weeks after Wilkins left Australia, Adolf Hitler invaded Poland and World War II began. Hitler had been eyeing Antarctica as a source of whale oil to lubricate his war machinery. In fact, while Ellsworth had been throwing his copper cylinder out of the window of the Northrop Delta, fifteen hundred miles along the coast to the west, German pilots were heaving javelins out of planes, over what they named Neuschwabenland. On landing, the javelins were meant to stand upright and, by waving a small swastika flag, proclaim Germany's right to the land for a future whaling station. World War II however, soon became such a drain on manpower and resources, that countries concentrated their ambitions closer to home and, just as with World War I, Antarctic exploration was temporarily put on hold.

AFTERWORD

After the stunt at Advance Base, which nearly killed him, Richard Byrd returned to Antarctica three times. The first was in 1940. Alarmed that various countries, including Germany, were making claims on Antarctica, the Americans formed the United States Antarctic Service (USAS), and sent an expedition south with the aim of establishing bases on the Ross Ice Shelf (West Base) and the Antarctic Peninsula (East Base), then flying across the continent to map it. Byrd was appointed commanding officer of the USAS, but his age and declining health made the appointment largely a public relations exercise. He returned briefly to Little America, but did not winter there. The work of the USAS was cut short when the U.S. entered the war in December 1941. At the end of the war, the USAS mounted Operation Highjump, with the aim of mapping as much of Antarctica as possible. Again Byrd was appointed commanding officer, although everyone understood it was an honorary title. On February 16, 1947, he flew over the South Pole a second time. Byrd went to Antarctica the final time during Operation Deep Freeze and spent February 1956 at Little America IV. He died at his home in Virginia on March 11, 1957.

A few months after Byrd's death, Bernt Balchen published his autobiography *Come North With Me*. In it, Balchen made no mention of his two trips to Antarctica with Wilkins and Ellsworth. He did, however, cast doubts on Byrd's claim to have flown to the North Pole in 1926. According to Balchen, the Fokker Trimotor, *Josephine Ford*, in which Byrd had made the flight, was not fast enough to have flown from Kings Bay, Spitsbergen, to the North Pole and back in fifteen and a half hours. Balchen started a controversy that continues to this day as historians debate whether Byrd actually reached the North Pole, mistakenly believed he had, or purposely faked his records. Balchen died on October 18, 1973. He is buried at Arlington National Cemetery, Washington, DC.

Herbert Hollick-Kenyon rarely spoke about, and never wrote about, his time with Lincoln Ellsworth. He joined Canadian Pacific Airlines and retired from flying in 1962. He died in Vancouver on July 30, 1975.

Shortly after he returned to America in 1939, Lincoln Ellsworth announced that he would spend the southern winter of 1941 alone at the South Pole. He wrote to Wilkins, asking him if he knew of any ships similar to the *Wyatt Earp* that were for sale. A few weeks later Ellsworth changed his mind and announced instead that he intended to fly from Enderby Land to the Ross Sea. Nothing came of that either.

In July 1941, the sixty-one-year-old Ellsworth was talked into joining an eleven-man expedition to Peru in search of Inca treasure. He went along, but the whole thing was little more than a hoax that Ellsworth was gullible enough to pay for.

In May 1943, he wrote to Wilkins asking for some excuse to get back to the polar regions. Wilkins, as always, placated him by sending him suggestions. Ellsworth continued to correspond with Wilkins, proposing this scheme or that. It was all fantasy. Harold Clark, Ellsworth's business manager and the man who had originally persuaded him to sponsor Wilkins's submarine expedition, regularly exchanged letters with Wilkins, as the two devised fictitious schemes to bolster Ellsworth's flagging spirits and indulge his dreams. Wilkins would write long letters, comparing the suitability of new airplanes for polar work, or suggesting areas that needed to be explored. Running out of ideas, Wilkins wrote to Clark, "I wish to goodness we could find something that Lincoln could do and which would interest him. The Antarctic potentialities will wear thin before too long."[1]

Ellsworth suffered a stroke in 1948. Since childhood, his one source of self-confidence had been his physical strength and fitness. Even in his fifties he had prided himself that he could do the work of younger men. Now, his body frail, he became increasingly despondent and difficult to be around. Mary Louise lived separately, unable to deal with his black moods, and Ellsworth's care was given over to professional nurses. He died on May 26, 1951 and is buried in Hudson, Ohio.

When Wilkins wrote his autobiography, he devoted only one paragraph to the six years he spent managing the *Wyatt Earp* expeditions. Philosophically, he came to see it as a period of transition:

> It was a fine partnership we had, Lincoln Ellsworth and I, and together, using our own ship and the Northrop plane . . . we did fine work on a bigger scale than was possible for me before. The star of the individual explorer operating with minimal equipment had set, and the day was dawning of the big expeditions, financed by huge sums of money, with a supply line and trained men stretching from the frontier of the unknown, all the way back to the sources of supply at home. In this period of transition, Ellsworth and I formed a kind of link between the old school type of expedition and the new.[2]

While he was magnanimous publicly, privately Wilkins was critical of Ellsworth's lack of generosity toward those who had served him so faithfully. He complained to John King Davis:

> Your enquiry about Ellsworth's legacies reminds me that he did not leave anything to any geographical society, any institute or fund. He did not even make provision for the occasional small sums, about $200 at a time, I used to worm out of him for one of our sailors [Lauritz Liavaag, who had his leg crushed on the fourth expedition] who, in an accident while on duty in the Antarctic, lost the use of one leg and who had been existing on the very meagre Norwegian sailors' disablement pay.
>
> Naturally he did not leave me anything at all—I did not expect or want him to, but about eight months after Lincoln died his wife did offer me something—an overcoat, which I

had helped Lincoln to buy four years ago and which, of course, would not have fitted me in any case.[3]

Wilkins was, perhaps, unfair in being critical of Ellsworth. There was nothing that Ellsworth had promised that he had not delivered. By the completion of the third voyage of the *Wyatt Earp*, Wilkins had assisted Ellsworth to cross Antarctica, and had thereby repaid whatever moral or financial debt he might have had. What their arrangement was for the fourth voyage is unknown, but at the end of that voyage the *Wyatt Earp* was sold to the Australian Government, which was clearly the plan before departure, and Wilkins had the opportunity to present himself as the potential head of any Antarctic program that Australia might instigate. That Mawson outmaneuvered him is hardly Ellsworth's fault.

Ultimately, Ellsworth and Wilkins should have shared any credit or accolades that might have been awarded for the first crossing of Antarctica. Neither man could have done it without the other. Ellsworth provided the money. But he contributed more than that. Ellsworth was driven partly by curiosity and partly by something haunting him from his past. That restless nature, which few people understood, drove Ellsworth again and again to seek out what was beyond the horizon—to go to a place where no one else had been, or perhaps where no one else was.

Wilkins, for his part, had the knowledge of Antarctica as a result of his previous trips. He had the skills and the experience to plan, organize, and implement the expeditions. He was also an experienced navigator, whereas Ellsworth was not. And Wilkins was on hand to see to the running of the expeditions, while Ellsworth avoided coming aboard the *Wyatt Earp* until the last minute and always left at the first opportunity.

Wilkins was driven by his past too. His glory days were the 1920s. In that decade, he had led three expeditions to the Arctic, two to the Antarctic, and had been involved in two others. But he had overreached himself with his submarine expedition and, by 1931, was financially ruined. Had he not gone to the Antarctic with Lincoln Ellsworth, it is difficult to imagine what else he might have done in the 1930s—a time when sponsorship for private exploration had dried up. Although Wilkins spent the decade talking about attempting another submarine voyage to the North Pole, he probably knew he could not raise the money for such an expedition. As he observed in the tent on Snow Hill Island, when he was camping with Magnus Olsen, "You will never gain anything without personal wealth, or government backing." In the 1930s, Wilkins had neither.

At the outbreak of World War II, Wilkins contacted the Australian embassy in New York and offered his services, but the Australian Government had little use for an aging polar explorer. Wilkins did, however, have friends in many countries, including Germany and Italy. He went to Europe on behalf of the American government (not yet in the war) and was involved in a series of diplomatic missions. He traveled extensively, sometimes performing tasks for the Office of Strategic Services, the forerunner of the Central Intelligence Agency. In 1942, he was employed as a climatologist and geographer with the U.S. Army Quartermaster Corps. He designed clothing, tents, and related equipment so that American soldiers in the field—be it desert or ice—would be more comfortable and more efficient. When, after the war, the Quartermasters Corps opened the U.S. Army Soldier Systems Center at Natick, Massachusetts, moving its central operation from Washington, DC, Wilkins followed. The center later took for its motto, *cum scientia defendimus* (through science we defend). Wilkins rented a room at the Grand Central Hotel in the nearby suburb of Framingham. He repeatedly went to the Arctic with the army, helping to design clothing and equipment.

Wilkins and his wife, Suzanne, never lived together, nor did the marriage produce children. Wilkins died in the hotel room he rented at Framingham. His body was found on the morning of December 1, 1958. The U.S. Navy, out of respect for Wilkins's pioneering effort to take a submarine under the Arctic ice, took his ashes to the North Pole aboard the nuclear submarine, USS *Skate*. The *Skate* broke through the ice and surfaced at the Pole on March 17, 1959. After a short ceremony, Wilkins's ashes were scattered over the ice.

With the outbreak of World War II any plans Sir Douglas Mawson had to return to Antarctica were put on hold. The *Wyatt Earp* was renamed HMAS *Wongala* and pressed into service by the Australian Government. In the latter half of 1939 it carried ammunition from Sydney to Darwin. From 1940 to 1945 it served variously as a "guard ship" at Port Pirie and

Whyalla in South Australia, and as a "mother ship" to the Naval Auxiliary Patrol. At the end of the war the *Wongala/Wyatt Earp* languished in the Torrens River, Adelaide. With no other purpose, it was made available to the Boy Scouts Association for Sea Scout training.

By 1947, Australian interest in an Antarctic program had reawakened. Although he understood he was now too old to go himself, Sir Douglas Mawson was still pushing for Australian Antarctic bases to be established on Macquarie and Heard Islands, and along the coast of the Australian Quadrant. Mawson's influence saw the Australian National Antarctic Research Expeditions (ANARE) get the official nod. Finding a ship for an expedition, however, proved a problem. Nothing suitable was available and nothing available seemed suitable. Then Mawson remembered the *Wongala/ Wyatt Earp*, tied up in Adelaide and being used by boys to learn sea craft.

Mawson suggested the ship to the ANARE Planning Committee. John King Davis, who was on the committee, was against the idea, just as he had been against purchasing it eight years earlier. The ship was old, wooden, rotten, underpowered, and a throwback to the days when polar exploration was undertaken with dogs and sleds. But Mawson was all for it. The *Wyatt Earp* had proven itself in four Antarctic voyages and could do so again. Mawson, as he often did, won the day.

The ship was placed in dry dock at Adelaide and rebuilt at an enormous cost of £195,000. An eight-cylinder diesel engine was fitted, rotten timbers were replaced, the bridge was raised for better visibility—even a small radar set was installed. Davis continued to argue that the money would be better spent on a more modern vessel, but he was ignored.

On July 16, 1947, the *Wongala* was officially renamed HMAS *Wyatt Earp* to continue its proud record as an Antarctic exploration vessel. The ship left Adelaide on December 13 and, after a miserable trip marked with continual breakdowns, reached Melbourne, where an airplane was taken on board. From Melbourne, it headed to Tasmania. Phillip Law, a scientist on board, recalled:

> The first night out, the ship was a shambles. In my nineteen years of subsequent seafaring, I have seen nothing like it. It pitched violently, and rolled more than 50 degrees each side of the vertical . . .

Everything seemed to have come adrift. To the turmoil of the wind and the impact of the waves was added the sound of smashing crockery and the din of heavy objects sliding and bashing from bulkhead to bulkhead. Cupboard doors burst open and their contents were hurled horizontally to crash into the nearest vertical fixture . . . Men groaned and cursed and tried to salvage their more precious possessions . . .

And we were not even in the Antarctic! We weren't even in the Southern Ocean. We were in Bass Strait, less than a day's sailing from the Port of Melbourne![4]

After reaching Tasmania, and brief respite, the *Wyatt Earp* sailed from Hobart, bound for Antarctica on December 26. It didn't get far. Problems ranged from the trivial, such as a faulty valve in the toilet, which turned it into a fountain when the ship rolled and seawater blew the contents backward, to the major, like the hull leaking and the mountings for the new diesel engine cracking. Six days into the voyage the captain turned the HMAS *Wyatt Earp* around and returned to Melbourne. It went into dry dock at Williamstown, where the hull was repaired in an attempt to keep water out. After a month, the *Wyatt Earp* headed south again. This time, despite the discomfort, it reached Commonwealth Bay, Antarctica, briefly skirted a section of coast, and returned via the Balleny Islands and Macquarie Island. The voyage took seven weeks and the *Wyatt Earp* never went south again.

Within three months of its return the ship, which with refitting and repairs, had cost the Australian Government well over £200,000 since the war, was sold to the Pucker Shipping Company for £11,000. Its name reverted to *Wongala* and it became a trader between Victorian and Tasmanian ports. In 1956, it was bought by the Ulverstone Shipping Company and renamed again, this time, *Natone*, to honor a small Tasmanian town. After about eighteen months of service plying Tasmanian waters, the *Wyatt Earp/Wongala/Natone* was sailed to Queensland, where it continued to work as a coastal trader.

In January 1959, while en route from Cairns to Brisbane, it encountered two storms. It weathered the first, but sprang a leak during the second.

The pumps were unable to cope with the intake of water. With the engine flooded the crew rigged the sails and managed to reach Rainbow Bay, on Queensland's Gold Coast. When the moorings failed, the *Wyatt Earp/ Wongala/Natone* ran aground near Mudlo Rocks. The crew of eighteen reached shore safely. The date was January 24. Over the next few weeks, Lincoln Ellsworth's gallant little ship was smashed to pieces.

Wyatt Earp's cartridge belt, which Ellsworth carried across Antarctica, is in the New York's American Museum of Natural History. It is not on display. Visitors to the Museum can, however, climb the stairs to the first floor to discover a bust of Ellsworth along with a small display of artifacts and a map of his flight across Antarctica.

During the International Geophysical Year (1957–58) Vivian Fuchs (later Sir Vivian) led a Commonwealth party of nineteen men who crossed Antarctica from the Weddell Sea to the Ross Sea, via the South Pole, where America had established a permanent base. The book of the expedition, *The Crossing of Antarctica*, stated:

> Men have long dreamed of crossing the vast frozen wastes of the Antarctic, but not since Shackleton's last attempt to reach the Pole from the Weddell Sea in 1914 has anyone embarked on this great adventure. In turning the dream into a reality Sir Vivian Fuchs has taken his place alongside Shackleton, Amundsen, and Scott, with a feat of courage and endurance that has rightly been called one of the truly heroic and magnificent achievements of the century.[5]

The book made no mention of Lincoln Ellsworth.

PROBLEMS IN POLAR NAVIGATION

L incoln Ellsworth was not an expert navigator. Bernt Balchen, Umberto Nobile, and Leif Dietrichson all claimed he was incompetent in this area. Nevertheless he did, along with Hollick-Kenyon, manage to bring the *Polar Star* 2,200 miles (3,500 km) across an unexplored continent to within sixteen miles (25 km) of Little America, which was about the size of a football field and hidden beneath the ice. Had his plane not run out of fuel it is likely that Ellsworth would have flown directly over it. Therefore his flight, from Camp III, high on the Antarctic Plateau, when he knew he was (a) lost and (b) his sextant was set wrong, was pinpoint accurate. How did he and Hollick-Kenyon manage it? Was he guided by some metaphysical force, as polar explorers often claimed they were? Did he manage to navigate the last part of the flight accurately, or was it simply blind luck, or possibly a combination of these factors? To appreciate what a remarkable feat this was, it is necessary to have a basic understanding of the problems of polar navigation in Ellsworth's time.

Navigation is about angles and imaginary lines on the surface of the Earth. Establishing where they were, in terms of latitude and longitude, along with the direction in which they had to travel, navigators used the techniques and instruments developed for mariners at sea level.

Establishing longitude

The Earth rotates through 360 degrees every twenty-four hours. This means that every four minutes it rotates one degree of longitude. Establishing which line (or meridian) of longitude they were on, or near, sailors had to know two things accurately: when it was midday where they were and how many hours and minutes had elapsed since it was midday at a place from where their lines of longitude originated. Today this is the Greenwich section of London, and most maps are drawn (as Ellsworth's were) with lines of longitude expressed as degrees east or west of Greenwich. Knowing Greenwich Mean Time (GMT) for sailors meant carrying one or more accurate timepieces, which were permanently kept at GMT. When ships were in port, or passed other ships, the captains would compare their timepieces for accuracy. By the 1930s radio signals were broadcast exactly on the hour to help navigators check their timepieces. (Ellsworth, in his diary, mentions getting "three pips from Buenos Aires.")

Establishing exact midday at sea was a practiced art for sailors. It was the time when the sun was highest in the sky. They measured this using a sextant. The angle of the sun's elevation was measured repeatedly, starting before midday. Elevation and time were noted until the sun stopped rising and began sinking. If they determined, for example, their midday was three hours and four minutes after midday at Greenwich, then they knew they were at 46° West. For sailors, once they had timepieces capable of remaining accurate during the rigors of long sea voyages, the puzzle of longitude was solved.

Nevertheless, longitude held special challenges for the polar aviator. First, in the polar regions, the meridians of longitude converge until they ultimately meet at the North or South Pole. At the equator each degree of longitude is a little more than sixty-nine statute miles (111 km) apart. At the Antarctic Circle (66°33' South) this separation has halved to a little more than thirty miles (55 km). At 80° South, where Ellsworth was flying, it is reduced to twelve miles (19 km). The closer proximity of the meridians makes accurate observations more critical.

Observation of the sun is more difficult in the polar regions. The low angle of the sun on the horizon increases the chance of refraction. The navigator cannot be sure he is looking at the sun and not some refracted image. Wilkins, on his flight across the Arctic in 1928, described the sun "dancing" just above the horizon as a result of refraction. Over the equator the sun arcs from the horizon to high in the sky. Halving the interval between sunrise and sunset gives an approximate midday, and the observer can watch the sun's arc rise and fall. In the polar summer, however, there is no sunrise or sunset; just one long polar day, during which the sun circles the sky. Determining midday accurately is extremely difficult.

Observations for sailors were aided by the fact they traveled so slowly. Captain Cook's *Resolution* needed strong winds to reach five knots (5.8 statute mph). When he circumnavigated Antarctica in 1775–76 he would take hours to go from one meridian of longitude to another. Flying, Lincoln Ellsworth did it in minutes. Landing to take observations was the only sure way for Ellsworth to do so.

Timepieces were also difficult to use in the polar regions. Wilkins wrote that on his flight across the Arctic Ocean his stopwatch ceased to function because it became too cold. He adopted the practice of keeping it under his fur jacket, near his body, to keep it warm.

Establishing latitude

Lines of latitude run horizontally around the Earth. Unlike lines of longitude, which converge at the North and South Poles, lines of latitude run parallel. They are measured from the equator, which is zero, to the North and South Poles, which are 90° north or south respectively.

To establish latitude the navigator needed to measure his angle north or south of the equator. He did this by measuring the angle of some heavenly body, such as a star or the sun. The polar aviator is flying (at least Ellsworth was) during the long polar summer. There are no stars out. The best astronomical method available, which uses the sun and is relatively simple to employ, is known at the Marcq St. Hilaire method. Using a nautical almanac (a kind of astronomical calendar produced each year) the navigator can determine that the sun is directly above (in its zenith) a certain point of the Earth's surface. By finding the latitude of that point from the almanac, the navigator can, using a sextant, determine how far he is from it. He measures the angle of the sun with a sextant. He knows the "height" of the sun in the sky, which gives him the length of one side of a right-angled triangle. His sextant has given him the acute angle of that triangle, so using cotangent tables he can determine his distance from the point on the surface of the Earth, directly below the sun. If he knows his meridian of longitude he can establish his latitude.

When the navigator is only able to take sun sights at low elevations, as in the polar latitudes, accuracy becomes paramount. The slightest error in angle read from the sextant is magnified by interpolation of figures from published tables of cotangents. These are least precise at the lowest angles, giving the greatest error for the estimated position on the ground.

This method was devised for sailors who were, obviously, at sea level. The surface of the sea is (ignoring for a moment the curve of the Earth) one side of the right-angled triangle. If the navigator is, for example, at an altitude of 10,000 feet (3,000 m) he must make an allowance, or know the angle from his point of elevation to the point where the sun is directly above sea level (his angle of declination). To measure this angle he needs to know his exact altitude. In an unexplored area, where the heights of mountains has not been established, the only way he can know this accurately is by using a barometer. This measures air pressure, and the higher the navigator, the less air pressure he is experiencing. In the polar regions, the extreme cold and the vagaries of air pressure make barometers unreliable. In short, Ellsworth had no way of accurately knowing his altitude on the Antarctic Plateau, and therefore, even the Marcq St. Hilaire method of establishing latitude could not be relied on.

Establishing direction

Knowing where he is on the imaginary grid of lines that encircle the Earth does not enable a navigator to know which way to travel to reach the desired destination. Before the days of radio-direction finding (and, more recently, GPS) there were two ways of doing this. One was using astronomical bodies, such as the sun or the North Star, to establish direction. The other method was the magnetic compass.

The magnetic compass does not, of course, point to the Geographic North Pole, but to North Magnetic Pole. In the northern hemisphere the Magnetic Pole is more than 400 miles (640 km) from the Geographic Pole. In Antarctica, the South Magnetic Pole is some 1,700 miles (2,700 km) from the Geographic South Pole. The position of the South Magnetic Pole was known. But that did not mean Ellsworth could simply use a magnetic compass that would accurately point to the South Magnetic Pole. Being so close to the South Magnetic Pole meant that compasses were highly susceptible to variation. One of the first things polar explorers did when they reached unexplored areas was to chart the magnetic variation. Scott, Mawson, Byrd, and Shackleton all took magneticians to the Antarctic, whose job it was to chart the directions in which the compass needle pointed. Most of the area over which Ellsworth flew was unknown. He knew, once he passed Hearst Land, that he would be flying roughly in the direction of the South Magnetic Pole which, fortunately for him, lay beyond Little America, but how much magnetic variation he would find along the route, he could not be sure.

An additional problem is that magnetic compasses are not attracted to a position on the surface of the Earth. They are actually trying to point to a place somewhere inside the Earth's core. Near the equator this is not so much of an issue. The difference between Geographic Poles and the Magnetic Poles is known, mapped, and allowed for. Near the Magnetic Poles, however, the compass needle, in an effort to align itself with the lines of the Earth's magnetic field, actually tries to point downward, into the centre of the Earth. It's known as magnetic "dip." The tendency to dip, pulling the compass needle to one side or the other, as it tries to point downward, resulted in the manufacture of the "dipping compass," which allowed the needle to tilt downward, as well as to the left or right. Ellsworth carried a "dipping compass," but its accuracy could not be relied on.

His only other means of establishing direction was the sun, which Ellsworth knew at midday would be directly north. He also knew that the sun's angle changed at an even rate, from which he could approximate north.

In addition to using sun sights and magnetic compasses, Ellsworth had another method of navigating; dead reckoning. Dead reckoning is based on speed, time, and direction. A navigator could set off in a certain direction and, providing he accurately knew his speed and the time he had been flying, and as long as he did not drift off course, he could calculate how far he had traveled, and therefore where he was.

In addition to direction, the other critical factors for Ellsworth to measure for dead reckoning were the plane's ground speed and whether or not it was drifting to one side or the other.

The *Polar Star* was fitted with an air-speed indicator on its port wing. This consisted of a simple propeller that was turned by the air pressure as the plane flew. The faster the flight, the faster the propeller turned. Air-speed indicators could not compensate for wind. Head or tailwinds would mean an air-speed indicator could be used as a guide only. A more accurate way of measuring progress was the ground-speed indicator. The navigator looked forward at an angle of forty-five degrees to a point on the ground. That point would be the same distance ahead of the plane as the plane was above the ground. The navigator could start a stopwatch when the sight was taken, and stop it when the plane was directly above the sighted point. The distance traveled, being equal to the altitude, could be compared to the elapsed time, and the ground speed calculated. Ground-speed indicators needed the plane to be traveling over level ground and the plane's height above that ground to be known accurately. Ellsworth had no way of knowing the height of the mountains below, and therefore no way (even assuming his barometer was correct) of knowing the distance between the *Polar Star* and the ground. He was also flying over a featureless white landscape. Finding some point ahead from which to take a sighting was almost impossible. Therefore, for his estimates of ground speed, he was forced to rely on the known performance of the *Polar Star*. Bernt Balchen, the only man to have tested the plane over a long distance, said it cruised at 150 mph. By the time they had reached the Eternity Range, Ellsworth and Hollick-Kenyon knew this was wildly inaccurate. They realized that they would not be making the flight in fourteen hours. Their estimates of time and position, so carefully worked out before the flight, were useless. The discrepancy between the *Polar Star*'s performance and what Balchen said it was capable of, has never been explained.

Finally, Ellsworth had no way of knowing if wind was causing him to drift to the left or the right. A drift indicator allows the navigator to look forward to a fixed point directly ahead, then notice if he is drifting to one side or the other. With the featureless landscape below him, Ellsworth had few, if any, fixed points.

All these factors conspired against Ellsworth, who was, to begin with, an inexperienced navigator. The flight across Antarctica, by guess or by God, remains an incredible achievement.

NAVIGATION INSTRUCTIONS PREPARED BY SIR HUBERT WILKINS

N ote: Wilkins prepared these instructions for the 1934–35 flight, which was to leave from Snow Hill Island. Once they reach the Ross Ice Shelf, Wilkins instructs Ellsworth and Balchen to look for Byrd's ground parties. The instructions were found among Sir Hubert Wilkins's papers. He may have recalculated the course and positions for the 1935 flight, but if he did, those instructions have been lost. On the other hand, he may have simply used these instructions and had Hollick-Kenyon and Ellsworth start fifteen minutes earlier (which they did), to allow for the extra distance from Dundee Island.

The compass course will be practically constant during the whole flight. 190° for the first twelve hours and 200° for the remainder. The sun's bearing to the true course will change from 171°—three hours out and to thirty-two [when] twelve hours out. At the time when the course is in the middle of the unknown area the position line is parallel to the course. Any observed altitude difference will then give a direct indication of distance off the course.

In order to have the line of position parallel to the course around eight hours out the sun will have to be about 30° west of north or 2:00 P.M. local time. The corresponding longitude to eight hours is 91° West or six hours and five minutes. To obtain the correct takeoff time, eight hours is deducted from 2015 GCT [Greenwich Civil Time] giving 1215 GMT or eight hours, seventeen minutes local time in Longitude 57° West.

For the first three-and-a-half hours the route lies along the eastern side of Graham Land and Palmer Land, already explored by Sir Hubert Wilkins on December 20, 1928. This part gives good opportunity to check the ground speed and navigational data. After crossing Stefansson Strait and entering Hearst Land the coastline between Hearst Land and Charcot Land can be located as to the direction and approximate latitude. Between the fifth and eighth hours out the direction of the extended Queen Maud Range should be seen. (If islands exist to the south and west of Charcot Island, these should also be seen.)

If no indication of land has been seen out toward the eastern side of the course, the course can then be laid more southerly; the mountain range picked up and the direction and character of it determined. Between the eleventh and twelfth hours out the southernmost end, as reported by Amundsen and Byrd, should be located if the course and speed has been maintained. About thirteen hours out the Rockefeller Mountains should bear to the north and the crevassed area described by Amundsen and Byrd should be seen on the horizon to the southwest. Shortly afterwards the ridges in the Barrier [Ross Ice Shelf] from the southeast, leading into the Bay of Whales should be picked up and Byrd's camp located. Thirteen hours out the Tractor Party of Byrd's expedition should be seen.

Up to the eighth hour of the flight the crew of the plane should be able, in case of a forced landing and unable to continue by air, to reach the coastline by traveling on the barrier.

The farthest distance they will be away at any time from the coast up to the eighth hour will be 300 miles. From the eighth hour onward they must depend upon the facilities of the Byrd expedition in case of a forced landing.

Flight Data for Great Circle Course: Snow Hill Island to Bay of Whales

GMT	Hour	Lat. S	Long. W	Course	Mag. Var.	Mag. Course	Sun Bearing
0817	Start	64°25'	57°00'	202°	-14°	188°	196°
0917	1	66°25'	59°00'	204°	-17°	187°	
1017	2	68°23'	61°21'	206°	-19°	187°	
1117	3	70°19'	64°11'	209°	-22°	187°	171°
1217	4	72°11'	67°33'	212°	-25°	187°	
1317	5	74°00'	71°41'	216°	-29°	187°	
1417	6	75°42'	76°49'	221°	-34°	187°	122°
1517	7	77°16'	83°13'	227°	-39°	188°	
1617	8	78°39'	91°16'	235°	-46°	189°	
1717	9	79°45'	101°15'	245°	-52°	193°	76°
1817	10	80°28'	113°10'	256°	-63°	193°	
1917	11	80°45'	127°06'	270°	-80°	190°	
2017	12	80°28'	141°02'	284°	-93°	191°	32°
2117	13	79°45'	152°57'	296°	-100°	196°	
2217	14	78°39'	162°56'	305°	-105°	200°	3°

APPENDIX C

WYATT EARP CREW LISTS

1933-34

L. Ellsworth—Commander

H. Wilkins—Manager

B. Holth—Captain

M. Olsen—First Mate

L. Liavaag—Second Mate

M. Johnannessen—Bosun

I. Strom—Carpenter (Norway)

R. Berg—Sailor and Doctor (Norway)

J. Holmboe—Sailor and Meteorologist

H. Holmboe—Chief Engineer

C. Braathen—Second Engineer and Aircraft Mechanic

H. Bigseth—Third Engineer

O. Dahl—Steward

B. Larsen—Mess Boy

W. Lanz—Wireless Operator

B. Balchen—Pilot

A. Robison—Sailor (Taken on board at Dunedin NZ
to Ross Sea and returned.)

1934-35

The crew was the same for the second voyage with the exception that R. Berg was replaced by Dr. Dana Coman (United States) and A. Duthie—Sailor (New Zealand), who was taken on board at Dunedin, New Zealand, and returned home from Montevideo.

1935-36

L. Ellsworth—Commander
H. Wilkins—Manager
M. Olsen—Captain
L. Liavaag—First Mate
O. Valderhaug—Bosun
B. Larsen—Able Seaman
P. Howard—Sailor and Aircraft Engineer
T. Schlossbach—Sailor and Doctor
H. Holmboe—Chief Engineer
H. Soeraa—Second Engineer
H. Sperre—Third Engineer
M. Johannessen—Steward
K. Jensen—Messboy
H. Hollick-Kenyon—Pilot
J. H. Lymburner—Pilot and Mechanic
W. Lanz—Wireless Operator

1937-38

L. Ellsworth—Commander
H. Wilkins—Manager
P. T. Johansen—Captain
L. Liavaag—First Mate
A. Norseth—Second Mate
J. Hvitfeldtsen—Carpenter
J. Bakker—Able Seaman

P. Berg—Sailor

T. Berg—Sailor

H. Ronnebarg—Sailor

H. T. Rhoads—Sailor and Doctor

J. R. Trerice—Pilot and Aircraft Engineer

F. Seid—Wireless Operator

A. D. Schroeder—Chief Engineer

O. Hjelseth—Second Engineer

H. Sperre—Third Engineer

O. Dahl—Steward

A. Dahl—Messboy

J. H. Lymburner—Pilot

BIBLIOGRAPHY

Amundsen, Roald and Ellsworth, Lincoln, *First Crossing of the Polar Sea*, George H. Doran, New York, 1927.

Amundsen, Roald and Ellsworth, Lincoln, *Our Polar Flight*, Dodd, Mead & Co., New York, 1925.

Amundsen, Roald, *My Life as an Explorer*, Doubleday, Doran & Co., New York, 1928.

Amundsen, Roald, *The North-West Passage*, Dutton, New York, 1908.

Amundsen, Roald, *The South Pole*, L. Keedick, New York, 1913.

Ayres, Philip, *Mawson: A Life*, Melbourne University Press, Melbourne, 1999.

Balchen, Bernt, *Come North with Me*, E.P. Dutton & Co., New York, 1958.

Botting, Douglas, *Dr. Eckener's Dream Machine*, HarperCollins, London, 2001.

Bowie, Walter Russell, *The Master of the Hill*, Dodd, Mead and Company, New York, 1917.

Byrd, Richard E., *Alone*, G.P. Putnam's Sons, New York, 1938.

Byrd, Richard E., *Discovery*, G.P. Putnam's Sons, New York, 1935.

Byrd, Richard E., *Little America*, G.P. Putnam's Sons, New York, 1930.

Byrd, Richard E, *Skyward*, G.P. Putnam's Sons, New York, 1928.

Cross, Wilbur, *Ghost Ship of the Pole*, William Heinemann, London, 1959.

Davis, J. K., *High Latitude*, Melbourne University Press, Melbourne, 1962.

Ellsworth, Lincoln, *Beyond Horizons*, William Heinemann, London, 1938.

Fuchs, Sir Vivian and Hillary, Sir Edmund, *The First Crossing of Antarctica*, Cassell, London, 1958.

Glines, Carroll V., *Bernt Balchen: Polar Aviator*, Smithsonian Institution Press, Washington, 1999.

Goerler, Raimund E., (ed.), *To the Pole: The Diary and Notebook of Richard E. Byrd 1925–1927*, Ohio State University Press, Columbus, Ohio, 1998.

Grierson, John, *Challenge to the Poles*, Archon Books, Hamden, Conn., 1964.

Grierson, John, *Sir Hubert Wilkins: Enigma of Exploration*, Robert Hale Ltd., London. 1960.

Holland, Clive (ed.), *Farthest North*, Carroll & Graf, New York, 1999.

Huntford, Roland, *Shackleton*, Little, Brown and Company, London. 1996.

Huntford, Roland, *The Last Place on Earth*, Modern Library, New York, 1999.

Law, Phillip, *The Antarctic Voyage of the* Wyatt Earp, Allen & Unwin, Sydney, 1995.

McKee, Alexander, *Ice Crash*, Granada, London, 1979.

Maynard, Jeff, *The Unseen Anzac*, Scribe, Melbourne, 2015.

Maynard, Jeff, *Wings of Ice*, Random House Australia, Sydney, 2010.

Montague, Richard, *Oceans, Poles and Airmen*, Random House, New York, 1971.

Nobile, Umberto, *My Polar Flights*, Frederick Muller Ltd., London, 1961.

Nordenskjöld, Otto, *Antarctica*, Hurst and Blackett Ltd., London, 1905.

Olsen, Magnus L., *Saga of the White Horizon*, Nautical Publishing Company, London, 1972.

Ommanney, F. D., *South Latitude*, Readers Union Ltd., London, 1940.

Page, Dorothy G., *Polar Pilot: The Carl Ben Eielson Story*, Interstate Publishers Inc., Danville, Ill., 1992.

Paine, M. L., *Footsteps on the Ice: The Antarctic Diaries of Stuart D. Paine, Second Byrd Expedition*. University of Missouri Press, Columbia, Mo., 2007.

Pool, Beekman H., *Polar Extremes: The World of Lincoln Ellsworth*, University of Alaska Press, Fairbanks, Alaska, 2002.

Rodgers, Eugene, *Beyond the Barrier: The Story of Byrd's First Expedition to Antarctica*, Naval Institute Press, Annapolis, Md., 1990.

Roosevelt, Theodore, *Ranch Life and the Hunting-Trail*, The Century Co., New York, 1911.

Rose, Lisle A., *Explorer: The Life of Richard E. Byrd*, University of Missouri Press, Columbia, Mo., 2008.

Shackleton, Ernest H., *South: The Story of Shackleton's 1914–17 Expedition*, Century Publishing, London, 1919.

Shackleton, Ernest H., *The Heart of the Antarctic*, William Heinemann, London, 1909.

Sherman, Harold M., *The Dead Are Alive*, Fawcett Gold Medal, New York, 1981.

Smith, Dean C., *By the Seat of My Pants*, Little, Brown & Co., Boston, 1961.

Thomas, Lowell, *Sir Hubert Wilkins: His World of Adventure*, Arthur Barker, London, 1961.

Wilkins, Captain George H., *Flying the Arctic*, G.P. Putnam's Sons, New York, 1928.

Wilkins, Captain Sir G. H., *Adventures in Undiscovered Australia*, Ernest Benn Limited, London, 1928.

Wilkins, Sir Hubert and Sherman, Harold M., *Thoughts Through Space*, House-Warven, Hollywood, Calif., 1951.

Wilkins, Sir Hubert, *Under the North Pole*, Brewer, Warren & Putnam, New York, 1931.

Williams, Marion D., *Submarines Under Ice*, Naval Institute Press, Annapolis Md., 1998.

ENDNOTES

I commenced this book in 2010 then put it aside to write another project. I returned to it in 2016. During that time some of the primary source material changed hands, making it necessary to explain certain references. Throughout his life, Sir Hubert Wilkins kept copies of his correspondence, along with the radiograms, telegrams, accounts, and written material relating to the Wilkins Ellsworth Trans-Arctic Submarine Expedition, as well as Ellsworth's Antarctic expeditions. On his death, those records were inherited by Wilkins's wife, Suzanne. Along with her partner, Winston Ross, Suzanne then destroyed many records that she did not want made public. In particular, references to other women in Wilkins's life were destroyed. In some cases, Suzanne and Ross retyped letters, omitting certain parts, then destroyed the originals. After Suzanne's death in 1974, Winston Ross inherited the Wilkins material. Ross sold some of the records to collectors of polar memorabilia. In 1985 he also sold a large portion of the material to the Byrd Polar and Climate Research Center (BPCRC). Still, Winston Ross had more records, and after his death in 1996 his son, Michael, held that material.

Although Lincoln Ellsworth kept artifacts and possessions, he was casual about keeping written records. Fortunately, however, much of Ellsworth's written material was collected by his friend and biographer, Beekman Pool. I met Beekman at the BPCRC in 1999 when I was researching Wilkins, and he was researching Ellsworth. We spent an enjoyable few days together discussing our projects and swapping information. Beekman held many original documents relating to Ellsworth. I stayed in contact with Beekman and, after his death, asked his wife, Elizabeth, what was to become of his records and artifacts. She explained that they had disappeared before Beekman's death, and she was unable to tell me what happened to them. Consequently, when I list a reference as "quoted from Pool," I am usually quoting a letter published in his biography of Ellsworth, but in some cases I am unable to say where the letter is currently held, if indeed it still exists.

One of the collectors of polar memorabilia who bought a quantity of Wilkins's correspondence from Winston Ross was Dr. David Larson. I met Dr. Larson at his home in Washington, DC, in 2013 and he generously let me copy his Wilkins correspondence. Shortly before his death in 2016, Dr. Larson gave some of his material to a fellow collector. After Dr. Larson's death his son generously donated the remainder to the BPCRC. I have not had the opportunity to compare my copies with what was donated to the BPCRC. If I quote a reference as "Larson," it may be held at the BPCRC or it may be held in a private collection.

Winston Ross's son Michael held thousands of Wilkins's documents for many years. I visited him at his home in Fremont, Michigan, in 2014, and he allowed me to copy his documents. Shortly after my visit he donated his material to the BPCRC. Michael Ross died in 2016. If I quote a reference as "Ross," the source material will be in the BPCRC.

The BPCRC at Ohio State University holds the records of Richard E. Byrd and Sir Hubert Wilkins. When I quote a reference as OSU, followed by numbers, it refers to the collection of the BPCRC and the box and folder number as it was catalogued on my visits in 1998, 1999, and 2013.

Finally, many of the radiograms received or sent from the *Wyatt Earp* (usually in the Ross Collection) were undated. The radio operator (Walter Lanz) simply penciled the message on a pad and handed it to Wilkins. I sometimes quote these original penciled messages without being able to specify a date.

PROLOGUE

1   *Wyatt Earp* radio message, Ross.
2   *Wyatt Earp* radio message, Ross.
3   *Wyatt Earp* radio message, Ross.

PART I: ALMOST HEROIC
I: THE ELF CHILD

1   Letter, M. Grouitch to Ellsworth, quoted from Pool, *Polar Extremes*, p. 19.
2   Quoted from Pool, p. 22.
3   Television documentary, *Hudson Profiles*, quoting J. Fred Waring.
4   Ellsworth, *Beyond Horizons*, p. 7.

5   Ellsworth, *Beyond Horizons*, p. 6.
6   Bowie, *The Master of the Hill*, p. 205.
7   Ellsworth, *Beyond Horizons*, p. 6.
8   Ellsworth, *Beyond Horizons*, p. 38.
9   Ellsworth, *Beyond Horizons*, p. 88.
10 Ellsworth, *Beyond Horizons*, p. 39.
11 Roosevelt, *Ranch Life and the Hunting Trail*, p. 100.
12 Amundsen, *My Life as an Explorer*, p. 66.
13 Amundsen, *My Life as an Explorer*, p. 67.

2: THE KINGDOM OF DEATH

1   Ellsworth, *Beyond Horizons*, p. 115.
2   Ellsworth, *Beyond Horizons*, p. 109.
3   Ellsworth, *Beyond Horizons*, p. 115.
4   Ellsworth, *Beyond Horizons*, p. 117.
5   Ellsworth, *Beyond Horizons*, p. 118.
6   Ellsworth, *Beyond Horizons*, p. 122.
7   Ellsworth, *Beyond Horizons*, p. 105.
8   Ellsworth, *Beyond Horizons*, p. 128.
9   Ellsworth, *Beyond Horizons*, p. 128.
10 Ellsworth, *Beyond Horizons*, p. 104.
11 Ellsworth, *Beyond Horizons*, p. 128.
12 Ellsworth, *Beyond Horizons*, p. 131.
13 Ellsworth, *Beyond Horizons*, p. 138.
14 Ellsworth, *Beyond Horizons*, p. 147.
15 Ellsworth, *Beyond Horizons*, p. 147.
16 Ellsworth, *Beyond Horizons*, p. 149.
17 Ellsworth, *Beyond Horizons*, p. 150.
18 Ellsworth, *Beyond Horizons*, p. 151.
19 Ellsworth, *Beyond Horizons*, p. 159.
20 Ellsworth, *Beyond Horizons*, p. 163.
21 Ellsworth, *Beyond Horizons*, p. 170.
22 Ellsworth, *Beyond Horizons*, p. 177.
23 Ellsworth, *Beyond Horizons*, p. 11.
24 Ellsworth, *Beyond Horizons*, p. 180.
25 Ellsworth, *Beyond Horizons*, p. 181.

3: NO LONGER THE ONLY AMERICAN

1   Ellsworth, *Beyond Horizons*, p. 184.
2   Balchen, *Come North with Me*, p. 24.

3   Amundsen, *My Life as an Explorer*, p. 93.
4   Quoted from Pool, p. 100.

4: JUST A PASSENGER

1   Amundsen, *My Life as an Explorer*, p. 180.
2   Amundsen, *My Life as an Explorer*, p. 131.
3   Amundsen, *My Life as an Explorer*, p. 206.
4   *New York Times*, July 20, 1926.
5   Quoted from Pool, p. 115.
6   Quoted from Pool, p. 116.
7   Amundsen, *My Life as an Explorer*, p. 208.
8   Quoted from Pool, p. 121.
9   Quoted from Pool, p. 135.
10 Ellsworth, *Beyond Horizons*, p. 217.

5: NO OTHER WORLDS TO CONQUER

1   Ellsworth, *Beyond Horizons*, p. 221.
2   Letter, Bowman to Ellsworth, November 15, 1926, John Hopkins University Library, Baltimore.
3   Letter, Bowman to Clark, January 9, 1929, American Geographical Society Collection, University of Wisconsin.
4   Ellsworth, *Beyond Horizons*, p. 6.
5   Letter, Osborn to Clark, March 12, 1929, Stefansson Collection, Dartmouth College Library, Hanover, N.H.
6   Quoted from Pool, p. 144.
7   Letter, Ellsworth to Clark, June 28, 1929, Stefansson Collection, Dartmouth College Library, Hanover, N.H.
8   Undated Wilkins Manuscript, Ross.
9   Undated Wilkins Speech, *The Next Steps Towards Civilization*, OSU 20/12.
10 Undated Wilkins Speech, Untitled, OSU 22/32.
11 Ellsworth, *Beyond Horizons*, p. 231.
12 Ellsworth, *Beyond Horizons*, p. 230.
13 Ellsworth, *Beyond Horizons*, p. 231.

6: THE SACRIFICE I MUST MAKE

1   Quoted from Pool, p. 13.
2   Quoted from Pool, p. 14.
3   Pool, *Polar Extremes*, p. 14.
4   Ellsworth, *Beyond Horizons*, p. 223.

5   Pool, *Polar Extremes*, p. 113.
6   Quoted from Pool, p. 153.
7   Ellsworth, *Beyond Horizons*, p. 226.
8   Telegram, Bowman to Wilkins, American Geographical Society Collection, University of Wisconsin.
9   Quoted from Pool, p. 150.
10 *New York Times*, January 31, 1931, p. 1.
11 Letter, Ellsworth to Wilkins, February 1, 1931, Larson.
12 Letter, Ellsworth to Wilkins, February 26, 1931, Larson.
13 Letter, Ellsworth to Wilkins, February 26, 1931, Larson.
14 Letter, Ellsworth to Wilkins, March 31, 1931, Larson.

7: THE THRESHOLD OF GREATNESS

1   Ellsworth, *Beyond Horizons*, p. 232.
2   Quoted from Pool, p. 153.
3   Ellsworth, *Beyond Horizons*, p. 233.
4   Ellsworth, *Beyond Horizons*, p. 233.
5   Ellsworth, *Beyond Horizons*, p. 233.
6   Ellsworth, *Beyond Horizons*, p. 234.
7   Pool, *Polar Extremes*, p. 154.

PART II: WYATT EARP LIMITED
8: THE LONE EAGLE

1   Transcript of O.K. Corral Inquest, November 16, 1881, www.famous-trials.com/earp
2   *San Francisco Examiner*, August 2, 1896.
3   Ellsworth, *Beyond Horizons*, p. 239.
4   Ellsworth, *Beyond Horizons*, p. 240.
5   Quoted from Glines, p. 98.
6   Ellsworth, *Beyond Horizons*, p. 240.
7   Ellsworth, *Beyond Horizons*, p. 240.
8   Pool, *Polar Extremes*, p. 164.
9   Ellsworth, *Beyond Horizons*, p. 241.

9: THE MAYOR OF ANTARCTICA

1   Rose, *Explorer*, p. 287.
2   Letter, Byrd to Ellsworth, April 16, 1932, Larson.
3   Letter, Byrd to Ellsworth, April 24, 1932, Larson.
4   Quoted from Rose, p. 317.
5   Letter Byrd to Ellsworth, May 2, 1932, Larson.

6 Letter, Byrd to Ellsworth, May 21, 1932, OSU 15/36.
7 Byrd, *Discovery*, p. 12.
8 Ellsworth, *Beyond Horizons*, p. 349.
9 *Wyatt Earp* Memorandum of Understanding, OSU 16/19.

10: CLOUD KINGDOMS OF THE SUNSET
1 Quoted from Pool, p. 166.
2 Quoted from Pool, p. 166.
3 Letter, Wilkins to Suzanne, August 12, 1933, Larson.
4 Letter, Balchen to Emmy Balchen, undated, Larson.
5 Telegram, Ellsworth to Wilkins, September 21, 1933, Ross.
6 Letter, Wilkins to Suzanne, September 23, 1933, Larson.
7 Ellsworth, *Beyond Horizons*, p. 245.
8 Quoted from Pool, p. 177.
9 Ellsworth, *Beyond Horizons*, p. 221.
10 Letter, Wilkins to Suzanne, November 11, 1933, Larson.
11 Letter, Wilkins to Suzanne, November 26, 1933, Larson.
12 Radiogram, Byrd to Ellsworth, November 20, 1933, Ross.
13 *Auckland Star*, November 21, 1933, p. 8.
14 Letter, Wilkins to Suzanne, November 26, 1933, Larson.
15 Olsen, *Saga of the White Horizon*, p. 63.
16 Letter, Wilkins to Suzanne, December 5, 1933, Larson.
17 Ellsworth, *Beyond Horizons*, p. 239.

11: THE UNIVERSE BEGAN TO VIBRATE
1 *Auckland Star*, December 11, 1933, p. 8.
2 *Wyatt Earp* radiogram, December 16, 1933, Ross.
3 Shackleton, *The Heart of the Antarctic*, p. 73.
4 Amundsen, *The South Pole*, p. 49.
5 *Wyatt Earp* radiogram, January 7, 1934, Ross.
6 Olsen, *Saga of the White Horizon*, p. 94.
7 Ellsworth, *Beyond Horizons*, p. 249.
8 Olsen, *Saga of the White Horizon*, p. 99.
9 Olsen, *Saga of the White Horizon*, p. 106.
10 Olsen, *Saga of the White Horizon*, p. 107.

12: ALONE
1 Letter, Wilkins to Suzanne, February 9, 1934, Larson.
2 Letter, Wilkins to Suzanne, February 17, 1934, Larson.
3 Letter, Wilkins to Suzanne, February 27, 1934, Larson.

4 Letter, Wilkins to Suzanne, February 27, 1934, Larson.
5 Byrd, *Alone*, p. 3.
6 Letter, Wilkins to Suzanne, February 15, 1934, Larson.
7 Telegram transcript, Wilkins to Ellsworth, undated, Ross.
8 Letter, Wilkins to Suzanne, September 2, 1934, Larson.

13: THE STARS FORECAST STRANGE THINGS
1 Paine, *Footsteps on the Ice*, p. 109.
2 Paine, *Footsteps on the Ice*, p. 159.
3 Byrd, *Alone*, p. 160.
4 Byrd, *Alone*, p. 183.
5 Byrd, *Alone*, p. 288.
6 Byrd, *Alone*, p. 295.
7 Letter, Wilkins to Suzanne, September 2, 1934, Larson.
8 Letter, Wilkins to Suzanne, September 2, 1934, Larson.
9 Letter, Wilkins to Suzanne, September 14, 1934, Larson.
10 Letter, Wilkins to Suzanne, September 18, 1934, Larson.

14: THE THIRD MAN
1 Ellsworth, *Beyond Horizons*, p. 255.
2 Byrd, *Discovery*, p. 325.
3 Quoted from Pool, p. 182.
4 Ellsworth, *Beyond Horizons*, p. 261.
5 Radiogram, Byrd to Ellsworth, November 20, 1934, Ross.
6 Undated report, Ellsworth, Ross.
7 Nordenskjöld, *Antarctica*, p. 60.
8 Ellsworth, *Beyond Horizons*, p. 266.
9 Ellsworth, *Beyond Horizons*, p. 267.
10 Ellsworth, *Beyond Horizons*, p. 268.
11 Ellsworth, *Beyond Horizons*, p. 268.
12 Quoted from Pool, p. 268.
13 Byrd, *Discovery*, p. 325.
14 Ellsworth, *Beyond Horizons*, p. 273.
15 Olsen, *Saga of the White Horizon*, p. 122.
16 Radiogram, Wilkins to Bowman, December 29, 1934, Ross.
17 Ellsworth, *Beyond Horizons*, p. 273.

15: A HIGHER TYPE OF COURAGE
1 Undated press release, Ross.
2 Radiogram, Ellsworth to Byrd, January 8, 1935, Ross.

3   Ellsworth, *Beyond Horizons*, p. 275.

4   Ellsworth, *Beyond Horizons*, p. 276.

5   Ellsworth, *Beyond Horizons*, p. 279.

6   Radiogram, Byrd to Ellsworth, undated, Ross.

7   Radiogram, Wilkins to Nelson, undated, Ross.

8   Wilkins's report to Hector Whaling Company, Larson.

9   Olsen, *Saga of the White Horizon*, p. 194.

10 Wilkins's report to Hector Whaling Company, Larson.

11 Olsen, *Saga of the White Horizon*, p. 148.

12 Undated note, Ross.

13 Letter (in Norwegian): Balchen to Emmy Balchen, February 30, 1935, Larson.

14 Letter, Wilkins to Suzanne, February 27, 1935, Larson.

15 Letter, Wilkins to Suzanne, February 15, 1935, Larson.

16 Letter, Wilkins to Suzanne, February 15, 1935, Larson.

17 Letter, Wilkins to Paramount News, February 9, 1935, OSU 15/39.

18 Olsen, *Saga of the White Horizon*, p. 151.

19 *New York Times*, August 11, 1935, p. 3.

PART III: THE HEART OF THE ANTARCTIC
16: THE GREAT UNKNOWN

1   Press release, undated, Ross.

2   Letter, Wilkins to Suzanne, February 13, 1935, Larson.

3   Letter, Wilkins to Holm, April 5, 1935, OSU 15/39.

4   Letters, Byrd and Innes Taylor to Wilkins, April 6, 1935, OSU 15/39.

5   Letter, Wilkins to Suzanne, September 4, 1935, Larson.

6   Olsen, *Saga of the White Horizon*, p. 167.

7   Letter, Byrd to Ellsworth, October 20, 1935, OSU 17/35.

8   Ellsworth, *Beyond Horizons*, p. 283.

9   Olsen, *Saga of the White Horizon*, p. 167.

10 Olsen, *Saga of the White Horizon*, p. 167.

11 Olsen, *Saga of the White Horizon*, p. 167.

17: CHASING THE SUN

1   Undated manuscript, Ross.

2   Undated manuscript, Ross.

3   Undated manuscript, Ross.

4   Ellsworth, *Beyond Horizons*, p. 294.

5   Ellsworth, *Beyond Horizons*, p. 295.

6   Ellsworth, *Beyond Horizons*, p. 296.

7 Ellsworth, *Beyond Horizons*, p. 296.

8 Ellsworth, *Beyond Horizons*, p. 296.

9 Ellsworth, *Beyond Horizons*, p. 296.

10 Ellsworth, *Beyond Horizons*, p. 297.

11 Ellsworth, *Beyond Horizons*, p. 43.

12 Ellsworth, *Beyond Horizons*, p. 298.

13 Ellsworth, *Beyond Horizons*, p. 300.

18: LOST

1 *Wyatt Earp* radio message, Ross.

2 Undated manuscript, Ross.

3 Hollick-Kenyon diary (copy), Ross.

4 *Wyatt Earp* radio message, Ross.

5 Hollick-Kenyon diary (copy), Ross.

6 Ellsworth, *Beyond Horizons*, p. 302.

7 Ellsworth diary (copy), Ross.

8 *Wyatt Earp* radio message, Ross.

9 Hollick-Kenyon diary (copy), Ross.

10 Ellsworth diary (copy), Ross.

11 Ellsworth diary (copy), Ross.

12 Hollick-Kenyon diary (copy), Ross.

13 Hollick-Kenyon diary (copy), Ross.

14 Ellsworth, *Beyond Horizons*, p. 305.

19: THANK GOD YOU'RE DOWN THERE

1 Ellsworth, *Beyond Horizons*, p. 308.

2 Radiogram, Ross.

3 Note (copy), Ross.

20: MAYBE IT'S ALL TO TRY US

1 Ellsworth diary (copy), Ross.

2 Ellsworth diary (copy), Ross.

3 Ellsworth, *Beyond Horizons*, p. 356.

4 Ellsworth diary (copy), Ross.

5 Ellsworth diary (copy), Ross.

6 Ellsworth diary (copy), Ross.

7 Ellsworth diary (copy), Ross.

8 Ellsworth diary (copy), Ross.

9 Hollick-Kenyon diary (copy), Ross.

10 Ellsworth diary (copy), Ross.

21: A FRIENDLY GESTURE

1   Letter (copy), Mawson to Casey, December 5, 1935, Larson.
2   Letter (copy) Davis to Casey, undated, Larson.
3   Radiogram, undated, Wilkins to Davis, Ross.
4   Ommanney, *South Latitude*, p. 171.
5   Ommanney, *South Latitude*, p. 171.
6   Ellsworth diary (copy), Ross.
7   Ellsworth diary (copy), Ross.
8   Ellsworth diary (copy), Ross.
9   Ellsworth diary (copy), Ross.
10 Ellsworth note, OSU 16/14.
11 Ellsworth diary (copy), Ross.

22: A SILENCE THAT COULD BE FELT

1   Letter, Wilkins to Suzanne, December 15, 1936, Larson.
2   Letter, Wilkins to Suzanne, undated, Larson.
3   Ellsworth diary (copy), Ross.
4   Ellsworth diary (copy), Ross.
5   Ellsworth diary (copy), Ross.
6   Ommanney, *South Latitude*, p. 196.
7   Douglas Family Papers, National Library of Australia.
8   Ommanney, *South Latitude*, p. 203.
9   Ommanney, *South Latitude*, p. 204.
10 Ellsworth, *Beyond Horizons*, p. 332.
11 Ommanney, *South Latitude*, p. 209.
12 Olsen, *Saga of the White Horizon*, p. 132.

23: CHUGGING ON

1   *Sydney Morning Herald*, February 21, 1936.
2   Letter, Wilkins to Ellsworth, March 1, 1936, OSU 16/31.
3   Letter (draft), Wilkins to Byrd, undated, OSU 17/35.
4   Letter, Byrd to Wilkins, September 19, 1936, OSU 17/37.
5   Ellsworth, *Beyond Horizons*, p. 299.
6   Letter, Northrop to Wilkins, May 25, 1937, OSU 15/41.
7   Letter, Wilkins to Ellsworth, June 1, 1937, OSU 15/35.
8   Letter, Ellsworth to Wilkins, July 25, 1937, OSU 15/41.
9   Letter, Ellsworth to Wilkins, undated, Larson.
10 Letter, Wilkins to Ellsworth, undated, Larson.
11 Note, undated, Ross.

12 Report of Ellsworth Antarctic Expedition Flight, OSU 16/32.
13 Press release, undated, Ross.

AFTERWORD
1 Quoted from Pool, p. 244.
2 Thomas, *Sir Hubert Wilkins: His World of Adventure*, p. 272.
3 Letter, Wilkins to Davis, June 5, 1953, Larson.
4 Law, *The Antarctic Voyage of the* Wyatt Earp, p. 53.
5 Fuchs and Hillary, *The First Crossing of Antarctica*, jacket flap.

ACKNOWLEDGMENTS

This book has evolved over a number of years and, during that time, some of the people who assisted me have died. I would like to acknowledge the late Beekman Pool for sharing his information and research regarding Lincoln Ellsworth. Michael Ross and Dr. David Larson, who lived in Michigan and Washington, DC respectively, both died in November 2016. They were gracious hosts during my visits to them and without their assistance and willingness to let me copy their records, this book would never have been written. Laura Kissel, the polar curator at the Byrd Polar and Climate Research Center (BPCRC), at Ohio State University in Columbus, Ohio, has cheerfully tolerated my requests for information (along with my visits) over many years, and I have to express my thanks, yet again, for her marvelous assistance. Many people have answered my emails and questions, but I would like to highlight the help given me by Kathie Bell, Stephen Carthew, Laraine Daly Jones, Donal Duthie, Ann Kirschner, Steve Kalvar, Jon Larson, Melba Matson, Rob Mulder, Mark Pharaoh, Saskia Raevouri, Kaye Ridge, Dick Smith, Bess Urbahn, Judith K. Thome, Christine Venema, Thomas Vince, and Hal Vogel. Richard Pearl valiantly tried to explain navigation to me in layman's terms and any errors in my explanations are mine, not his. My literary agent, Andrew Lownie, is always astute in his judgement, and I thank him for introducing me to Claiborne Hancock and the brilliant team at Pegasus Books, who have done a wonderful job with the production of this book. My friend and editor, Rebecca Green, steered me through the many drafts of the manuscript and continually provided valuable insights. As always, my wife, Zoe, and my family provide the support to make this work possible, and I can never thank them sufficiently.

INDEX

ABOUT THE AUTHOR

Jeff Maynard's books include *Niagara's Gold*, *Divers in Time*, *Wings of Ice*, and *The Unseen Anzac*. He is a member of the Explorers Club and a former president of the Historical Diving Society. He lives in Victoria, Australia, with his wife Zoe and their family. www.jeffmaynard.com.au